Modern Hungarian Poetry

Modern
Hungarian Poetry

Edited, and with an Introduction, by
MIKLÓS VAJDA

Foreword by WILLIAM JAY SMITH

COLUMBIA UNIVERSITY PRESS

New York   1977

Columbia University Press
New York   Guildford, Surrey
Published in Hungary by Corvina Press, Budapest
Published in the United States by Columbia University Press

Copyright © 1977 by Miklós Vajda
Printed in Hungary

Library of Congress Cataloging in Publication Data

Main entry under title:
Modern Hungarian poetry.
Includes index.

1. Hungarian poetry — 20th century — Translations into English. 2. English
poetry — Translations from Hungarian. I. Vajda, Miklós.
PH3441.E3M6   894'.511'1308   76-2453
ISBN 0-231-04022-9

ACKNOWLEDGMENTS

Modern Hungarian Poetry has been sponsored by the Translation Center, Columbia University, jointly with *The New Hungarian Quarterly*, Budapest. The aim of the Translation Center, funded by the National Endowment for the Arts, is to improve the quality of literary translation.

Most of the poems in this anthology appeared originally in *The New Hungarian Quarterly*. For those which have appeared elsewhere the editor is grateful to the following publishers and publications for permission to reprint:

Collins–Knowlton–Wing for the five poems of Gábor Devecseri, translated by Robert Graves, copyright © 1970, 1971, 1972 by Robert Graves. All rights reserved. Oxford University Press (Canadian Branch) for "Power of the Flowers," "The Boy Changed into a Stag," "Crown of Hatred and Love," by Ferenc Juhász, which appeared in Ferenc Juhász, *The Boy Changed into a Stag, Selected Poems 1949–1967*, translated by Kenneth McRobbie and Ilona Duczynska, copyright © 1970 by Oxford University Press.

Oxford University Press (London) for "The Coalmen," "Fair in Frosty May," "Squared by Walls," "Without Mercy," translated by Tony Connor; and "Love of the Scorching Wind," translated by Kenneth McRobbie from László Nagy, *Love of the Scorching Wind, Selected Poems 1953–1971*, translated by Tony Connor and Kenneth McRobbie, with a foreword by George Gömöri, published by Oxford University Press and Corvina Press, Budapest, 1973, copyright © 1973 by László Nagy. Penguin Books (England) for "Gold" and "Silver" by Ferenc Juhász, translated by David Wevill; and "The Lost Parasol," "Monkeyland," "Queen Tatavane," "Internus," translated by Edwin Morgan in Sándor Weöres and Ferenc Juhász, *Selected Poems*, 1970, copyright © 1970 by Penguin Books.

CONTENTS

Foreword by William Jay Smith   xv
Introduction by Miklós Vajda   xix

LAJOS KASSÁK (1887–1967)
Craftsmen *(Mesteremberek)*   1
Baffling Picture *(Érthetetlen)*   2
Young Horseman *(Fiatal lovas)*   2
Like This *(Így)*   2
Snapshot *(Gyorsfelvétel)*   3
I Am With You *(Veled vagyok)*   4

MILÁN FÜST (1888–1967)
"If My Bones Must Be Handed Over"
("Ha csontjaimat meg kelletik adni")   5
Old Age *(Öregség)*   6

LŐRINC SZABÓ (1900–1957)
Prisons *(Börtönök)*   8
The Dreams of the One *(Az egy álmai)*   9
All for Nothing *(Semmiért egészen)*   10
From Cricket Music *(Tücsökzene, részletek)*   12
    Farewell *(. . .búcsú. . .)*   12
    . . .on the outlook tower. . . *(. . .kilátón. . .)*   12
    . . .in the big blue meadow. . . *(. . .a nagy, kék réten. . .)*   13

GYULA ILLYÉS (1902–   )
How Soon. . . *(Milyen hamar)*   14
The Wonder Castle *(A kacsalábon forgó vár)*   14

Complaint on Solipsism *(Panaszdal a szolipszizmusról)*   21
It Is Five Years Now *(Öt éve...)*   21
At the Turning Point of Life *(Az élet fordulóján)*   22
Grass Snake and Fish *(A sikló és a hal)*   23
Consolation *(Vigasz)*   23
Aboard the Santa Maria *(A Sancta Mariá-n)*   24
Logbook of a Lost Caravan *(Megtalált karaván-napló)*   25
Ruler *(Uralkodó)*   25
Brazilian Rain Forest *(Brazil őserdő)*   26
Tilting Sail *(Dőlt vitorla)*   27
A Record *(Jelentés)*   28
While the Record Plays *(Lemez-zene közben)*   29
The Approaching Silence *(Közelgő csönd)*   30
Early Darkness *(Korai sötét)*   31
Work *(Munka)*   31
The Maker *(Teremteni)*   32
A Wreath *(Koszorú)*   39

ZOLTÁN ZELK (1906–)
And And *(És és)*   41
October *(Október)*   42
Man Falling *(Zuhanó)*   42
Cry *(Kiáltás)*   42
Moment *(Pillanat)*   43
Alone *(Egyedül)*   43
More Powerful than the Sea *(Tengernél erősebb)*   43
Petrified Minute *(Megkövült perc)*   44
The Way *(Ahogy)*   44
Salt and Memory *(Só és emlékezet)*   45
Echo *(Visszhang)*   46

ANNA HAJNAL (1907–)
Song of the Plain *(Ének a síkságon)*   47
Separate Time *(Külön idő)*   48
The Felled Plane Tree *(Kivágott platán)*   49
Fear *(Félek)*   49
Half Past Four, October *(Fél öt, október)*   50

AMY KÁROLYI (1909–)
From The Third House *(A harmadik ház, részletek)*   52

ISTVÁN VAS (1910–   )
  The Grand Finale *(Így lett vége)*   56
  Budapest Elegy *(Pesti elégia)*   62
  On Approaching Fifty *(Ötven felé)*   64
  The Etruscan Sarcophagus *(Az etruszk szarkofág)*   69
  Gods *(Istenek)*   71
  It Doesn't Count *(Nem számít)*   72
  The Mad Town *(Az őrült város)*   75
  Boccherini's Tomb *(Boccherini sírja)*   77
  Saint Médard *(Medárd)*   79
  Nagyszombat, 1704   80

LÁSZLÓ KÁLNOKY (1912–   )
  De Profundis   84
  Despair *(Kétségbeesés)*   85
  Instead of an Autobiography *(Önéletrajz helyett)*   86

GYÖRGY RÓNAY (1913–   )
  The Teaching Staff Disbanded *(A tantestület feloszlatása)*   87

SÁNDOR WEÖRES (1913–   )
  Antithin *(Anticingár)*   88
  The Lost Parasol *(Az elveszített napernyő)*   88
  Le Journal   99
  Monkeyland *(Majomország)*   105
  Queen Tatavane *(Tatavane királynő)*   105
  Landscape with Mountain *(Hegyi táj)*   110
  Internus   110
  Variations on the Themes of Little Boys *(Kisfiúk témáira)*   114
  The Seventh Garden *(Soha még egy kert)*   116
  Elan *(Iram)*   117

ZOLTÁN JÉKELY (1913–   )
  The Elegy of a Bronze Age Man *(Múzeumlátogatás)*   118

LÁSZLÓ BENJÁMIN (1915–   )
  Poem by an Unknown Poet from the Mid-Twentieth Century
    (Ismeretlen 20. századi költő verse)   122
  Cave Drawings *(Sziklarajzok)*   124

GÁBOR DEVECSERI (1917–1971)
The World Awoke Me *(Reggeli perc)*   126
The Bath in Pylos *(Polükaszté kádja)*   126
His Life *(Akivel az élet)*   127
Odysseus in Phaeacia *(Odüsszeusz a Phaiákok szigetére érkezik)*   127
Women and Masks *(Anyó és maszkok)*   128

IMRE CSANÁDI (1920–   )
Silent Prayer of Peasants *(Parasztok fohásza)*   130
Holiday-Afternoon Rhapsody *(Ünnepdélutáni rapszódia)*   131
Confession of Faith *(Hitvalló)*   134
Small Craftsman *(Kismester)*   135

GYÖRGY SOMLYÓ (1920–   )
Tale about a Flower *(Mese a virágról)*   136
Tale of the Double Helix *(Mese a kettős spirálról)*   137
Tale about A/An *(Mese a/az ról/ről)*   138

SÁNDOR RÁKOS (1921–   )
Pheasant *(Fácán)*   140
Interrogation *(Kihallgatás)*   140
Creature *(Vadállat)*   141

JÁNOS PILINSZKY (1921–   )
Under the Winter Sky *(Téli ég alatt)*   142
Sin *(Bűn)*   143
Passion of Ravensbrück *(Ravensbrücki passió)*   144
The Desert of Love *(A szerelem sivataga)*   144
Apocrypha *(Apokrif)*   145
Postscript *(Utószó)*   148
Fable. Detail from "KZ-Oratorio" *(Részlet a "KZ-oratórium"-ból)*   149
As I Was *(Amiként kezdtem)*   159
Celebration of the Nadir *(A mélypont ünnepélye)*   150
I Shall Be Watching *(Majd elnézem)*   151
Metronome *(Metronóm)*   152
Exhortation *(Intelem)*   152
Every Breath *(Minden lélegzetvétel)*   153
The Rest Is Grace *(A többi kegyelem)*   153
Meetings *(Találkozások)*   154
Cattle Brand *(Marhabélyeg)*   154

All That Is Needed *(Elég)* 155

ÁGNES NEMES NAGY (1922–)
Statues *(Szobrok)* 156
I Carried Statues *(Szobrokat vittem)* 157
Between *(Között)* 158
Defend It *(Védd meg)* 159
A Comparison *(Hasonlat)* 160
The Shapelessness *(A formátlan)* 160

ISTVÁN KORMOS (1923–)
I Am Being Dragged by Red Dolphins *(Vonszolnak piros delfinek)* 161
The Lament of Orpheus *(Orpheus panasza)* 161
Voyage 162
After Us *(Utánunk)* 162
Deep Sea *(Tengermély)* 163

MIHÁLY VÁCI (1924–1970)
Before I Die *(Mielőtt meghalok)* 165
The Most-Age *(Leg-korszak)* 166

LÁSZLÓ NAGY (1925–)
Frosts Are Coming *(Fagyok jönnek)* 168
The Coalmen *(A fekete fiúk)* 168
The Bliss of Sunday *(A vasárnap gyönyöre)* 169
Fair in Frosty May *(Deres majális)* 176
The Ferryman *(Ki viszi át a Szerelmet)* 177
Prayer to the White Lady *(Himnusz minden időben)* 178
Squared by Walls *(A falak négyszögében)* 180
Without Mercy *(Amikor nincs kegyelem)* 181
The Break-up *(A hűtlenség napja)* 182
The Peacock Woman *(Álmok játéka)* 182
Love of the Scorching Wind *(A forró szél imádata)* 183

ISTVÁN SIMON (1926–1975)
Rhapsody on Time *(Rapszódia az időről)* 188

JÓZSEF TORNAI (1927–)
You Must Hand Over *(Oda kell adni)* 192
We Say This Prayer *(Mondjuk a könyörgést)* 193

To Die for Something *(Meghalni valamiért)*   194
Mr. T. S. Eliot Cooking Pasta *(Mr. T. S. Eliot tésztát főz)*   194

FERENC JUHÁSZ (1928–   )
   Gold *(Arany)*   196
   Silver *(Ezüst)*   196
   Power of the Flowers *(A virágok hatalma)*   197
   The Boy Changed into a Stag Cries Out at the Gate of Secrets
   (A szarvassá változott fiú kiáltozása a titkok kapujában)   206
   Crown of Hatred and Love *(A gyűlölet és szerelem koszorúja)*   218

MARGIT SZÉCSI (1928–   )
   Love's Fool *(Szerelem bolondja)*   221
   Only with Radiance *(Csak sugárral)*   221
   The Burning Ship *(Az égő hajó)*   223
   Man *(Ember)*   224

GÁBOR GÖRGEY (1929–   )
   From Interview *(Interjú, részletek)*   224

GÁBOR GARAI (1929–   )
   A Man Is Beaten Up *(Vernek egy embert)*   229
   Calcutta *(Kalkutta)*   230
   Vigil at Dawn *(Hajnali virrasztás)*   231
   In Hungarian *(Magyarul)*   232

SÁNDOR CSOÓRI (1930–   )
   Golden Pheasants Flying *(Szálltak az aranyfácánok)*   233
   Barbarian Prayer *(Barbár imádság)*   234
   Ague *(Váltóláz)*   234
   Whispers, for Two Voices *(Súgás, két hangra)*   235
   I Would Rather Run Back *(Futnék inkább vissza)*   236

ISTVÁN EÖRSI (1931–   )
   When Things Fall Upwards *(Amikor fölfelé hullnak a tárgyak)*   238
   Generations *(Nemzedékek)*   239

ÁGNES GERGELY (1933–   )
   Crazed Man in Concentration Camp *(Bolond munkaszolgálatos)*   240
   With Lamp in Hand *(Lámpással kezemben)*   241

Sign on My Door Jamb *(Ajtófélfámon jel vagy)*   242

MÁRTON KALÁSZ (1934–   )
Legacy *(Örökség)*   244

MIHÁLY LADÁNYI (1934–   )
We Just Sit about Quietly *(Nyugodtan üldögélünk)*   246
Lenin   247
When All's Said and Done *(És végeredményben)*   248
Inventory *(Leltár)*   249
About the Hero *(A hősről)*   249
For the Record *(Jegyzőkönyv)*   250

OTTÓ ORBÁN (1936–   )
Galety and Good Heart *(Derü és vidámság)*   251
To Be Poor *(Szegénynek lenni)*   252
Concert *(Koncert)*   252
Report on the Poem *(Jelentés a versről)*   253
The Apparition *(A jelenés)*   254
The Ladies of Bygone Days *(A régi idők hölgyei)*   256

JUDIT TÓTH (1936–   )
To the Newborn *(Az újszülötthöz)*   258
Dead Embryos *(Halott embriók)*   260
Notes on Saint Maurice *(Saint Maurice-i jegyzet)*   261

ISTVÁN CSUKÁS (1936–   )
The Macadam Road Remembers *(Az emlékező makadámút)*   263

DEZSŐ TANDORI (1938–   )
"And Brief, Good Mother? For I Am in Haste? Whither??"
("S gyorsan, anyám? mert nagyon sietek? Hova??")   265
Homage   266
Details *(Részletek)*   267
Sadness of the Bare Copula *(A puszta létige szomorúsága)*   267

ISTVÁN ÁGH (1939   )
The Dead of My Songs *(Dalaim halottai)*   268

MIKLÓS VERESS (1942–   )
   Self-Portrait at Thirty *(Önarckép harmincéves korából)*   270

GYÖRGY PETRI (1943–   )
   You Usually Come in the Morning *(Reggel szoktál jönni)*   271
   With the Thin Girl *(A vékony lánnyal)*   272
   Song *(Dal)*   274

SZABOLCS VÁRADY (1943–   )
   An Outsider, If There Were Such a Man *(Egy kívülálló, ha volna
   ilyen)*   275
   Chairs Above the Danube *(Székek a Duna fölött)*   276

Biographical Notes   279
Index of Poets   287
Index of Translators   288
Co-Translators   289
Illustrations follow page   162

FOREWORD

How account for the magnificent and varied concentration of poetry in so small a nation as Hungary? Robert Graves has said that wherever horses and cranes still exist as indeed they do in that country poetry is certain to thrive. Situated in the center of Europe, Hungary has maintained for over a thousand years the integrity of its language and its culture. (Gyula Illyés, in his profoundly moving tribute to his native tongue in the poem "A Wreath," gives some idea of the price that has been paid for that integrity.) Whatever else it has been, Hungary in a sense has constituted an island in Central Europe, and it is the nature of islanders to turn inward—to seek in themselves the roots of legends, tales, and songs centuries old—and in this seeking there is always poetry. The writing of poetry in this instance has meant not only purifying, but literally keeping alive, the words of the tribe. A people living surrounded by other languages and cultures learns to listen more carefully to the sound of its own voice, to probe more keenly its tragic depths, to allow black humor—with its crystal surface—to bubble up from the deep. Islanders not only turn inward, they also reach out; and poetry is the most enduring of bridges, whether based on the Oriental philosophy of Sándor Weöres or the urbane European meditations of István Vas.

There is a buoyancy in the air of Budapest which must have something to do with the creation of its poetry. The city's concentration of mineral springs working their way through cracks and cavities in the bed of dolomite on which the city rests may have something to do with it. The Romans certainly found it a fine place to be, as did the Turks. The gusto and effervescence characteristic of great poetry are naturally there. Poets in all countries have always gravitated to springs; fountains are emblematic of their art. There is immediately a feeling of great activity in the city: everybody is on the move, rushing about in an intent and determined way. One expects this in any great capital, but in Budapest it seems ingrained, an inner buoyancy that demands expression. It is said that the inhabitants of Budapest stop for only two reasons—for an accident or when someone asks the way. Perhaps the third reason is when compelled to put down a few lines of poetry.

I firmly believe that only poets should translate poets, but how does one translate from a language of which one knows not a word? It may seem madness, and probably is; but poets are not to be put off by madness. I have tried it a few times—with the aid fortunately of trustworthy advisers who did know the language—but never on the scale that I have attempted recently with Hungarian poetry. My association with it began in June 1970 when on my first visit to Budapest I met Miklós Vajda, the literary editor of *The New Hungarian Quarterly* and the editor of this anthology. Mr. Vajda is a talented, intelligent, and very persuasive man. His English is impeccable, and his feeling for poetry in a number of languages is remarkable. In his introduction he describes how from rough literal versions he obtained from his translators polished, and often brilliant, results.

Like a number of the contributors to this anthology, I returned to Hungary at the invitation of Dr. László Kéry, Secretary General of the Hungarian P.E.N. Dr. Kéry is another of those remarkable men of letters that his country seems to produce, one keenly aware of Hungary's poetic heritage and at the same time widely read in English, American, and European literature. Budapest was immediately congenial to me; and what poet would not feel at home there—in a city where a workers' quarter on the banks of the Danube (why, I never discovered) is called the "Field of Angels?" The poets I met spoke directly and unhesitatingly, whatever language they used. I had been with Gyula Illyés only a minute or two when he remarked on my slightly Oriental eyes. When I explained that they were no doubt the legacy of my Cherokee forebears, he welcomed me at once as a brother. "We had the same ancestors," he said, "yours went one way out of Asia and mine another."

In the work of Illyés I found the vigor that one would expect from the author of *People of the Puszta*. His prose poem "Work" is a magnificent expression of his inborn sense of craft, inherited from his wheelwright grandfather. And this sense of craft is carried to a point of extreme sophistication and subtlety in the poems on creation, which one feels might have come from the pen of Paul Valéry. If I read them correctly, I find in the poems of István Vas deep feeling and profound terror under what seems a light, and at times even casual, surface. There is, of course, this same kind of gentle but forceful directness in the man himself. And when I encountered Sándor Weöres perched like a gnome beside the electric coffee-maker in his plant-

and-book-lined parlor, I was convinced—whether it took the form of a child's speech or that of a Chinese coolie—that the language he used was magic.

Wherever in the world one meets Hungarians of prominence in any profession, one quickly discovers how passionately they feel about the poetry of their country. That poetry has recently begun to travel; there have been excellent translations into French, German, and other European languages. Illyés and Weöres have both been mentioned for the Nobel prize. W. H. Auden called "The Boy Changed into a Stag Cries Out at the Gate of Secrets" by Ferenc Juhász "one of the greatest poems written in my time." Surely anyone who has read that brilliant metaphorical synthesis of man's primitive roots with modern technological society will not easily forget it. Although after several visits I still know little Hungarian, I do have the mad confidence shared by the other poet-translators of this volume that most of the poems assembled here by Miklós Vajda are of a rare beauty in the original and deserving of the best life they can be given in English.

William Jay Smith

INTRODUCTION

The background of some of the best poems in this collection is nothing less than five hundred years of unjust and debilitating history, with all its inevitable consequences. While Hungary shares the fate of the small nations in Central Europe and the poems necessarily reflect this history, no one should be deterred from reading further, for very little of the actual events appear in the poems themselves. Hungarian poets long ago passed the romantic age of national self-pity. What remains and still inspires Hungarian poetry is an awareness of history as a constant presence, pressure, and challenge.

Throughout the last five hundred years this nation, together with its culture and poetry, has been tormented, humiliated and toughened by a history which we think of as savage even by Central and East European standards. As a consequence, its best artists, writers, and poets sooner or later found themselves and their art yoked to the service of history and the struggle against the oppressor of the day, either directly or as the voice of some national, social or collective cause. This formidable burden, as everyone knows, can undermine art, and it did indeed in some cases produce parochial and didactic work of the sort Robert Penn Warren has called "diagnostic and therapeutic." But the truly great poets were able to transform their burden into a part of the universal human experience, and they did so with the same immediacy that the burdens themselves imposed.

The first lyrical poet of importance, who wrote his charming and personal songs in Hungarian instead of Latin, was a charismatic, full-blooded womanizer, bully, adventurer and soldier-poet, Bálint Balassi. By the time he died at the age of forty fighting the Turks, he had already inspired imitation, or, in modern terms, had made a fashion of expressing what was in the air and in his heart.

But then, Balassi was also writing in the language of a nation in mortal danger. It was not the first traumatic blow to Hungary. Internal power struggles had allowed the Mongols to invade in the mid-thirteenth century and destroy an advanced and rich medieval kingdom. But it recovered with relative ease, and in fact soon reached the peak of Hungarian history when, in the latter half of the fifteenth century, the country enjoyed a few decades of development in all walks of life that was unprecedented in scope and pace. In the hands of a brilliant Renaissance king, Matthias Corvinus, the country quickly caught up with the rest of Europe, but the period, so rich in cultural achievement, came to an end in disruptive anarchy, and meanwhile the Turks were already slowly pushing their way up the Balkans toward the heart of Europe. Following the ruthless suppression of a peasant war that originally started as a holy campaign against the Turks, the biggest, central part of the weakened country, including its capital Buda, easily fell into Turkish hands and stayed there for 150 years. The poet Balassi died in 1594 at the siege of Esztergom, the same city overlooking the Danube that had seen the coronation of the first Hungarian king some six hundred years before. But now it was the Turks who held it, and the Hungarians who attacked it. The Turkish occupation and its consequences gave Hungary a history from which it was never able to recover.

This all has a direct bearing on Hungarian poetry and the writers in this book. As T. S. Eliot says in *Tradition and the Individual Talent*: "No poet, no artist of any sort, has his complete meaning alone. His significance, his appreciation is the appreciation of his relation to the dead poets and artists." Hungarian poets in particular were subject to the relentless vicissitudes of their country's history, involving very real and immediate questions of the nation's existence, her fights for independence against foreign oppression and exploitation, her struggles against internal backwardness, poverty and conformity. Such was the life of the nation, such was the heritage of "the dead poets and artists," themselves part of the material to be fashioned into poetry throughout the centuries. Poetry had to meet the historical challenges of the political and armed conflicts of Reformation and Counter-Reformation, four hundred years of an uneasy forced marriage to the Habsburgs, an Enlightenment carried out like a conspiracy, and two world wars in which Hungary was on the losing side, and as a consequence lost two-thirds of its territory and more than half of its population. One of the most interesting features of Hungarian poetry as a whole is, in spite of all this, the variety of individual approaches, the poetic power and the validity beyond topicality of the poetry and the unique blending of life and work that characterizes the poets.

Since the end of the eighteenth century Hungary has always had at least one poet who, had he written in a language less isolated than Hungarian, we feel would now be revered wherever poetry is read. The Enlightenment produced Csokonai; mid-nineteenth century romanticism produced Vörösmarty, and populist-realism, its offspring, included Petőfi and Arany. At the beginning of this century there were Ady and Babits, and later, Attila József and Miklós Radnóti. Included in this volume are also at least two or three who now, in their own lifetimes, may be compared to the greatest of the past.

Jonathan Swift once asked, not without malice, "Say Britain, could you ever boast / Three poets in an age at most? / Our chilling climate hardly bears / A sprig of bays in fifty years." In our historically and geopolitically chillier climate, the crop of bays can be considered continuous and abundant. But, and Swift did not have to point this out, Britain had also developed the novel and drama to go with its poetry, while in Hungary it was poetry alone that produced an unbroken line of immortals. With a few notable exceptions, like Bartók in music, none of the other arts, fiction or drama ever rivalled the level of poetry in this country. In the chaos and destruction following the Renaissance, most Hungarian cities were destroyed, thus preventing urbanization for several hundred years. Poetry was witness to all of this, and indeed, flourished on the turbulence that submerged the other arts. It even expanded and toughened itself to bear its solitary burden. Its cohesive powers grew; romanticism, for instance, which quickly arrived from England originally as a backlash from the vulgarity of the Industrial Revolution, was dressed by Hungarian poetry in fancy national garb. It gave some confidence to a nation which had to go centuries on end without the slightest sense of success and historical achievement. The giant revolutionary seer, Endre Ady, turned French symbolism into a cloak. And it was poetry which best kept alive what some sociologists call the super-ego and define as the commonly shared sense of the existence of a higher community interest reaching beyond the individual: the assumption that society is, or ought to be, an organic and continuous common enterprise, expanding horizontally in space and vertically in time, as everyone makes his contribution from generation to generation. In Hungary, however, the kind of philosophy that could be distilled from a lifetime to be passed on from one generation to the next was the rather gloomy but useful advice to survive, adjust, save, keep silent, mistrust. Poetry, which cannot be shelled like a city, or whitewashed like murals, crushed like sculpture, closed like theaters, or even banned and censored as easily as novels and journals, can spread and be influential even without print or manuscript. And so it dominated the literature of a people that had to live under difficult conditions, luring the best talents and forcing them to lead dangerous lives and produce extraordinary achievements.

The two greatest Hungarian poets, Sándor Petőfi and Attila József, died before they could have completed half a life's work in any field but poetry. Petőfi had only five years to grow from a miserable childhood as the son of a village butcher into one of the greatest poets of the nineteenth century, to write his several hundred lyric poems which transformed Hungarian poetry; to write also epic poems, a play, a novel, letters, articles, travelogues; to acquire a sound working knowledge of several foreign languages; to translate Shakespeare's *Coriolanus;* to travel all over the country, edit a paper, take part in politics, intrigues, and quarrels, make friends, marry, father a child, almost literally trigger the 1848 March revolution in Pest with one of his fiery poems, fight in the army against the Austrians, and die in battle at the incredible age of twenty-six. His life itself was a phenomenal performance while his work embodies sensibility and lucidity—the perfect match of a great role played properly and spontaneous self-realization.

Less than a hundred years later, out of the depth of a more complex society came the son of a soap-factory hand and a washerwoman: Attila József. His childhood, like Petőfi's, prepared him as if by some plan for what he was to become. Misery, starvation, humiliation, solitude and disillusion dogged his life, but at least he was allotted somewhat more time than Petőfi. Visions of the modern industrial proletariat, bleak urban landscapes of factories and industrial suburbs, underground communist activity, antifascism and looming social revolution appear in some of his poems, organized into superbly compressed and tangible images and metaphors. All this is achieved in a language that can boldly apply terms and concepts of Marxist philosophy, Freud, modern science and sociology, and still remain gentle, poetic and highly individual. And—once more the perfect blending of life and work—there is a harrowing tension in his late poetry, coming from the anguish of a man who was left totally alone in a country rapidly succumbing to fascism and imminent war. Forsaken by his love and his party, which was unable to understand the kind of political poetry he wrote, he was tormented by nightmares and fits of madness, unalleviated by analysis. The pressure and tension that were eventually to crush him produced a crystalline condensation that seems to verge on the ineffable. There is a retrospective quality here that includes the angle of someone already far beyond and above the human condition and capable of speaking for man. With deadly accuracy and utmost simplicity, the totality of a life is revealed in which absolutely everything existed to produce suffering. He foresaw and described his own death, the way it finally happened, when, in

1937, at the age of thirty-two he threw himself under the wheels of a freight train.

But the most dramatic death of all came to Miklós Radnóti, at the end of World War II, when he was thirty-three. He began his career as a mediocre surrealist with strong political inclinations. And then, as the pressure of fascism and war began to mount, Radnóti started his own poetic fight against inhumanity. Using classical forms which he chiselled and hammered into perfection, he wrote time capsules to encase the essence of everything that was dear to him, memories and landscapes of childhood, love, the quiet happiness of reading and writing, the atmosphere of friendly gatherings over a glass of wine, the small everyday things that make up human civilization. As a Jew, he was first sent in a labor battalion to work in a copper mine in occupied Yugoslavia, then was taken through Hungary in a forced march towards Germany. He was offered chances to escape, but refused and stayed on, continuing to write in the same condensed, classical manner, now about life in the labor camp and the execution of his comrades. In his last poems it was already his own death he was describing: the men next to him were shot; their blood splashed on his face while he dug their graves. And then he too was shot. His last poems were found on his body after the war, in a mass grave.

His friend, István Vas, one of the poets in this book, wrote of him: "These poems are among the rare masterpieces that combine artistic and moral perfection... Radnóti left us not just an exciting body of work, not just truly great poems, but also an example of human and artistic integrity that is as embarrassing and absurd as it is imperative."

The reader would be entirely wrong to believe that all Hungarian poetry is political and patriotic odes and poems. Not at all; it is just that—as with some other nations—certain conditions made great poets write political poems, thus elevating the genre but also involving the poets in politics, sometimes to the point where it killed them. By now the reader will, I hope, understand why a poet noted for a clarity totally devoid of illusion, like István Vas, would see his city become a battlefield little more than ten years after World War II, and write in 1957 (in "Budapest Elegy," included in this book):

"I lived here and never wished to live any place but here"

—for being Hungarian and being a Hungarian poet may mean terrible burdens, dangers and pitfalls, but also attraction, beauty, and possible sublimity.

This anthology was designed to survey post-war, that is to say, contemporary Hungarian poetry in the variety of its attitudes and approaches, its richness of themes and styles, with a strong emphasis on the most important poets. Forty-one, the number of the poets represented is, however, quite arbitrary, for it could have been thirty-five, fifty-five or seventy-one. Similarly—except for the poets who are presented with a special emphasis—the number of poems by individual poets in the book, be it six or just one, is equally difficult to justify and does not necessarily indicate proportionate importance. This collection is selected from the pages of *The New Hungarian Quarterly* and put into English by poets who live thousands of miles away. The magazine has been carrying out a program of surveying living Hungarian poetry, but once the chance to bring out a book arose, the still incomplete survey had to be sampled. There are good poets writing today who deserve to be included, and are not. Others ought to have had more space but could not, as they had not yet had a second chance to appear in the magazine. And, of course, the selection had to be made primarily with the quality of the translations in mind. Not all poetry travels, in general, and in particular not all Hungarian poets have as yet found their proper translators. Translation is, needless to say, infinitely more than a linguistic and technical exercise, and sometimes beyond what even maximum affinity, sympathy and technical brilliance can achieve. It is also replantation, in the real sense, from one culture to another, and there is a limit to what poetry can endure in different cultural subsoils and climates. Furthermore, English and American poetry like Hungarian are subject to their own inherent development, and mutual contact might produce phase shifts that at times can kill something as brittle as a poem, making it seem different, naive, outdated, even ridiculous. And then, there are the translators themselves, who are subject to all sorts of inherent differences, added to the necessarily limited capacity for laborious identification that translating other poets' work requires. Translations are of necessity approximations—but there is no limit to how close they can get.

Those poets who did not live to see the end of World War II are not included, and that explains the omission of József and Radnóti. Separate and concentrated efforts will have to be made to present these two poets properly in English, for attempts thus far at translation have been largely unsatisfactory. And two much older poets, Lajos Kassák and Milán Füst, have been included, for though they were important initiators of modern poetry early in the century, they both survived the war and died only in 1967. Most poems in the book were written some time in the last twenty-five years, and for any exceptions the date is given. The date is also given of those few poems for which it has some significance.

The forty-one poets in the book may roughly be grouped into four generations: the two great forebears: Kassák and Füst, who were still writing after the war; poets who are considerably younger but began publishing before or during World War II; those born before World War II who began publishing only after World War II; and a few of those who grew up under socialism. Sometimes more important than generational classification is the background they came from, rural or urban, which has a special meaning in Hungarian literature.

Among the few poets there is room to discuss here, Gyula Illyés is the oldest. The son of a farm mechanic, he was born on a huge estate in 1902. His formative experience was bridging the gap between his impoverished *puszta* childhood and the eminence to which he rose in Hungarian cultural life. Up to now I have deliberately avoided the term "committed." Neither Petőfi nor József can be called committed poets, for commitment is the result of a a specific decision based on deliberation and choice. Illyés did have such a chance to choose when, after the fall of the 1919 Republic of Councils—in whose army he served—he fled the country, settled in Paris and wrote his first poems in the environment of the French surrealists who had befriended him. He could have become an experimental modernist, an avant-garde poet, for which he was eminently qualified. But his childhood and the loyalty he felt to that world eventually made the decision for him. He returned and committed himself to Petőfi's ideals and style. He is a realist poet with a strong social and moral passion, a master of the political poem, who carries out a mission, a mandate, as it were, from the people he represents. Visiting him one summer several years ago at his house on Lake Balaton, I casually mentioned that an experimental theater company was to be formed in Budapest. He looked at me sharply, and said abruptly, "Damn, that will cost the peasant another two eggs." And then he broke into an impish smile. He still instinctively measures everything in terms of cost to the people, and rightly so, because this has always been a country where everything has to be done at the expense of something else; priorities are of supreme importance. Moreover, at the time of our conversation in the mid-sixties, memories of the forced industrialization of the fifties were still fresh in people's minds. It was primarily the peasantry, then still the largest social class, that had to bear the cost of that tremendous economic venture.

Illyés does not share Petőfi's soaring, extroverted optimism, for his elevated diction blends a kind of shy classicism with irony and subdued passion; there is even at times a scepticism infused in his philosophical poems. His work also incorporates elements of his early surrealism as well as the lessons of numerous brilliant translations and his extensive knowledge of French culture. His fine nonfiction includes, among many other subjects, a life of Petőfi and the semi-autobiographical *People of the Puszta*, in which the detailed, shocking account of peasant life on the estate where he was born perfectly blends sociology and literature. Both are considered classics and have appeared in English translation. In this anthology a long, passionate poem, "The Wonder Castle," shows the glowing but subdued rage of his pre-war poetry; a ride on the cogwheel railway up to an elegant district of Budapest is the occasion for an accurate tableau of society's parasites. One of his recent poems, "A Wreath," is a declaration of love in the form of an ode addressed to his mother tongue by one of her prodigies. Few writers are more aware of the limitations of a language spoken by only fifteen million people, of whom a third live outside the country. He sees it as almost a miracle that poems are still being written in that language today, and that there exists a public for them as well.

István Vas comes from the Jewish lower middle class of Budapest, and had to bridge the wide gap that his friend Miklós Radnóti's fate bears witness to. He began writing poems under the influence of Kassák, the socialist poet, novelist, and constructivist painter, but soon went his own way. There is a strange tension in his poems, created by the contrasting inclinations of ruthless sincerity and shyness as well as rational analysis, and an almost naive longing for belief and capacity for wonder. He combines an unyielding, exact wording with the soft, warm melody that sometimes awkwardly but captivatingly lurks in his rhythm—as if the compulsion to be accurate and objective had suppressed an innermost self that found expression finally only behind the words, in the music and finer interior gestures of the poem, like a contrapuntal melody. He almost never resorts to similes; perhaps he thinks they are inaccurate and therefore possibly obscure and even immoral. His most important contribution to Hungarian poetry is perhaps his total lack of illusion, his ability to face and name anything in a purely intellectual way even if it visibly hurts his suppressed irrational self. Whether he writes on intellectual subjects as in "Gods," on mankind's cultural heritage as in "The Etruscan Sarcophagus," observes his own aging self as in "On Approaching Fifty," or turns to poetic reportage as in "The Grand Finale," he always manages at once to be highly personal and objective, lyrical and intellectually inspiring, austere and warm, direct and insecure. The same qualities blend in his essays and criticism, and in the successive volumes of his prose autobiography, a slowly unfolding, rich panorama still in progress, showing his own development against the background of his life and the ups and downs of the fertile Budapest intellectual climate. Lately he has become something of a highly respected father figure for young writers and poets who seek his encouragement and advice, which he provides with the same sincerity he has always applied to himself.

The great exception, whose very existence refutes almost everything I have said so far about Hungarian poetry, the critics' constant headache (because he fits none of their categories), is Sándor Weöres, the magician and prankster who can spin mankind's entire culture like a striped ball on the tip of a finger, a boyish-looking, sixty-four-year-old, cheerful, smiling, puckish man with a high-pitched voice. He was a fully developed, ripe poet at the age of fourteen. If Hungarian poetry ever happens to become fashionable in a major language, Weöres will be the first to be famous. His poetry, unburdened by things Hungarian, travels well, and his only restriction seems to be that he happens to write in Hungarian. Floating high above reality in regions of total detachment, he views the universe and man and himself in it as mere manifestations in ephemeral and accidental shape of the endless process of time, nature and matter, all ordained by a mysterious will. Seen from such a vantage point, the concerns and values of individuals and civilizations shrivel: time and history merge into a single gigantic flood and appear as just another aspect or dimension of nature's existence. With his formidable representational powers, Weöres conjures up the gods and idols, charms and rhythms of ancient primitive mythologies. The sophisticated and the primitive, good and evil, joy and suffering, black and white, possible and impossible overlap and become interchangeable, as his imagination and language spell out the unspeakable, drawing on a seemingly limitless stock of ideas, forms, rhythms, rhymes, and devices, all used with great facility. There is no conceivable form and rhythm he could not write in if he chose, and probably already has used. He is capable of both total identification and extreme, almost inhuman, abstraction and indifference. He never writes directly about himself and his life; he views himself as a mere medium through which the poem, like a transcendental afflatus, is transmitted. He was among the first Hungarian poets to make use of Oriental philosophy and primitive myths.

It is as if in Weöres Hungarian poetry were making up at once for everything it had to miss throughout the centuries simply by being Hungarian. His unique quality is a magic virtuosity manipulating the poetic self, shifting the poem's focus back and forth in time and space, up and down the scale of human emotion, while narrowing and widening his poetic lens at will to include microcosm or macrocosm or both. Anyone or anything can be made abstract or concrete, sublime or intimate, infantile or prophetic, sarcastic or hymnlike, infinitely simple or infinitely complex. He writes sweeping philosophical poems and virtuoso light verse, simple songs of folksong-like perfection and ancient heroic pseudo-sagas. His charming children's poems have taught generations to enjoy rhythm, rhyme, grotesque wordplay, and to know what a poem is. With all these qualities it is not hard to imagine his deft handling of translation from among the dead and living languages of East and West. His recent longer work is the autobiographical cycle of an apocryphal Hungarian female poet of the early nineteenth century. Her intimate revelation of amorous adventures and suppressed emotional life are a masterpiece of empathy and charm, the female impersonation done with ribald humor and spirited linguistic persiflage—unfortunately totally untranslatable.

László Nagy and Ferenc Juhász, though very different in poetic character, are best treated together. Similar in career, background and age, they are naturally friends and rivals. With village backgrounds, they grew up in close contact with folk poetry, before and during World War II. They joined many thousands of peasant and working-class youths in the enthusiastic belief that with liberation society would be immediately transformed.

It is important to make this clear: the end of World War II saw the final collapse of a totally rotten, anachronistic, and reactionary social structure. Hungary's ruling classes, among the most narrow-minded in Europe (even from their own point of view), had chosen a path that inevitably made them Hitler's last allies and brought the country to the brink of total destruction. The great majority of the population lived at a subsistence level and was practically denied any chance of social or cultural improvement. Centuries-old needs and demands cried out for fulfilment—largely the same that had been written in blood on the banners of crushed wars of liberation and failed revolutions. Only knowing this background can one understand the tremendous zeal and energy of the young people who then filled the institutions of higher learning.

At the start both Nagy and Juhász wrote simple and frank folksong-type poems, and Juhász also wrote narratives, supporting change with revolutionary fervor. But when the pure optimism of those first years began freezing over at the end of the forties, both poets underwent fundamental transformations. They completely abandoned direct political poetry and gradually developed their own rich and vast poetic worlds that are completely their own and entirely different. What remains common to them both is their firm adherence to their background and their beginnings. Their entire work expresses and suggests the transformation of this country, so full of suffering and tragedy, in a way that is neither simplistic nor merely descriptive. Both have created powerful metaphors, rich in wild beauty and meaning, to tell of the rapid decline and disappearance of the

village way of life, once their own, the source both of social backwardness
and the artistic perfection of ancient folk art. They both witness and
sense this transformation in their own and their families' lives. Having been
born intellectually, if not literally, into the world of socialism, grudgingly
and sometimes uneasily, they still view it as their own, and live through
both its achievements and its crises with an insider's attitude in a different,
perhaps more sensitive, way than previous—or future—generations. Their
work takes cognizance—in quite a different manner—of the technical and
scientific revolution, with all its enormous changes and complexities,
which reached this society as part of the socialist transformation and interacts
with it.

Juhász is a myth-maker and self-tormentor; Nagy considers the poem as
magic, prophecy and incantation, a mysterious force that can preserve,
destroy and cure. The cosmic and human suffering emanating from the
Juhász poem overwhelms and excruciates; the solid and ancient power, the
soaring belief in the Nagy poem soothes and elevates. Among the Juhász
poems in this book, "The Boy Changed into a Stag Cries Out at the Gate
of Secrets," written in 1955, compresses into a single, powerful central
metaphor all that has happened, and is still happening, to this country and
to the poet and his generation in it, in a way that manages to encompass the
essential drama of history and human life. Images of modern technology and
biology stream into the ancient folk ballad, and the dialogue of the mother
and her son suggests the ruthless inevitability of change, development and
human fate. The boy transformed into a stag cannot make himself understood by his mother any more, he cannot enter the house that once was his
home, lest he destroy it with his magnificent antlers; he cannot and must
not return. The poem makes all the pain, the sublime tragedy and the
inevitability of this condition directly, emotionally, and visually accessible,
and also, in the meantime, universally valid. Juhász achieves this by the
power and pitch of his diction, and the irresistible wild strokes of his
imagination. The central metaphor, laden with manifold compressed meaning, is supported, as it were, by a linear torrent of words and images. Juhász
has ever since been fascinated by images of death, decay, and transformation,
visions of the beauty, horror, and suffering that go with birth and death, and
the pointless and unceasing processes of nature that still suggest to him hope
and order. They have come to occupy a great number of his poems—mostly
of great length—leading him into hitherto unexplored territory. On its
first publication in English—in Kenneth McRobbie's translation—in an
anthology of Hungarian writing published in 1963, W. H. Auden said in
his foreword: ". . . though no translation can ever do justice to a poem, I am

convinced that "The Boy Changed into a Stag" by Ferenc Juhász, is one of the greatest poems written in my time."

László Nagy's long poem, "The Bliss of Sunday," written in 1954, contains an altogether different, though no less complex and meaningful, vision. Juhász's poems are mostly jeremiads, huge laments; whereas basically Nagy's poems are always hymns and exultations, even when—as in this case—they also contain defiance and anger. This poem is a passionate glorification of the life of simple people, *the* people, an ode to life's everyday banalities. Simple joys and pleasures, the objects and utensils of life, insignificant actions by insignificant people acquire a brilliant inner glow and a higher meaning as the poet, with his magical powers stretching beyond words, makes us recognize that the ultimate source of all beauty, value, and power is life itself, as it manifests itself here, in the opulent images of the people's boisterous, colorful and noisy lives. This Breughelian vision, itself a metaphor of great depth and complexity, is saturated with understanding, warm humor and also an unspoken, defiant anger. The latter comes from the bitterness felt by the whole nation in the early fifties, when a deeply mistaken policy, followed in the name of the people, barred those very people from what they had achieved with so much sacrifice. László Nagy's poetic development has since then taken him much further along the same lines. His work continues to radiate the preserving, soothing, elevating power of poetry with ever more sophisticated and concentrated expression, regardless of whether his poem is a hymn, a curse, or an exultation.

All the poets discussed have had an impact throughout contemporary poetry, not so much as direct inspirations but as guides to new territories and possibilities. The confrontation between rural backgrounds and a changing modern world produced committed realism with Illyés, magic poetry with Nagy, and myth with Juhász; these continue to appear in individual variations and syntheses, some of them producing very different results, as in the works of poets like Imre Csanádi, István Kormos, József Tornai, Sándor Csoóri, Margit Szécsi, Márton Kalász. István Vas is not the only poet to come from an urban middle-class background and have access to sophisticated culture and the advantages of urban life without painful struggles and self-transformation. Likewise, Sándor Weöres is not the only poet to turn towards universal and philosophical themes while ignoring national and social ones. Among the older generation, we have recently been witness to a second blossoming of two poets, Zoltán Zelk and Anna Hajnal. Zelk was a leading representative of official political poetry in the early fifties, but with an entirely convincing metamorphosis, has grown into a fine poet of time *perdu*, the nostalgia for childhood, youth—and perseverance.

Beyond traces of the Hungarian avant-garde of the twenties, his poetry incorporates the experience of a man who received his education in the political trials and tribulations of the century. The poems are mostly about everyday subjects and radiate a bitter-sweet fondness for the small pleasures and niceties of life. They are given an added emotional charge that derives from a painful personal history of persecutions, humiliation, and blunders. Anna Hajnal's chief poetic gift of empathy and identification produces quiet painful visions of the way all that lives and strives toward self-realization is thereby condemned to die.

Of the poets of the middle generation, Ágnes Nemes Nagy has produced a new individual synthesis out of the fertile tension between strong intellectual passion and a craving for cool objectivity. Her poems avoid direct personal experience, but are rich in striking, sombre imagery. The struggle, going on and superbly described in the poems, to satisfy a desire for some sort of order and reason in a hostile and mysterious but ultimately sublime universe, is as much an intellectual process as it is a profoundly moral concern, an obligation. Her fine essays reveal one of the sharpest and most sophisticated minds thinking about the writer's craft today, with a deep sense of irony and an eye for detail, and the assured authority of the practicing artist. The taciturn and infrequent output of János Pilinszky reveals with sophisticated simplicity an angelic personality and moral sensitivity akin to that of a tortured, medieval ascetic saint. This modern Catholic metaphysical poet strips a poem down to the bare minimum, forcing almost more from the silences than from the words themselves. Precise images acquire a manifold meaning as the self in his poems confronts the ruthlessness of existence with only naked sensitivity and gentleness. Among contemporaries sometimes given to overstatement, pompousness and verbosity, his terse and lucid poems stand out in genuine contrast.

The younger generation, whose members began publishing in the second half of the fifties, knew the war as part of their childhood. This experience—as István Csukás's poem, "The Macadam Road Remembers" shows—is entirely different from what those of the same age went through in Britain. Hungary was on the losing side, of course, and saw itself torn with bitter fighting and devastation for many months, but more importantly, the end of the war was also the end of a long period of Hungarian history, and an entirely new and different era immediately began. The work of the poets who were still children in the heroic days of the new order displays feelings that are more direct and personal but also more sceptical than before. Myth and magic, nostalgia and sentiment are gone. In place of cosmic philosophical visions or gentle verse-music comes a tough, new, inquisitive voice of sober objectivity. In different forms, this considerable change is evident in the work of the three most gifted poets of the younger generation. Ottó Orbán shows it as irony and self-mockery, deflating the inclination towards rhetoric of such an intellectually high-powered poet. He is one of those still viewing the world and himself in terms of history. In "The Apparition" a brilliant ironic metaphor connects the family scene to the European past: "...the whole piss- and blood-smelling novel / which Central Europe works up / from the Verona balcony-scene." In the name of the original idea and vision of Communism, the poet Mihály Ladányi keeps contrasting revolution with the evidence of a society that is at present engaged in enjoying the fruits of revolution. With Dezső Tandori, scepticism turns against poetry and language themselves. His recent poems, mainly about journeys, walks and banal memories, give the impression of a poetic diary written in short-hand, full of abbreviations, words cut in half, suffixes standing alone, words italicized and capitalized, question marks and exclamation points in brackets. The poet is trying to reconstruct reality in its entirety, but does not be-lieve in the possibility of distinguishing any longer between the important and the unimportant. The outcome reveals the struggle to grasp reality in a supremely organized, pseudo-scientific way. Not unlike electronic music, pop art and the *nouveau roman*, it emphasizes the infinite complex-ity of reality and the power of circumstance and accident over man and his choices.

This anthology is the result of ten years' hard work—mine and others'. For fourteen years now I have been literary editor of *The New Hungarian Quarterly*, a periodical started in 1960 in painful recognition of our stifling linguistic isolation. The main part of my job has been to find the literature that can withstand translation and replantation into another culture from among works we consider important and interesting. I knew right from the start that poetry, our most important message to the world, required special treatment, but at the beginning we had to depend on unsolicited translations by non-poets that arrived in increasing numbers but were no good. Neverthe-less, we had to use some, in lieu of anything better. Whole books of this kind of dilettante work occasionally appeared abroad under the imprint of important publishers, and did more harm than good. Something had to be done, and so the *Quarterly* decided to start a program of recruiting American and British poets to translate Hungarian, mainly contemporary Hungarian, poetry. From the start we kept in mind the idea of an anthology—and this is it.

The indefatigable and brilliant Scottish poet, Edwin Morgan, for whom nothing seems untranslatable, was the first to join us. Trips to Britain and the United States, random meetings, visits by poets to Hungary, persuasion, discussion, and also the self-generating effect of the work already published, did the rest. I met the poet Daniel Hoffman by chance at a Columbia University faculty dinner in 1967, and persuaded him to do some translations—neither of us realizing at the time just how many. Kenneth McRobbie's attachment to Hungarian poetry is an old one. His version of Juhász's "The Boy Changed into a Stag," published in Canada in 1963, was among the first translations I came across that confirmed my belief in the possibility of adequate translation into English. The Hungarian P.E.N. Centre did important recruiting by inviting poet-translators to come for visits and work on translations in collaboration with experts and sometimes the poets themselves in the milieu in which the poems were written. Iván Boldizsár, the Editor of the *Quarterly*, helped formulate, fully encouraged, and gave an entirely free hand to our poetry translation program. The result is the collaboration of a considerable number of the best poets writing now in Britain, the United States, and Canada, who have produced an abundance of good translations which we have published over the years—in fact, only about two-thirds of the material could be included in the book.

And last but not least, William Jay Smith, the gifted and versatile American poet, had a lion's share in everything. In addition to his own important contributions, he has paved the way for this book on the other side of the Atlantic by assisting in the selection of translations and by offering invaluable advice.

Most of the work itself was done by airmail. I selected the poems and was one of a number of people who prepared rough translations. Only those who have seen a literal prose version of a poem which tries to follow the word order and sentence structure of the original with lots of alternative suggestions, question marks in brackets, and even footnotes can know what this is like. They strip from the poem exactly what makes it a poem—even more so when a Danube-size gap exists between the original language, Finno-Ugric Hungarian, and Indo-European English. Rough translations were always accompanied by explanations of rhyme and rhythm structures, a glossary of unfamiliar terms, background information, short characterizations of the poem, its style and diction, as well as its creator. Then the whole thing, together with the original text, was put in an envelope, and disappeared. A few weeks later, a miracle suddenly happened: another airmail envelope arrived, and out of it came something totally different from what was sent: poetry that in satisfyingly many cases had an authenticity that made it seem to have been written originally in English, a feat, of course, that could only have been accomplished when the translators are poets of the stature of those who have produced this book.

Talking to friends in Britain, and even more in America, I have often heard the observation that Hungary, a country small in size and population, seems to produce a disproportionate number of great individual talents, mainly in music and the various sciences. The culture itself, the background out of which these men grew, was, however, totally unknown to my friends, and they looked at me with some understandable suspicion when I mentioned poets with all sorts of strange-sounding names. This book will, I hope, help fill in part of the gap and show something of that culture in which poetry, that infinitely brittle and volatile wonder, has such great significance.

Miklós Vajda

Modern Hungarian Poetry

LAJOS KASSÁK
(1887–1967)

CRAFTSMEN

We are neither scientists nor abstracted priestly Chrysostoms
nor are we heroes driven with crazy clamor to battle
and left sprawling senseless on sea-floor and sunny hilltop
and all over the thunder-beaten fields, all over the world.
Now the hours bathe in bad blood under the blue firmament...
But we are far from everything. We sit deep in the dark peace-barracks:
wordless and undivided as indissoluble matter itself.
Yesterday we still cried and tomorrow, tomorrow maybe the century will
                                            admire our work.
Yes! Because quick force jets from our ugly stubby fingers,
and tomorrow we shall toast our triumphs on the new walls.
Tomorrow we shall throw life onto the ruins from asbestos and iron and
                                            titanic granite
and away with the gilded dream-swags! the moonlight! the music-halls!
We'll soon set up great skyscrapers, an Eiffel Tower will be our toy.
Basalt-based bridges. New myths from singing steel in the squares
and shrieking blazing trains thrust onto the dead tracks
to shine and run their course like meteors dizzying the sky.
New colors we mix, new cables we lay undersea,
and we seduce ripe unmarried women to make earth nurse new types
and the new poets can rejoice as they sing the face of the new times
                                            coming:
in Rome, Paris, Moscow, Berlin, London, and Budapest.

(1918)   (Edwin Morgan)

LAJOS KASSÁK

BAFFLING PICTURE

Where did I see this region before with its bleak earth
its blind stars at the back of the clouds?
It all shakes and shimmers on butterfly-wings
and yet everything is so surely in its place.
Beyond the reed a Gypsy keeps playing his hook
and while the wind cries for its wild brood
the moon is a silver raft and drifts, drifts
dead it drifts on the black mirror of the lake.

(1940) *(Edwin Morgan)*

YOUNG HORSEMAN

The horse he sits on is saddleless
and he himself is naked.
Marvellous boy
as his thighs tighten
and his sunburnt chest
heaves up and down.

My mate whom I
can't sing well enough ever.
Burning youth unconscious pride
let me praise you!

(1945) *(Edwin Morgan)*

LIKE THIS

Neither the interminable patches of land
nor crags with frozen stone-geometry
my true home is the city
with its gangrened damp-walled houses
with its chimney-stacks to scrawl the sky black

with its endlessly swarming crowds
with its knots of children yelling and squealing
with its half-bald dogs
with its amorous cats
with its rats emerging from nocturnal sewers.
And I love the feverishly clattering machines
bathed in oil
gorged on flames
workmen's wood and iron constructions
looking like fearsome fireside pets.
Idols of my early days
that made me leave my birthplace
my school my church.
I have served them and praised them.
They became
goal of my vagabondage
seed of my verses.
Day and night I drum out their rhythm
and write my books
with my brain's eternal discontent.

(Edwin Morgan)

SNAPSHOT

Everything but everything
has to be smashed
including even
what lurks in the dark walls of the womb.

The fury inside me has reached flashpoint.
Impotence hour.
Redhot.
Icecold.
My ashen faith's
in a cave of my heart
crouching.

LAJOS KASSÁK

If I open the window
of my room nothing happens.
No wind.
No din.

Beside the tram-rails
an old dog lies
dead.
His right eye
and his muzzle
gape.

(Edwin Morgan)

I AM WITH YOU

In front of you I go
you in front of me
the early sun's gold chain
jingles on my wrist.

Where are you going—I ask
you answer—how do I know.

I speed up my walk
but you speed all the more.

I in front of you
you in front of me.

But we stop in front of a gate.

I kiss you
you give me a kiss
then without a word you vanish
and spirit my life away.

(Edwin Morgan)

MILÁN FÜST
(1888–1967)

"IF MY BONES MUST BE HANDED OVER"

This wild carriage hurtles at a wild canter.
And as if it aimed at safe shelter, leaving me under a good roof-tree:
It runs upon the zones of old age, sickness, toothlessness
And then it stops among the happy natives of nonexistence.
I am not troubled, I am not crying.—Oh, run, wild horses
And gallop with me till the forest of men is like thunder,
Let me see nothing, hear nothing. Let my heart be all wild like the hunter's
When he goes out to kill without fear—he has no thought for any
heavenly Maker,
And why should he watch his Maker's face for frowning clouds, to be
judged for the flight of that bullet?...
But says: here is reality!—I am sacrificed, I am a man dying,
I was starving like the serpent,
Torpid like the crocodile
And deadly-tempered like the yellow Apocalypse horseman,
With wild spots of greed in my eyes flickering.
Why grieve over your own bad fortune?
Look at the bird in the air, when she shrieks whoever comes to help her?
Think of the giant oak when it snaps in the hurricane, shuddering,
Consider the calf that would suck at the very slaughterhouse doorstep
And everything else which goes down in unhappy last reluctance...
And then write out your hymn in this world about the screaming vultures
And how a shattered eye was preferred in beauty to a shining one.

(1933)   (Edwin Morgan)

MILÁN FÜST

OLD AGE

O my eyes where are you, you that found a face so wonderful?
And o my marvelous ears where are you, you that grew sharp as a
                    donkey's from some bitter-sweet laughter?
And where are you my teeth, ferocious teeth that drew blood not just from
                    strawberries but from richer and redder lips also?
And where are you, dreadful song in my breastbone?

And where is the pain and where is the delight I go after emptily in
                    my distraction, clutching a crooked stick as I wander?
Mad helter-skelter? Chasing the deer, the deer-footed, lying down
                    somewhere to whisper to her, not her but the moonlight...
About the enigmas no one unravels beyond their changeless name—
                    anguished happiness...
Where are you swirlings, sooty oaths? Everlasting scuttlings?
Where is the ravening mouth and where is my laughter?
God, where is my laughter, where too is the great motiveless sobbing:
When again and again—O blood-drained webs of reverberating
                    daybreaks!—
I groveled in the darkness before you!

Listen to me o youth. Remember the old Greek who lifted
Both hands like a statue and calling for his youth to return to him
Cast that Aeschylean curse on the one who gave old age to the living.
Half blind he stood on the hill, wrapped round with radiant light,
                    his hair blown back with the wind and
The tears coming down from his stammering eyes at the steep feet of
                    the Deity.
And still his voice roared, his words transfixed the mill-wheel, shook the
                    hill-side.
And even made the five-year ram lift up its head.—But the Deity
Did not look at him, said nothing to the old man, nothing.
The Deity wept. For it was like drums beating in his ears, a dull
                    drumming,
And the drumming answered by the landslide and the landslide answered
                    by the sea-surge...
The immemorial wretchedness of old age had swept up so huge before
                    him, and so sacred.

For he was standing there by his own grave and arguing with the wind
                                                        incessantly
And aching to declare his truth once again before he crumbled...

And then of course he moved on—silence at last took that territory.
But by then everything in his heart was also silent, we should not
                    forget, and another still vaster attention...

And round his head the wan half-daylight.

(1940)   *(Edwin Morgan)*

LŐRINC SZABÓ
(1900–1957)

PRISONS

Still in one body, locked and barred?
Still me? Never a new image?
Nowhere a thoroughgoing change?
How do you all endure these bars?

A different man! Why for once
can I not be my anti-self!
My soul, what is out there? It spells
other days, another order, other skies.

My brain is like the shell of a hall,
the word flies through it and returns;
and unless my fate concurs
even dying's impossible.

I am an engineer who sits
in the prison of his own works
fumbling blindly, and in the dark
some day will throw a fatal switch.

(1930)   (Edwin Morgan)

THE DREAMS OF THE ONE

Since you are this way and they are that
and his interests are different
and truth's a sort of nervous fact
or verbal front
and since nothing out there pleases me
and since the crowd still has supremacy
and of the framing of rules I am utterly
innocent:
it is high time now
that I escaped your net.

What should I go on waiting for any longer,
timidly scanning days to come?
Time hurries past, and whatever lives
is true to itself alone.
Either I am sick, or you are; and
am I not to recognize the weapons in the hand
of love or hate that comes to stand
before my face?
If I am forever only to understand,
where is my own place?

No! no! no! How can I bear to be
no more than a thread in a mad web:
to understand and honor the guard
and share his pain, his pain!
All who could, have long got out of the snares,
they go freely through and about the wires.
I and the world, there go the two of us,
captive in the cage,
the world with the limelight on itself,
like me on my own stage.

We're escaping, my soul, we've sprung the lock,
the mind has leapt away
but is careful to paint itself
with the bars of appearance.
Inside it is one that outside's a thousand fragments!

Who knows where the man ever went
that saw the fish, and still the net
intact?
Forbidden? By someone else! Sin? To them,
if caught in the act!

Within us, inside, no divisions or frontiers,
nothing is forbidden;
we are only what we are, each one a solitude,
not bad, not good.
Hide in the depths of yourself! For there,
the great and free dream, you'd swear,
lies abandoned still, as where
our mother the unbounded
sea appears like a memory
in the sharp taste of our tears and blood.

Back into the sea, into ourselves! Only
there we can be free!
We needn't look out yonder to see
anything coming to us from the Many.
If ever we are hucksters with the crowd,
truth crumbles down to powder;
only the One is our home ground,
never undone:
let us dream, if we still can,
the dreams of the One!

(1931)   (Edwin Morgan)

ALL FOR NOTHING

It is terrible, I admit that,
            but it is true.
To love's to have your own heart
kill or nearly kill you.
You will never see me pause
for today's people, today's laws;
within, the man is master who

was prisoner out there,
and I take gladness only through
the law I own and cannot share.

You are not mine till you are yours:
            in love?—not yet.
If it's still me-for-you you choose
you hang weights upon my neck.
Business, though sacred, is business: the thing
I need now is: All for Nothing!
Anything else is two selves running
            a hidden fight;
I want more: you, becoming
part and parcel of my fate.

I am tired, I am sick, I am suspicious
            of one and all;
my faith has given up its patience
though I perhaps desire you still.
If you would allay my fears,
all my disgusts, this is for your ears:
show me how the last humility
            and sacrifice
are for joy, show me your ability
to contradict a world I despise.

For until you need one minute
            with yourself alone,
till you dare think you could win it,
till you regret the life you've known,
till you stop being an object,
lying there dead and abject:
till then you are no better, no more
            than all the rest,
till then a stranger at my door,
till then irrelevant at best.

Let the law save those who are
            good as their fellow-men;

beyond the law, like an animal,
be like that, I'll love you then.
Like a lamp that's turned off, you
mustn't be if I don't need you to;
don't complain, don't even see
            a prison that's invisible;
and I in my mind will guarantee
that you forgive my ruthless rule.

(1931)   *(Edwin Morgan)*

From CRICKET MUSIC

Farewell

What happened? My dear, don't cry. The thing
I felt was: moulting. There's been a dissolving
of the threads in my fate, and now I am spun
by a hundred spaces and times (in the old days one),
destroying-and-building. Turtle-doves coo up there,
have sung four days above me; but I'd despair
of telling you fearful wars have raged here too.
Even to myself it is hard to believe this is true,
although my senses branch out each minute. Your pain
is new, looks through me, asks where I remain.
In a million places every inch of me!
What is it then? Love, electricity?
I'm in the dark still. Maybe gold-gas-atom,
maybe heat-ray-nucleus. Light on Saturn,
space-living light. It's strange. But that
the Universe is only a Poet's Brain I grant
seems true.—Are you going? I feel night's touch.
And since at one time I loved you very much,

. . .on the outlook tower. . .

I will take you now again to Balaton,
to the tower above the lake. Kisses float on

your face from the wind: from me! Huge, full,
the moon sails over rough Badacsony hill,
its bright watery bridge almost at our feet.
Can you hear the chirping of this holy night?
The soul swings open: it is vigilant,
but still the nerves of space envelop it
and between the infinities above and below
crickets strike up a fortissimo:
zither-twangs of *u* and sparks of *i*,
rich and thick, *u-ru-kru* and *kri-kri*,
ringing out loudly and ringing round
like rings of foam that encircle an island,
richer and richer, as they did last year and before
and always will: weave it into your soul,
weave yourself into its warp and weft and
you will become a sigh, and understand,

       . . . in the big blue meadow . . .

and you are already that, you are all rustling,
earth and sky, fire-conjuring, dream-dancing,
and you close your eyes for the wind's kiss once more
and inner and outer diffuse into each other
and sounds resound and the grass swims and hums
and as your heart takes that measure and succumbs
the Self leaves you like something exploded off
on the light-wide skin of a sphere and runs rough
up through the sky expanding, and only then,
when it has encapsulated the world of men,
only when it makes the earth its kernel, can
you begin to see yourself again, and
see a vanished particle, yourself the frame
of everything and everything the same
as your own inwardness . . . : comfort comes sudden,
heavenly, as your earth-mind goes unconscious
and in the big blue spaces of the meadow
the stars start up their cosmic cricket-concert.

  (1947)   *(Edwin Morgan)*

GYULA ILLYÉS
(1902–   )

HOW SOON...

How soon you take quite naturally
the leaves on all
the trees: how soon you take it naturally
that leaves fall;
how easily you take summer
and winter to be final;
how easily you would take
life to be eternal.

(1923–37)   *(William Jay Smith)*

THE WONDER CASTLE

I'd arrived the previous night from the country.
Next morning, my eyes were casting about anxiously
for (like an old coat
the body feels easy in) the run-down countryside
where I'd lately been on a four-week visit,
so familiar and roomy, floating in sunshine,
where I feel at home, where in the rag-fluttering dust
man and beast lick parched lips;
but enough said
on that subject
—why go on about my home in the country?

In a word, I'd only been back in Budapest
a day, still feeling a trifle
awkward like one just
come up to town on his first trip
—a little awed, not yet used
to the everywhere apparent more-of-everything.
I wore it uneasily like a newly starched shirt
next to the skin, when
I had to go out visiting
—or, let's say, up the Rácz Hill on an excursion.

Then home and its memories
would buzz in my ears, get in my eyes,
so that I felt I was climbing
up the Hill straight from the puszta's
evening fields, where many times
I'd written out day-laborers' schedules.

I'll tell you why I thought that way,
looking at the ticket in my hand
in my seat on the Cog-wheel Railway:
for should a peasant have a mind
to take the self-same ride,
he'd dig for his ticket an entire working day.
At home seventy fillers is a whole day's pay.

There we were, some hundred or more
in comfort, legs crossed, for the full
price of a vineyard worker's labor
gliding up the back of the Hill.

A villa, a flower garden
floated past; on a sand-strewn
flat roof two young women taking sun;
further off in the shade of a walnut
someone dealt cards on a green table;
somewhere a radio was humming.
The higher we got
the cooler the air, the less dust;
faces were a carefully even tan.

It was as if, from the hell of the plain below us,
we were borne up from circle to circle
into some present-day Turkish heaven.
Or, with the old look-out tower
it was like a magic castle,
the terrifying or happy
seat of some Asiatic deity
found only in Hungarian and Vogul folk-tale,
called Castle Spinning on a Duck's Leg: Wonder Castle.

Over a hedge flew tennis balls
and as though in competition after
them, like invisible flights of birds,
balls of happy girlish laughter,
laughter that rose the higher.

—And this no weekend, but a working day.
The afternoon was half-way to summer sunset
in a blue sky with faint silver streaked,
heat glowed only in the green light
of the tree-tops' dying lamp, smokily.
It was a weekday, but suffused with peace
and brimming with luminous grace
such as no religion ever gave in a week of Sundays.
Across lamplit leaves
to faint music, where trees afforded shelter,
glimmering like a dream
a knot of girls circled, pirouetted, weaving
the spell of an unattainable, tender future
over the hearts of rapacious nomads,
like Dul's daughters once in Meotian marshes.

Paper lanterns flashed on in a plane-tree
setting another scene—a gent in pyjamas,
somewhat paunchy, leaning back with cigar
in the wine-tinged light—a figure
reclining in the ease of Property
like some cartoon for the Communist Party.

By then the whole Hill
sparkled with lights, and still
it rose every minute higher.
I alone recalled the landscape's flat table
far below, perhaps now underground even, the people,
the country
which just might have heard some story
about it, yet
like a blind plodding horse still drives the mill
—this modish sleek curvature,
this real live Eden of a Hill
where electricity flames more lavishly,
for instance, than in all of Tolna County.

I looked about me. A hill further
off lit up, and then another
like brother beacons.
Soon, will o' the wisp-like hundreds beckon
shrieking, dancing; they all spun
around upon swamps of blindest misery
in each of the universe's regions.

Very beautiful, I thought; but I am too tired
to join the choir
providing this glittering merry-go-round's music.

The outdoor restaurant's
seventy or more tables of idly chattering
diners will consume at one sitting
as much as, even at a rough count
—such were my thoughts, grinding underfoot
the stubbornly unyielding material, as in my poetry
I'd always grappled with raw reality
in the hope that someday it would fuse and shine.
Supper here would cost a week's wages
I reckoned, expertly; almost enthusiastically
I pictured to myself the pumps,
delicate piping, capillaries
sucking all this up, for there's no surplus,
well-kneaded, boiled,

mashed, several times cooled,
over from those
who swallow their spittle at home with us.

Outside the garden—where daily
a crunched bridge and hospital
melt on the tongues of this charmingly
cavorting throng, not to mention thirty thousand
stillborn infants—
a parade was on: the milling casual
lookers-on applauded, laughed.

In the moon-shading bushes
were silent couples making love on benches,
dreamily (spooningly, I'm inclined to call it)
in pastry-shops others chatted,
and whatever cares they had
were triple-distilled,
delicate as angels' wings.

Oh poet! Be on the look-out
for wonder, for the unusual
that delights the eye and heart
just because someone points a finger at it:
a swineherd among this happy lot, for example,
a reaper, a shepherd
nonchalantly sipping iced pineapple
in a reclining chair, or leisurely
picking broken straw from between his toes
—some new color, some new face amid this uniformity
that for a millennium has bored us, heaven knows!
A potter, a miner, a baker
who, I'm sure, would like to see just what
his creations are up to out in the world, like a mother
wonders about her children who are far from her
—but I saw not one of those I sought.

The monotonous crowd reclined, stretched, ambled;
like moon-blazed foreheads in a herd of horses
here and there went revered personages
well-known to all,
as among us the count, the priest and judge.

And others hard at their heels:
with such dignified mien newspaper hacks,
squeamish mass-circulation tycoons
who pay hard-working loyal goons
to do their blackmail behind their backs.

With a girl on each arm, an employment
agency boss erect, with smiling face
strutted with a paper in his pocket
certifying he was a mental case.

There, with face pensive and woebegone
lifted towards the moon
(as if to take a swig from it)
having polished off a large chicken,
sat the celebrated playwright;
you'd swear that in no time at all
he might say something original.

Under a sunshade (much like a market woman's)
a very proper gentleman, noted for this,
was offering his wife for sale
—discreetly covered with a veil—
we nibbled at her apricot smile
as if we'd been offered a bowl of fruit.
However, no one fancied the deal.
And... why go on? The faces were so alike,
as I've said, that being unable to tell them apart
is quite disturbing for a lover of art.

As they talked, marriageable maidens
fluttered the whitest of hands
whose long nails seemed to indicate
that they had never cleaned a grate.

So I took a good look
at God's chosen ones, these fairy folk
in suits and shirts of silk
that permitted glimpses of hairy arms and chests,
and meekly
—with heart so long barred from feeling passionately,
only humbly, and with a servant's wisdom—
for my spirit was above
envy or incitement;
mine was a reputation for being peaceable, quiet
and so patient that I blush for it

(I do not judge, I merely watch, the world)

not to mention being rich,
or regarded as such
with regular meals and a bed to sleep in.

Well—like a scout surveying new territory
lately emerged from archetypal slime,
during that glistening evening
I was thinking about just this one thing
as I looked about me, quietly:

Once the marsh rises
—were it ever to rise—to topple
the myriad towers and huge axle
of this glittering miracle
all coming to pass as in the old tale,
that "grass grow not, nor stone remain on stone"

I would even then
stand aside, still play the quiet man,
so that when all came tumbling down
order might be kept,
and calmly, impartially, I should
be able to give account
of how life was before the flood
in this pre-historic period.

(1937)   (Kenneth McRobbie)

COMPLAINT ON SOLIPSISM

Between myself and the apple tree
there stood my desire.
It was not the apple tree I saw—
But only my desire.
It was not the apple that I ate;
What I wished with all my soul—
An sich—has never been mine.

It is myself that I get back
from being's slot machine.
Wherever it is that my steps lead—
bits of my past come in the way
and not my future: That's why I'm poor
in an ever-rich today.

If only I had, in place of my head,
my liver instead—
. . . .
(1938–39)   *(William Jay Smith)*

IT IS FIVE YEARS NOW

It is five years now that you've been dead,
but from the grave you find your way—
nothing has changed—to the old café
where I waited for you, where last you waited
in the smoke-thatched gloom, in a corner where
you shivered as in some field lean-to;
the rain came down: we fought, we two;
and you were mad, but I didn't know then.

You're less than mad now; nothing has remained:
on the floor where time that danced so bright
has flown away, I sit mute, alone.

Absurd it is since you have gone:
the whole world seems to have gone mad—
and you, being mad, have won the fight.

(1942)   (William Jay Smith)

AT THE TURNING POINT OF LIFE

Night envelops us: clouds rest, darkness drizzles—
outside, the branches are bare and glittering wet;
as the wind sweeps by, they let fall their tears—
youth is passing.

Before my window two swallows dive, dip down,
almost hand in hand like fish at the bottom of the sea.
One is love, I thought, and the other, secret hope.
All that accompanied me flees, quietly retreating to a truer homeland.

And now in her loose robes, with large, disproportionate
limbs, monster Melancholy sits down beside me,
drawing my head to her moist breast,
and mocks me: "Weep if you dare, weep, unhappy one...

Mourn if you have anything to mourn for: Examine your life:
Around you autumn rain pours down and mist covers the wooded hills;
frothy, filthy water rushes toward you down the sloping road
where once with secret intent you led your beloved."

Like prayer beads drops run down the windowpane.
O you nimble minutes, seasons, centuries:—Autumn twilight covers the
                                                                paper
over which I lean as to a mirror, twilight that soon will cover my young
                                                                face.
Through trickling drops I watch the brown trees swing, reaching into the
                                                                mist.

(William Jay Smith)

GRASS SNAKE AND FISH

Among pebbles, at the pond's edge,
  in limpid shallows whose water
flows as transparent as the atmosphere,
  suddenly visible

in that world made for other lungs,
  living purity, where
the stone wavers in the drift
  of the reflection, a branch in air;

into that shut Eden, slides the snake,
  guided by the oldest law;
a fish palpitates hanging from its fangs
  howling what no one can translate.

(Charles Tomlinson)

CONSOLATION

Your sorrow overflowed you; I let the stream
running across the pebbles
bathe my hands; and that
was how I heard you.

Clear, the water glided
between my fingers, time
without color fled
almost alive, between my fingers.

I listened to time
caressing my palms and
murmuring out its flight:
it was your flowing sorrow I handled.

I was sad... and yet
already beneath the bruising
of spent time, my hands
foretold appeasement.

(Charles Tomlinson)

ABOARD THE SANTA MARIA

A dirty fog is swirling in the wake
Of a lonely house perched out above the lake.

The trunk of a tall fir tree stands like a mast
but even its very tip in the fog is lost.

Buttressed forth, a hanging garden there,
the terrace like a ship divides the air.

A table of stone, a rickety chicken coop
emerge through holes within the shifting fog;

and farther on, a friend withdrawing from the road,
a *ritirato* made of pre-Columbian wood.

And now when the pounding waves reach up to me,
I feel I am centuries ago at sea.

On some Santa Maria I sail off through the air,
but I, its master, am wondering to where.

Lurching up and down the deck I go,
drugged by medicine, not alcohol.

We speed ahead: tatters of fog flutter and play
in the trees, signals that time is speeding away.

And now and then a gull sweeps through the fog—
but black it is; and crows a pitiful caw.

(William Jay Smith)

LOGBOOK OF A LOST CARAVAN

Only the compass, keeping hope alive,
            stuttered on, uttering its paralyzed
directions; with something somewhere beyond
            to which to respond.

            And for another long day
we struggled ahead through desert sand.

Then to the edge of stone cliffs
            covered with hieroglyphs.

Line after line, incoherent, they read—
            wrinkles on some mad forehead.

            An ancient age
struggled there in desperate tones—

With nothing more to say—

            And only the wind moans.

Sand in our eyes. Between sweating fingers, and
            ground between teeth, sand.

We slaughtered the camel who knew the way...
            had our final meal today.

                              (William Jay Smith)

RULER

I wanted without delay to give order to the world, so I put first my boxes
in order, then my votive pictures, then my stamps. The latter I considered
most effective in carrying my will even to the most insignificant islands
in the farthest parts of the world. What purpose, what peace of mind,
what plans—at the end of each day! What good will!

Nor was ruthlessness alien to me. Whose eyes blink less at the sight of death and torture than a tyrant's? A child's.

And what pleasure in granting pardon!

At Simontornya, on the far bank of the Sió, in the Dzindzsa quarter, before the open oven door in a peasant kitchen, with an album of my own making opened in my lap, when spring had already released its clouds on a still cold sky. On the side of Mózsé Hill—the name of everything there was unique—yes, then it was. . .

Today, exiled—dethroned, and even ushered out of my own mausoleum—I weep for the magic of lost power.

(*William Jay Smith*)

BRAZILIAN RAIN FOREST

In Old Buda, a street almost as wide as a square
coming down from Újlaki Church. The one-storey
houses here are even lower than usual. The pavement
once swelled to the level of the windows, and remained
there as in some frozen flood. From such a house,
a tavern still privately owned, a tall slender young
woman who is well-dressed comes out into the Friday
twilight. Her eyes are glazed; she is dead drunk.
She sways gracefully. The basalt cobble-stones of the
broad street mock her by pretending to be the stepping
stones across a mountain stream, and that's why she
may only step on every second one. Since the stones are
wet, the scene is made all the more probable. It is raining,
fully and evenly, as in the tropics, although it is
November. The pouring rain is broken into threads
by the light of the street lamps. The woman's dishevelled
hair drips also into so many threads. She is soaked
to the skin.

She is soaked to the skin, but does not feel a thing.
Otherwise she would not push away the threads of rain
as if she were parting the reeds of a marsh or thrusting
aside the bead curtain of some southern barber shop.
But after this bead curtain comes another and then
another, ten, twenty, a hundred, thousand upon
wondrous thousand.
    All this, of course, is illusion. The situation and reality:
the woman walks amid the lianas, the hanging tendrils
of a Brazilian rain forest, and above her are trees teeming
with bright-colored parakeets, snarling monkeys,
serpents, and other creatures that do not even exist
in South America, but have come here only for this
occasion. At such a time who would not think of coming
to her aid? As Chateaubriand says, this is how the most
exciting adventures with native women really begin.
Yes, but there is something rarely taken into
account—the distances in a rain forest! Between the
two of us, my sailor's eye tells me, a thousand
miles at least.

(William Jay Smith)

TILTING SAIL

The tilting sail careens;
    scything the foam,
the tall mast creaks and leans—
    the boat plows on.

Look—when do mast and sail
    fly forward most
triumphantly? When tilted
    lowest.

(William Jay Smith)

A RECORD

It was easy then to catch
the flow of a stream: it murmured
at once through the pulsing
rhythms of my poems—
the mountain, the meadow—whatever
our words touched took human form.

But then came the bleak
country, the Alps of slag,
the barren soul of mining
towns, lunar gray.
The waste from tanneries,
hell-born, black as the Styx.
Red-brick barracks
through which again and again—
like the striking of obstinate, mad
clocks—crackled firing squads.

And then this:
purple smoke and ash
floating in place of sky
over a land of chimneys
thicker than vineyard poles.

And we recorded this:
for here our forces passed,
children and dogs at our heels,
bent more and more by the weight
of our useless belongings.

(William Jay Smith)

WHILE THE RECORD PLAYS

They heated hatchet blades over gas fires in roadside workshops and hammered them into cleavers.

They brought wooden blocks on trucks and carried them across these new provinces grimly, quickly, and steadily: almost according to ritual.

Because at any time—at noon or midnight—they would arrive at one of these impure settlements,

where women did not cook nor make beds as theirs did, where men did not greet one another as they did, where children and the whole damned company did not pronounce words as they did, and where the girls kept apart from them.

They would select from these insolent and intolerable people twelve men, preferably young ones, to take to the marketplace,

and there—because of *blah-blah-blah* and moreover *quack-quack-quack* and likewise *quack-blah-quack*—would beat and behead them,

of historical necessity—because of *twaddle-twiddle* and *twiddle-diddle*,
and expertly, for their occupations would be different one from the other,

agronomist and butcher, bookbinder and engineer, waiter and doctor, several seminarists, cadets from military academies, a considerable number of students,

those familiar with Carnot, Beethoven and even Einstein, displaying their finest talents,

because, after all, nevertheless, *blah-blah-blah* and *twiddle-dee-dee*,

while through loudspeakers records played—music and an occasional gruff order, and they, the zealous ones, wiped their foreheads and turned aside every now and then to urinate since excitement affects the kidneys;

then having washed the blocks and hauled down the large tricolor which on
   such occasions always waved above their heads,

they too would march on into the broad future,

past the heads, carefully placed in a circle,

then out of the settlement where now also

and forever and ever,

reason, comfort, and hope would be no—

wrr-wrr-wrr—that is to say—we-ep, wa-rp, the sound (by now the only one

without music or words) that the needle makes as the record grinds on.

(William Jay Smith)

THE APPROACHING SILENCE

Lightly clad, on tiptoe, the little rain has just run into the garden
through the gate. Is the sunlight here? The rain stops, listens,
gazing at itself in the glass balls, shifts its weight; draws away.
But it is still here; now and then its drops continue to fall.

Whom is it looking for? The plants have now all resumed
their allegiance to the sun; the wettest enjoy the light with all
the more brilliance. Yet there is one fewer bird, one fewer, now
singing. That one has got wind of things; he is sharp. Or can it be
mere politeness?

I am old, and feel even older, sensing how light is the
passing of the rain. Another bird stops. I sense even this slight
encore of silence. A silence that feels close even though already part
of all that is boundless. But it creates a stage for what light
graces around one who darkens and grows heavy.

(William Jay Smith)

EARLY DARKNESS

Before autumn's swift clouds the moon bounds to and fro,
wishing to see itself reflected in the cool well water before
departing—torn away. It holds out like an obstinate woman,
but not for long. The corn shucks rattle. After the mad chase,
the last hare sits on its haunches, pricks up its ears, and
gradually stiffens into sculpture as catastrophe approaches.

(William Jay Smith)

WORK

They stuck pigs in the throat. Might I not have done
it myself? They tossed chickens with their heads cut
off out into the courtyard. With a child's thirst for
knowledge, I watched their final spasms with a heart
hardly touched. My first really shattering experience came
when I watched the hooping of a cartwheel.
From the huge coal fire, with pincers at least a yard
long, the apprentices grabbed the iron hoop, which
by then was red hot up and down. They ran with it to
the fresh-smelling oak wheel that had been fixed in place
in the front of the blacksmith's shop. The flesh-colored
wooden wheel was my grandfather's work; the iron
hoop, which gave off a shower of sparks in its fiery agony,
was my father's. One of the apprentices held the sledge
hammer, the other the buckets. Places, everyone.
As on shipboard. As at an execution. The hoop, which
in its white-hot state had just expanded to the size
of the wheel, was quickly placed on it; and they began
to pry it out with their tongs. My father swung the
hammer with lightning speed, giving orders all the while.
The wood caught fire; they poured a bucket of water
on it. The wheel sent up steam and smoke so thick
you couldn't see it. But still the hammer pounded on,
and still came the "Press hard"! uttered breathlessly
from the corner of the mouth. The fire blazed up again.

Water flung again as on a tortured man who has sunk
into a coma. Then the last flourishing bush of steam
evaporated while the apprentices poured a thin trickle
from a can on the cooling iron which, in congealing,
gripped lovingly its life-long companion to be.
The men wiped the sweat from their brows, spat,
shook their heads, satisfied. Nothing—not the slightest
flicker of a movement—could have been executed
differently.

(William Jay Smith)

THE MAKER

1
Like a voyeur
I watched their coming together
among the springs,
the watchmaker's gaze
of pointed steel, and
his tweezers—
the way they were testing one another!

It was all explained to me in advance,
anxiously I watched
as under the cover of a blue flame
in the test-tube, two thoughts
of the chemist were gladly becoming
better acquainted.

A stirring among the golden springs,
a tentative whirr of a new creature
trying its wings,
teetering on the twigs
of the nest's rim.

More ardent
than two lithe bodies dancing
together, embracing,
those two
thoughts so different from each other
frolicked and turned
struggling
for life, for death,

finding their fulfilment
in a third.

2
As a babe in the hands of a midwife
begins to live, a success,
tiny, naked,
powerful,
it kicked among the wheels and springs,
a deed that has been given
life and body almost
like our own.
It came with me,
came as my perpetual
dog, my master
on my leash,
myself on leash.

3
With eyes more screwed-up than an ant's,
on the nib of my pen
it turns, spying
on my work—
it lurks, waiting to find
a gap,
a split-second only, to rush
through space
exchanging its message
for another.

4
Glistening,
the file slid back and forth;
shrieking as though
by its own light,
the copper rod, thick
as a finger in the vise;
jammed,
jumped, it too
wanted to do something
by itself.

Then from that oily palm
like a tiny fish
rushing with purpose from the instant of its birth,
it wanted to leap
among companions,
into its element,

knowing its place from the start.

5
What a fate. We have no
director to guide us, no
thread to follow, only
this work in our hand,

this quivering little compass.

This is the oldest
god, a dog sniffing
the long trail to where we are

from the time when islands
floated and the mountains rose
ever so slowly,
as though to show there is direction:
an order needs something
more than itself,

needs companions.

6

What humiliation!
What a spur to pride,
that the premiere bit of good counsel
for our far-famed human
mind—to tell the truth its
most brilliant argument—was
the original gift of
the exchanges between
the two thumbs and the index
fingers . . .

7

Nothing's sweeter than the ecstasy
of such revenge!
No god, no leader
protects me,
only that ardor,
frailer than an inchworm
at my fingertip
—what does it accomplish?—
to set
something right.

This purpose
is no longer mine alone,
this challenge
risen from the dust, that says
go on, and

the stars will change places!

—By our will.

8

To grasp the first clue
of a puzzle, the neck of a net,
the purpose of my being alive here on earth,

of my servitude,
from what work whispers to me,
and then the network of the planets,

whatever is confused, obscure
even in the tissue of the light,
or in my mind,
—that is servitude; perdition;
dying.

To stand face to face, to grapple
head on like a pair of wrestlers
locked in the fight to the death, yes,
to fight it out with
death, with
fear,
although smeared with mud, to carry to safety
something pure.

The order, the order that suits me.

9
What poverty is this,
what wealth,
never to have known a handshake
more stirring to the heart,
more stimulating than the touch
of the Lord
—it was no longer my hand guiding
hammer and wedge
but His on mine.

10
Well, I create too.
I can make things.
Since then, the Rival hasn't shown
his spectral face.

Jealous, eh? Put to shame?

That time I had to spread the sheaf of reeds
between four stakes to make a roof,
the heavens began to fall,
tumbling, thundering, uncontrollable—

fell in hail on the front garden.

O.K., that one died.

But not its longing
to be eternal, nor
its memory.

11

All the mines, blast furnaces, atomic piles
of Europe, America, all the continents
and planets yet to be reached
in the future
cannot squeeze
into one fist as much power, as much knowledge
as you,
the first

to swing an axe-handle,
sky-crushing.

12

How sad it is to be an orphan,
to have no step-father
but the one I raise.

It is pitiable to be alone,
the one whom nobody can love
but she whom I can teach
how to love.

Facing nothingness,
hell simmering with its secrets?
The labyrinth of our fears.

Taking in hand, at last, slowly,
assiduously, moving well,
our face, too,
the divine.
The one which faces itself.

In our children
reunited.

13
With these mortal eyes
to learn what I am here to do,
the job that waits for me to do it,
for which somewhere,
a peasant, hoeing, sends me this
glass of wine,
a worker touching down his soldering-iron
sent light
into my room,
to find with mortal eyes
the eternal task:
Make the future speak!
—already it is quarreling with death,

skillfully, intelligent,
bustling, with
authority.

To do the job
well, to our liking
—yes, like good
love-making.

Almost stroking its face
in gratitude.

To leave it there,
to look back a few times
on the one who lies there satisfied;
she keeps my riches,
conceiving my future,
the meaning, maybe forever, of all
I was here for,

mortal, imperishable.

                                        (Daniel Hoffman)

A WREATH

You can no longer
soar. And yet you blaze,
wind-slit Hungarian tongue, sending
your snakelike flames along the ground, hissing
at times with pain,
more often with the helpless rage of the humiliated,
your guardian angels forsaking you.

Again in grass,
in weeds, in slime.
As through all those centuries, among
the stooped peasants. Among
the tight-lipped old, keeping their counsel. Among
girls trembling under coned reeds as
the Tartar hordes swept past. Among
children lashed together
while mute lips shaped their words,
for the Turks, if they heard a sound,
would bring whips down in their faces.
Now you show forth
truly—and to me as well—your use,
your pedigree, your coat-of-arms, the stone-biting
strength in your veins.

Language of furtive smiles,
of bright tears shared in secret, language
of loyalty, lingo
of never-surrendered faith, password of hope, language
of freedom, briefly-snatched freedom, behind-the-prison-guard's-
                                                back-freedom,
language of master-mocked schoolboy, sergeant-abused rookie,
dressed-down plaintiff, of little old ladies boring clerks,
language of porters, odd-job hired men, being a language
of the no-good-for-the-factory, no-good-for-test-passing proletariate,
language of the veteran stammering before his
young boss; testimony—
rising from depths even greater
than Luther's—of the suspect
beaten up on arrival at the station;
language of the Kassa black marketeer, the Bucharest servant girl,
the Beirut whore, all calling
for mother, behold your son, spittle
on his rage-reddened face,
master of many tongues,
held worthy of attention by other nations
for what, as a loyal European,
he has to say:
he cannot mount any festive platform,
cannot accept any wreath,
however glorious, which he would not, stepping quickly down,
carry over to lay at your feet, and with his smile draw forth,
on your agonizing lips,
your smile, my beloved, ever-nurturing mother.

                                        (William Jay Smith)

ZOLTÁN ZELK
(1906–)

AND AND

When I came into the room I saw
my murderer
chatting in a shell-shaped chair
sneaking dumbstruck through the walls
drenched in electric light—
How I pitied him! Does he remember,
he who killed? He reaches out his hand,
I take it and sit down beside him and
 how've you been Oh still alive and kicking
 it's twenty years well time does pass
 but we're still full of piss and vinegar
 in spite of troubles when it rains it pours
 in spite of dentures and a coronary and
and and
talking
and the needle scrapes the record
and coffee and sandwiches and drinks
and cigarettes and a few cigars
and sofa and bunk-bed and ticking full of straw
and blizzards and blighted appletrees
and forest fires and rivers flooding
and it's after midnight and the words drop off
and the guests put down their drinks
propping up the wall of night
that kept the world from crashing on them.

        (Daniel Hoffman)

ZOLTÁN ZELK
OCTOBER

With crumpled leaves flung in his face
and bloodshot eyes
the first autumn morning turned into our street.

(Daniel Hoffman)

MAN FALLING

Autumn sky between the leaf and bough
The void between the moments then and now
In vain from twig to twig you clutch and thrash
While heaven's branches crack, snap off, and crash.

(Daniel Hoffman)

CRY

The cry reverberates across the water,
smashes the fragile window of the sunset,
glass slivers screech—
The moon rises in the frogs' bewildered eyes.
A wordless terror in the landscape howls
from sleepless throats of baying dogs,
                              then
wide-eyed, you'd raise your head, and listen
to the annoyed murmur of the silence.

(Daniel Hoffman)

MOMENT

As at the railing of a bridge
leaning on September's afternoon,
a glimmer of the cleavage between minutes,
the moment brims with fullness,
the self-sufficient triumph of the trees—

I would prolong it
though all I have is words.

(Daniel Hoffman)

ALONE

Desert afternoon.
Impenetrable part of the day.
And the sunset coolness? And the night?
To whom does that disheveled servant,
your widowed shadow, open the door?

—The tatterdemalion horde
of your memories.

(Daniel Hoffman)

MORE POWERFUL THAN THE SEA

In the courtyard where young Lajcsi, limping,
pulled the paper box by its string,
through iron gates opening on two streets
how many seas went rolling!

Shores, skies of how many countries have caved in
but these church walls still stand,
and no sea will ever wash
children's shadows from the walls—during
our lives we do live, but childhood
is indeed more immortal than God!

                                        (*Barbara Howes*)

PETRIFIED MINUTE

In the big room my father stands
in shirt-sleeves, before the wall-
mirror: slipped from his hand,
a stiff collar lies white on the
russet floor—
                    sixty years aren't time
enough for me to bend down for it.

                                        (*Barbara Howes*)

THE WAY

The way she told me about her home in Jászberény,
about the kitchen, which was also a shoemaker's shop,
the way she spoke of her father who hammered away
humming even when he had wooden nails in his mouth,
the way she came to Pest, orphaned, unmarried,
the way she once travelled to Paris,
the way she climbed on a streetcar in the morning,
the way she bought fresh peas in the market,
the way she straightened her dress
in the foyer of the theater,
the way she woke beside me in bed,
the way she stepped out, beautiful, from the bath,
the way she stared after me through the window

through fog for a thousand eight hundred miles,
the way she watched my anguished feet
while I dragged myself along the minefield,
the way she covered my face with her hair
so they could not see me, lifting me to her breast
she ran with me through the burning night
above burning walls, burning streets,
the way, when she had to, she became a flame among flames,
became a blade of grass, became shade,
the way a closed mouth, a susurrus,
the way Schubert's Ave Maria
when she sang it to me,
the way she, squeezed within four boards,
still managed to reach me through the wall of my cell,
the way she entered my room this morning,
with our dog at heel, who's been dead for twenty years,

because she knows where I walk, and where I live.

(Barbara Howes)

SALT AND MEMORY

A tribute to Marc Chagall

When you arrive in our town
I would like to sit on the roof
and play the violin, play the violin,
play—it is good that you live
sweet old man sweet sweet
sweet even as was my father
your sixty-six thousand colors glitter
on the walls of my sixty-six years
bearded sky bearded dawn
bearded smoke of my childhood
your candles burn in my window on
hills that grew from bones of the dead
bundle-carrying shadows carry

salt and memories in their headband
the calf steps out of the cow's belly
so it can lick your hand.

                                          (Barbara Howes)

ECHO

When it is only the echo,
when nothing else but echo,
when only silence-beyond-stars,
in the throat of this piercing silence an echo—

when in four season solitude
in leafless desert solitude
you hear rattle of ancient rain
and footsteps of old
on mired cobblestones of slanting years—

when the flies' autumn dance
of death on the old window
clatters, echoes above you so
there's no sound your ear can take in—

you can only hear what was once said,
you are fenced in by what collapsed;
wanderer of chasms, ramps,
abysses, the black Milky Way,
you sit, ears primed with echoes,
behind the barbed-wire of your memories.

                                          (Barbara Howes)

ANNA HAJNAL
(1907-   )

SONG OF THE PLAIN

You have many great sons and daughters, Lord,
under Your slow-revolving skies,
on Your slow-revolving earth:
the lion reposing under the bushes,
the men listening in their houses
to the oratory of Your rain.

On the island mid-ocean there is one,
who, having swum to a sunny spot, lies on a promontory,
reclining on his walrus tusks,
blinking at the sun,
and the brine rolls down his red beard
in round drops.

You have many great sons and daughters, Lord:
split in two yet fused together,
they beget according to Your holy sexes—
the male germinating the small
male within the woman
and the small woman within the woman
with pleasure again and again.

And I, walking alone on the plain,
am made to pause and sit by Your streams
with this happy thought:
I watch the wart-hog, grunting joyously,
run through the man-high grass,
the necklace of her eight
piglets swinging behind her.

And how good it is that I, a childless woman,
together with all things, can see
Your onward rolling and continuation.
You have many great sons and daughters, Lord;
in the terrible heat the elephant's giant ear fans for You;
the young man marble-hewn
is moved to tears by his joyous singing to You;
and even the howling monkey,
his cry swallowed up by the gaping throat of the giant lizard,
calls to You,
for we live and die with You forever and ever.

(William Jay Smith)

SEPARATE TIME

Broad Gulf-Stream, great stretch of time,
your silky current may be shimmering,
the shell of nothing seals my mind,
inside me a bubble-sphere is misery,
my separate time rolls separately,
you can spin my rainbow sphere at will,
but I can never step from it,
my separate time is my separate cell.

Uncouth monsters stare at me
wretched creatures, wretched men
with their weeping rainbow faces:
my separate time rolls separately.
Underneath chameleon shades
their wall-white sorrow gives them pain
my time runs down, runs out and fades,
again I am inside, separate again.

(Edwin Morgan)

THE FELLED PLANE TREE

Its trunk as of dead silver cast,
a statue, it lies,
within whose tufted crest ground-creeping
wind bubbles and sighs.
Its branches are lopped silver arms,
stubs that do not stir,
its tresses matted by the mud,
turned brown and grey.
Spirit high above it flies;
transparent vapor encircles
its many long-lashed
eyes, all shut.
Its lopped head dropped upon the earth,
giant tresses sprawling,
the smoke of dead breath rising,
in faded, soundless music calling;
rustling, whispering, it breathes,
voicing the vacant altitude's agony;
through changing shapes, the fallen tree
weeps silently from dead, fringed eyes.

(William Jay Smith)

FEAR

I am afraid I may be Ilia
the wild duck mired in the oil.

What if, instead, I'm Algernon
the white mouse in the maze,

or Pompilius, the dog in the laboratory
with the cancer graft under his skin?

I am afraid. What if the bull calf
with the new moon marking his forehead

—the one chosen for slaughter—
is really who I am? I have a fear

that maybe I am Bonnie
the chimpanzee who died

in the solitude of the spacecraft...
But no, I know I'm Anna, and afraid,

for knowing this, I know I live
until the debt I owe for this is paid.

(Daniel Hoffman)

HALF PAST FOUR, OCTOBER

Twilight. By now the genial sea of dusk
is lapping at the window. A rising tide
bears the plane-tree aloft and far away.
Above these undulations of the sky
on silky wings the wild goose floats unseen.
His cries we hear, and hear again
until the waves of dust rise over him,
but where will he be then? Where does he fly
southward with his strong companions?

How many planes and levels deep does dusk
hover in autumn? Deeper than the sea
where the wild saffron, purple sea-star blooms,
down to the cellar where the silken mole,
hardworking and secure, lives with his brood.
It seeps where the snake is drowsing amid dead leaves.

The dusk flows past us, turns on wings
noiseless as fins,
the owl, his eyes like bulbs, drifts by, a fish with ears;
the bat's wings wriggle like a slowly-swimming skate,
we grow sleepy too but cannot hang
head-downward from the plane tree's hollow all the winter long—
we know what would be good,
we live as best we can.

(Daniel Hoffman)

AMY KÁROLYI

(*1909–*)

From THE THIRD HOUSE

I
Like moon-hunted clouds, the two
fine houses of my life drift from me:
the lamb's-wool sky of youth,
my stifling, lightning-flickering summer years—
see me now crowned with vine-leaves,
a bunch of grapes plunged in the vat,
like that I step onto the porch of my death.

(The stairs deceive. They seem to soar
but stop in a ravine.
The old man mumbles his acorn on the valley floor.
His nose drips,
he sits propped on twigs.

O, where is noon, the milk-loaf heart?
The sun was devoured like a slice of bread.)

This porch still takes a friendly part,
the sun still bakes,
the stone still boils,
the full moon lights its linen shade,
but already it's a night with crickets shrilling,
the plum-scent has dissolved into a spirit—
O, transfiguration of things!

Jesus Christ is sleeping in the host
wafer-colored stripes gliding
under a round sky milled on the lathe
in our eyes its stripe keeps going
cool saliva from old women falling
dribbles down the apron of the year.
Now only the crust is left here,
the sun is devoured like a slice of bread.

. . .

3
I comb my hair.
I make my bed.
I wonder where the laundry-bill has gone.
And every one of my bones
is on a bill, to be read.

The vertebrae all billed
first this one clanks then that
the chain of vertebrae bursts
they string a fresh groove in the dust.
Out of the ensemble out of the bone-music
solitary voice
the knee looms
the knee-bone longs
to kneel
even under the loam
wax-yellow like a candle-end
trembling with phosphor-blue flame
the knee-bone longs to kneel
Where is the threshold that would be its home?
O, where is the stone for me to kneel on
that the knee of millennia has worn a bed in
doves' nest fluttering towards heaven
first step of God's stairway
o where is the stone

4

Once we had got the new flat habitable
and pressed our faces to all the windows
and hung all the walls with mirrors
and gone in and out through all the doors
(here my mother came in
there my father went off)
and lit candles and chandeliers
and sat under huge pictures
and snored under pashas' duvets—
and as the picture the duvet the chandelier
the life the song the lawn
clung to us like a second skin—
all of a sudden
the heart of the pictures blackened
and the gleaming holystoned honey-colored floor

whirlpooled up under our shoes there.

. . .

9

Only love surely is like this.
The tender dark compulsive force
rises out of strands of pearly nerve-knots,
of cells like coral-islands rising and sinking.
What happens to the gaze of animals
what happens to the mirror melting and panicking
a star soaring from it up to the sky
sharp dawning of March nights.
Green brown yellow fish-scales
circular weaves of living fibre
bitter almonds crafty hazelnuts
portholes made of mica plates
behind them a splash of mother-of-pearl
foaming sea-abyss
silver-secret.

Gallopers in the wheel-ruts of our fate
scramblers onto our wagon-frame
wranglers over us like red whips
liners of our path with weeds for tulips
demi-vegetables
unhurriable
voiceless children of our fables
if we don't speak
their fate swirls off as the leaf-fall crumbles.

A needle's eye will get you into heaven
if you like, but an animal's
melting-mirrored
terror-mirrored
eyes can let you in.

(Edwin Morgan)

ISTVÁN VAS
(1910–)

THE GRAND FINALE

February dawn spread across the sky.
Today at last we can cross over to Pest!
We cannot, though,
If the ice on the Danube won't let us go,
I thought, and just as the thought took
Hold of me, the neighborhood shook.
I was about to doze off again
When I began to hear
The sound of gunfire and rockets
Mounting, drawing near.
No, that cannot be—
The siege of Buda starting once more?
And then a bang from the second floor—
The Russians are packing:
The half-light and the cold are hard—
And everything on the move—
Horses, carts, automobiles.
Like children we plead: "Please don't go!"
"But we've got to go!
The Germans are breaking out of the Castle,
They're almost here!
We're leaving but not for long,
We'll be back—do not fear!"

The bang, the rattle increased outside;
Within us silence opened wide;
In our hearts, our room, the cold spread.
A scene bordering on madness:

Listening, the huge Academy courtyard
Across the way
Yawns wide.
Panic grows inside
Us: silence,
Mounting fear.
And what if the Germans come back here,
And Mrs. Leitgeb reports us again.

Lucky T.,
Who has not yet shed the disguise of his Premonstratensian
Garb; he
Walks around day and night
In violet cincture and white
Cassock!

Confusion is rife.
What will each do to save his life?
"It's crazy just to wait, that much is clear.
Even if they come for only an hour they'll kill us for sure.
Let's go where the Russians are going."
"Between the lines? This is the front line now.
You want to explain to their bullets, fool,
That you are a friend, not an enemy?"

O. cleans his pistol,
While another packs his bag,
And another stares vacantly into the yard,
Scanning the empty neighborhood.
And would prefer to read
Some leatherbound History of Fascism.

While we still can,
We munch some bread,
Sit in a circle; the women smile,
The men stare glumly all the while.
The window rattles, the sun shines:
Across the room a bullet whines,
Until, weary of its flight,
It zings into the stove, whizzing right

Between Géza and me,
Between Mari and Gyöngyi.

We jump to our feet: the shadows
Of helmets in the distant courtyard move over the snow;
Then opposite—in a gate
A green soldier looms.
Beside him a small, stocky
Sweat-covered square face pops up,
Made monstrous by hunger and fury;
They've managed to break through;
The taller one flings a grenade,
His muscles strain
As he heaves it, leaning to the right
In an eternal movement,
An athlete,
A Borghese Fencer,
But his face is hollow, pale—
How he must have starved
In the cellars of the Castle
But still he would not cave
In; he has survived to carry out his orders,
He has lived to kill and make others kill.
His ammuniton gone, he carries no
Weapon any more;
He lost his battle a while ago
And is ready to kill even now.
A symbol of stubborn resistance, he watches there,
Ready to hurl his grenade through the air,
His body a perfect arc, but
How long will he wait? He hurls it,
But the old grenade fizzles out;
The third one, though,
Hits below our window.

From behind a nearby villa
Three Russian soldiers appear.
They approach, jumping, ducking,
Cold afternoon sun flashing on their colorful persons—

Not on their helmets but on
The fur above
The green, yellow, and red
Of the caps on their heads.

These are the Sons of the Wondrous East,
Embodiment of a folktale past
And a dream
Future, and nearer they come.
One crawls below the window
And their Tommy guns rattle
Toward the place where moments ago
The messenger of doom stared up from the snow.

The man at the window can feel,
Through the winter landscape, the smell
Of smoke.
Heavy steps on the wooden stair;
We listen in fear,
Hoping. Three flamelike figures
Burst through the door.
Love, bravery, victory
Flash from each eye,
The light of the lovely war.

No time to stare
At them for long; we could not stay there.
We had to go down; they set up machine gun
Emplacements in the windows of our room.
And that night all
Crammed into the small
Downstairs kitchen, the stamping, the shouts,
The candle stump, flickering out!
Listening for steps, watching the dark—
Is it a friend arriving now,
Whose hand we can grasp,
Asking: how long will this go on?
Or a gun-barrel thrust among us,
The enemy sweeping wildly in,
A flashlight casting its enquiring beams

On the women sitting on the bench.
The slow night, dawn breaking through
The snow-covered scene, waking to
The noise of machine guns.
We soothed our hearts, our nerves by means
Of books instead of medicines.
T. read "Toldi,"* Irén the Bible,
And O. buried himself in a history of
Cabaret. In my hands, *The World
As Will and Idea.*

The sun is out, life is easy
Again; the rattle of arms dies down;
The Russians upstairs say goodbye;
We may return now; the apartment is empty.
The Academy is empty; light engulfs it from above. A few shots
Are heard, then dead silence.
While O. patches the pane,
Outside we hear the cawing of a crow.
And then we shave. The melted snow
Hurts our tired skin. Our teeth chatter:
When the room warms up at last,
Prisoners file past,
The grenade-thrower among them,
Without his helmet, wearing spectacles
Through which focusses
A cold, death-dealing mind.
What would he be in civilian life? Chemist, teacher,
An example of the "rational cognition"
I read about last night?
Satellite, guide of decay,
Stumbling block of wisdom,
The bloodless one, intoxicated by the smell of blood.

Next to him the short fellow who yesterday
Was planted there in such fury
Now trudges along resigned
Limping dumbly, half asleep;
We run down. The rest

* A nineteenth-century Hungarian epic poem.

Are not better as they file past,
The ruins of a world-conquering
Army. That's how the fiend
Europe produced
Came to its end.
It sinks now
Like a tired dirty crowd
No more elegant
Than the unarmed crowd they used to herd around
For more than a decade.
On the Hidegkúti Road one sees
Tank-flattened, green-uniformed corpses
Thrown against the trees
In the eccentric arrangement of
Terminal terror. And yet
Slowly in my heart the place of hate
Is taken by a sense
Of detachment and indifference.

Major Grigory comes back. Tonight
We'll shoot dice with him again,
A Viennese waltz on the gramophone;
Then we'll eat and drink some wine.
The Tokay shines in the glass. We rise to toast
The one-eyed young Russian soldier lost
In action. Ah, if he could only drink with us tonight!
But before the joy could go completely sour
Alexandr lifts his glass again,
His black eyes twinkling, and
Proposes a toast to the silly war:
"Voina prima, voina gut!"

Midnight. Tomorrow we may cross to Pest.
Can't sleep. My mind won't rest—
It pictures the city and the years to come.
And the history of this day sparkles clear
And the whole thing takes on meaning
And we believe that horror—
And all its causes—
Have been blotted out forever.

How many years has it been since then? What keeps me going still
Is having witnessed this grand finale.
Having seen how the big lie ended,
Having seen men
Take the mechanized monster
And tear it to shreds—
Having seen the infection-spreading flag
Sink into the mud,
Having seen what seemed iron and steel
Crumble like clay.

I saw all this and it was enough to remind
Me forever that what takes its place
Will in the end be likewise overthrown,
The stronger force will conquer
Fickle luck.
There is, after all, a difference
Between arms—
And although lies may go on blaring for years,
They can never win out, they will go down;
And into the old pits
New terrorists be thrown.

(1951)   *(William Jay Smith)*

BUDAPEST ELEGY

Ah what a town! Mud spurts up bursting with dirt.
February is busy laying slush on purple crape of the dead.
Soot sifts down ceaselessly thickened by sleet.

The compost-heaps of snow grow dark with grime.
The racked, hacked body of the town shudders in its mire.
Even deep in mud that body is one with mine.

Fog like poor wartime cottonwool hides the wounds of the Boulevard.
No more smoke from the Royal, the Emke, black and charred.
The New York's brand-new neons quiver by bombed-out shards.

This town has challenged the town-murdering fever,
its tortured gaieties are rekindled, it struggles to its feet,
declines again to drown in running mud, mortar, and fear.

Ten o'clock. The neons of life are quivering yet—just.
Despair, a helpless drunk, vomits in the mud.
Night cringes on Pest; sporadic car-revs thrust.

But oh what voices rose over the streets of the town!
Impossible hope with its fresh whistling sound,
utmost purity showering bright arguments around.

We flash eyes at each other and still remember its lights—
and it's everything we remember, my poor friends, am I right?
The dicky brickheart town beats to our own time.

The dicky brickheart misses beats but never stops,
and if fate should someday strip the town of stones,
it would rise again in time by the right it stores.

Its stones and beams and walls are not what make it,
a hundred demolitions could not break it:
its eternity is redeemed when death would take it.

The town has redeemed itself and it has redeemed me:
There my sins go swimming, in filth of February.
It was the time of the great Shriving, now and here.

And hell slips from my heart, repentance marked by solitude:
The town has redeemed itself, redeemed me for its good.
A strange forgiveness glimmers at me from its wounds.

Now every light is out; faith dawns through misty air.
I know this will be put on record, somehow, somewhere:
I lived here and never wished to live any place but here.

(1957)   (Edwin Morgan)

ISTVÁN VAS

ON APPROACHING FIFTY

An account of one day

I go to bed late these days,
Look up this and that, translate a bit.
Now I have just intoned Ben Jonson,—
The curious conceits, the wise words.
Each new task still excites me,
And the craft—
When suddenly I remember what awaits me;
A coward, I put out my cigarette,
And calm my disturbed imagination with sleeping pills.

I fall asleep quickly these days, but usually wake up
At three in the morning. In most cases, scared.
I calm down: I'm still at home;
But my mind is grinding out the morrow
When it occurs to me
That I must go on an empty stomach to have an X-ray.

And I know how far behind me everything is—
Affection, hatred,
Doubt, mysticism,
The desire to travel,
Love, faith, country—
Everything that could have been,
And everything that has been lost—
For I'm not living now; I live only in my cells,
My fluids, my organs,
As if there were nothing else at the core of me—
Narrowing, harrowing, shrinking,
As they begin to understand the situation.

Now there's no shower to wash off the nightly
Gloom, for there's no water on the fourth floor;
I have to make do with a quick shave.
It's still foggy outside. I haven't been out in the street
So early for a long time. I'm no longer a clerk,
And yet the singer in me is even more in the dark.

Singer and song narrow and shrink:
The season of love is over;
Tired of laments, the series of young
Elegies run down, the old heart
Yearns for new deception, for the sea again—
And yet the way of all flesh opens out instead.

At the clinic that lovely dark
Young woman is wheeled in
And looks up with eyes frightened and dimmed with pain
(This is what they mean by the way of all flesh.)
And the two old friends supporting each other
To the X-ray room, one still cheerful in spite of age.
"We'll wait for her to finish" says one, while the other slobbers with
                                                              morose
Indifference, and nods in his senile way.
And the man and wife, trembling,
Toddle, arm in arm—how can they bear it?
He who becomes prisoner of life and death at the same time
Why does he crawl along the way of all flesh?

What else can salvation mean to me,
Except to understand what heart and brain cannot?
What else is there that God can do to me?
But make me understand or damn me for it?

And now I'm the one who sends grotesque writhing curves on the
                                                              screen;
And the ray sends its light through the flesh
To the depths where the pain-wet machine
Of digestive shame keeps eating me up,
And the way is blocked by the old
Poorly healed scars of. . . a duodenal ulcer.

How did it go so long unnoticed?
When I suffocated in the forest of numbers?
Or later, once I had resigned
Myself to the life of a clerk,
And the attacks of

Gastric neurosis were the only signs of despair?
Or just when I tried to find relaxation in the small pleasures
Of a clerk's life?
Dropping in for a dish of goulash, a wine-and-soda in secret,
The quick lunch in the pub of the Újpest stadium;
Was the strong taste of food in the workers' quarter too much for
                                                          me?

The blood sausage, smoked sausage, pork chops, good peppery stews,
The fine fat-dipped pâtés before lunch,
The fire-bite of pointed paprika,
The heavy sauce of a peasant stew,
The cabbage soup eaten at dawn?
How pleasant it was to drink at a bar
Ordinary wines, home-distilled brandies;
And I keep the smoke of a Levente cigarette
Alive in a brain, whose fertile soil yearns continually for it!
If all this left its ravaging traces deep in my body,
Now, even in its crippled state, I say it was worth it.

"This is an ugly picture; what can I say?
Of course, it's no business of mine,
But an operation's not absolutely called for;
It can be worked on a bit."
Outside there is still a cold wet fog;
I inhale it deeply, as in my youth.

It's the same man who inhales the fog—
The same old mist but not the same old misty youth—
As in an old-fashioned novel
Which has one hero for all three volumes—
Who gropes his way along, and by the time he learns to live,
The way of all flesh has caught up with him.

Now I can afford doctors and medicines,
Not like long ago when for *her*
I was helpless, wanting to ease
Her final agony,
Oh, shameful, clumsy misery
When she started on the way of all flesh!

In the double imagination of memory and fear
Sensuality can be terrifying:
By the time I enter the familiar room of the café
My being is bathed in sweat.
I gaze out at the fair and dark heads,
The kind guffawing ones, those who will follow me.

If I'm not with them tomorrow, who will ask where I am?
Who will ask where I am if I must stay away for good?
Who has noticed the resignation, the shy, shivering farewell
In my quick nervous hello?
And those who dropped out for years, without saying good-bye?
I wander off alone, swaying in the cold wet dark.

I tremble as I feel life like a sea ebbing away;
And, depressed, get ready for the concert;
The waves of music will replace
The sea perhaps, and the concert will serve as a sentimental farewell
Before the knives, tubes, hospital beds.

But beautiful women, fine clothes, sham pleasures
Take up too much of the night
And the waves of Mozart somehow
Cannot catch up with my excited
Perception.

But after the intermission comes Schubert,
The Seventh, C-major.
And the *allegro* and *andante*
Suddenly bring together
All that has been: my youth.
And its intermingling themes, changing *motifs*,
Its strength and sweetness,
The trill of the idyll in the storm,
All that I wanted,
And all that was impossible.

And the horn of the second movement drones on,
Saying it is good this way and that,
And the interlacing of all the movements,
Returning to the main theme,
Resounding in the finale with the final ecstasy
Of life and death together.

While we sit inside, winter loses its force;
A light wind whistles through the city.
Above the deserted streets shine
The proud lamps, the pert new neon signs;
Swaggering light of Budapest,
Ever-fresh city, how I love you even now!

Big old rooms of the city's center,
How I love you, cavern colored with books!
In you I loved, wrote, lived for eight years,
Whichever way you turn, I want you, life.
Oh, to watch the lamplight in the Károlyi Garden!
To sense you, my last love.

To sense you and in you the blessing
And terror of the years, the embrace
Of all embraces, the integral calculus of our loves
During one single night,
Light shining on my crippled existence,
Illuminating continually,
Whichever way it turns, the way of all flesh.

Only this last cigarette—
This one Kossuth to inhale deeply . . .
Don't pity me in the hospital nor in the tomb.
I am forever the man who now gazes out into the night.
Do not believe me if I complain.
One more glass of Badacsony red wine,
This last one and then no more!
I sip it slowly—in farewell
To what was, is, and will be again.

Hell may be preparing within me, if not below me:
I know the better part of me is immortal,
And through all decay, all metamorphoses,
It will carry with it this night—
Amongst knives, tubes, pains and starlight—
And with this wine, this cigarette ends this night.

(William Jay Smith)

THE ETRUSCAN SARCOPHAGUS

Which is the more elegant I do not know: the woman's narrow,
long-pointed fashionable shoe, or the man's narrow, long-toed foot
and vaulted sole? The narrow, well-ordered feminine braids curling
from under the round, high hat, or the same kind of plaits over
the man's elongated, narrow face with his pointed beard, coming down
to the middle of his naked back? I do not know either what the
woman's half-opened hand holds—or does she vaguely raise it,
as if to bid farewell? To whom? To what? What is this long narrow
hand taking leave of? What is this beautiful woman somewhat
irresolutely looking toward? Nor do I know, of course, who they are.

All I know is that as the woman rests on her elbow and leans against
her husband's naked chest and he embraces her, love, together
with their beautiful chosen life, shines from the red stone: they lived,
or would have lived, as I wished to live with you. Were they like
that—as young—when they died? Or was that the moment they
thought to be eternal? How should we know what these figures with
their sign language mean? Or am I perhaps what I appear to be?
But they wanted to be seen like that when they crumbled to dust
down there under the red stone.

This is not a Christian sarcophagus, with its willed or achieved quietude,
nor Latin discipline applied to Roman ashes: it is love growing
more and more beautiful through all destinies and infernos. Death
can be solved by propositions of many kinds, and I have tried a few
formulas, but in my old age I am pleased with the present one that
does not ask where we came from and whither we go: nothing is more

worthy than our lives and what we can make and dare make of them;
the great meaning and adventure of our existence is this and all
the rest is mad or maddening humbug, for, where is that famous
Etruscan ecstasy that joins in marriage with death? No, they just love
each other and their beautiful lives, this married couple.

And the great Etruscan enigma so often talked about? Those famous
death-copulations? Where are they? I do not see them, wherever
I look among the graves, the vases, the designs, the fired clay figures,
I see only life and with it also its infernal monsters, of course,
because death is great. Yet it is even greater to outwit death, and there
is no neater formula for this than laughter.

So the Apollo of Veii laughs as he looks one in the eye—but at whom
does he look? I did not realize that I was the one he fixed with his
gaze when I looked at him. One could not see that in the reproductions,
nor did any of the professors write about it—and he laughs staring
fixedly into the world, and yet it is not the death call of mysteries,
and yet it is not the thing emitting evil fumes concocted of rotten
leftovers in my youth by the charlatans and dopes of the death
myths who had, in their impotence, grown tired of unrewarding,
slow work and especially of their own desiccated, tired brains;
by those sick of reason, those whose activities become more and more
questionable, a poor, deluded generation falling into the vapors
of death. But the story that would make your flesh creep I find
nowhere here: the Apollo of Veii flashes, the dark-faced light-bringer,
the life-daring, and his broken foot steps forward—laughing, he steps
beyond death as he looks me in the eye.

If I look him in the eye. Yes, just to see, to see! And still to look!
I am still curious to see you, old and new and newer life, the whole
world! Only he who sees knows. And do not abandon me, curiosity!
On and on!

Let me still look, let me still see! And trust you! And not believe
any delusion but only in my eyes. I so needed this Etruscan
sarcophagus and what it stands for! The hope that we still await
on foot that which somewhere starts out against us and is preordained
to win. And that I do not lose what I believed in. And he who laughs
last laughs best. And that we preserve life as long as possible,

perhaps even a bit longer. And if nothing else and nowhere else,
when we do not exist any longer, somewhere down there, our
desiccated skulls will laugh. And we do not give a damn, a damn,
about death.

(William Jay Smith)

GODS

Gods, arraigned so often and so often!

You beasts and monsters, rivers some, and stars,
Dog-headed ones and hundred-nippled ones,
Some marine, some subterrene, some nurtured
On the nursery-floors of underworlds, fen-dwellers,
Attendants of the departed, corpse-devourers,
And totems come of even older strains
Of noble stock, rearing up, stone-faced spirits,
Mounded a-tilt, tent-like, Inferno peacocks,

Never have I prostrated myself before you,
Never in your name gone through a hocus-pocus,
And yet I know you exist, I recognize you
In any form, in the fraudulent arguments
Of an allegedly science-based aesthetics,
In the peristaltic paroxysms of visions,
A consciously sombre rhetoric's sparse emissions,
Or in the ambiguously apathetic
Smile picked up unawares from a young physique,
I know you exist, and it may be, sooner or later,
You will contrive to get me in your clutches.

And yet perhaps—at heart this is what I hope for—
I have succeeded in slipping out of your grasp,
And you can whistle for me, unwieldy
Mask-wearers, prodigies tricked out hooligan-fashion!
And you, the light-bearers, archers, gazers at the sun,
You with the brains of fire, strainers of nerves,

Wearers of helms, shield-wielders, bearers of
Victory on the helm, on the shield the monster's head
Borne to the light, killers of dragons, good swordsmen,
The sunlight-bodied, the from-the-seas-emerging
From among the monsters to unprecedented pleasures,
The beautiful, the illuminations, the
Descenders to hell, overcomers of hell's forces,
Pilfering plunderers of the underworlds,
You have I never professed in hymns nor in
The covertly moustached and self-effacing
Erudite smile of a specialized monograph;
But you have I had with me in the combat.
How often was the shield not held before me, hiding!
How often has your spear not thrust for me!
How often have you not sent me the good enveloping
                        mist!

When I was imperilled, and when I fled, you were with me,
When I invented, when I overcame,
And you have been with me in many and many a bed.
Vigor-enduers you, and beauty-pursuers,
You of the bright hearts, you whom I have found,
Surely you know I am yours, and you will surely
Send me down the envoy, the attendant,
The god of poets and of thieves and secrets,
Him, the father of all stratagems,
To be my convoy on my slippery road,
To essay, when I must come to changing over
From form to form, his best wiles for my good,
When I shall step from the one into the other?

(Donald Davie)

IT DOESN'T COUNT

    The two are left alone
    now the others have gone.
    Every connection is snapped
    with every settlement.

The setting doesn't count.
In a moment the hill-top
is again unbuilt-on.
Connection has stopped.
The small stone house
stands alone, defenceless.
Replenishing their stocks
two distant strangers
reach the village from the hills.

The setting doesn't count.
The houses on the Danube
are suddenly a strange town.
They're here, throwing windows open.
What a fabulous Hat! But
what is the error they now
milk for their gain?
Quick, cross the bridge, go down
to the strange town, examine it,
remember we can only expect
to stay only a few days:
the error will slip out,
and an amateur pair of chancers
will vanish and leave no trace.

Time itself doesn't count.
Autumn, always autumn where they are.
Trees fading into red.
Their agitated crowns
mix and stream in the wind.
An autumn wind keeps blowing
wild, through a wild autumn garden.
Turn up your collar on the hill-top.
A fire blazes in the house.

No, time doesn't count.
Fog hugs the Danube.

As if in a lighthouse
they sit in the big room,
stand at the window
nosing the window-pane.
In front of them, gulls
hover and jab,
white gulls bob
on a grey sea. The flat
overhangs the water.

For time doesn't count.
Ten, twenty years back? No matter.
Even old age doesn't count.
Some old sin, some
undeclared sin
trails its wild cloak
fluttering behind them.

The setting doesn't count,
since time doesn't count.
Steep hill-top; castle;
two lonely torches flap.
In the yard two saddled horses wait.
Paper and seal don't count.
On uncharted seas
a wanted man, an old ship
adventure in full rig,
and that island of the setting sun.

The two are left alone
now the others are gone.
Connection has stopped.
Connection is discovered.
A sky half clouds.
A sky half stars.
Moonlight through clouds.

They keep watch on the hill-top
for humming leaf-messages.
They look embarrassed

they are old, after all.
They try out a smile.
"What romance, what freedom"
they say, so civilized
veneering the knowledge
that this is meaningless.

Veranda, light-switch: useless.
The others are already gone,
the two are now alone.
The connection that had stopped.
The connection that was discovered.
The moon at last rises,
wind whips up strong,
castle crumbles, house empties,
island and galleon founder,
something draws near in the garden,
every window is shattered,
they sit, they don't even blink,
as they smile at each other.

(Edwin Morgan)

THE MAD TOWN

Just for a cup of coffee? How exactly should one put it?
Be still, my heart, be still! Perhaps that's the way to put it.
When do we have dinner? We'll be ready by nine.
I can't really tell him
How exciting this trip is; and how afraid of it I am,
Or that I'm not even sure whether one should go back.
Go back. Challenge fate
And that town born of Bedlam.
                              Who would have believed
That the journey by car would be so boring? That speed
Would put you to sleep. I mean speed without danger;
The milestones, the red traffic lights,
The highway. Who would have thought

That one would dose off, rushing upwards? Why—upwards?
In vain did this height extended by towers,
Arches, lanes and steps open
The fearful stone hollows of its jaws: one cannot see it
From a car at night; all of a sudden we reach the top.
How did it happen so smoothly, without a jolt?
Did I sleep through it all? Here stands the unfinished
Cathedral, and the shell of the square below.

And where should we have our coffee? In the square, of course.
                                        Here or over there?
From here you can see better the steeple shaped
Like a pink bullrush topped with a big white stone flower.
Black coffee, ice cream. This young man
Confesses why he wanted to have coffee right here:
Here he'd lost his first girl whom he'd known for six years;
Now he likes to stop in this town
At night, after dinner.
                        Should I tell him
How I also said good-bye here? Even if I were on my own
I couldn't. And he wouldn't even understand it.
And what could I tell him about? The hot sun,
The frightening night, on the double torture-bed,
The dividing pain, the sobbing, yearning
In different directions, the sticking together in spite of all
Until death, even for a love that cannot be saved. Or the other night later,
The cold rain, the terror of
Losing a final shelter, the threat of the stone closing in on us,
In other words, the grip of two loves. And meanwhile the maze
Of circular lanes and alleyways, by day
And night, the unfinished
Cathedral, the shell-square below.
                            But all that
Is still present; it neither attacks nor threatens anymore,
It only looks at us, almost comforting—
The dread of that time turned to certainty.
And she is somewhere far away,
The beauty of her face stripped down to bitterness; she grits her teeth
And no one but the two of us knows anymore who she was.

Only be still, my heart, be still—this way perhaps,
After all, everything has calmed down. The grip of love—
It would be ridiculous for a cautious old man
To mention this sort of thing. And the great terror
That would have to be faced finally in a more familiar town.
Here there is nothing but *cassata*, *Campari*, coffee.
The popular tune behind us, comfortingly new
As well as excitingly familiar, and the madness turned to stone,
The deserted shell-square, the unfinished cathedral,
And the town's motto: *cor magis tibi pandit*,
It opens wide your heart—opens wide for what?
Right now only for dozing off while speeding
Amid the red-painted shining stones
Signalling in the illuminated dark.

(William Jay Smith)

BOCCHERINI'S TOMB

Shall we go there, too? Whatever for? Another half-Gothic
Small checkered church whose inside has been ruined.
Sub-baroque. We're lucky that it's dark.
Let's get away from here. But wait a moment, there's something white
showing over there,
A huge nose, a vaulted head, set in the wall. And a lute below?
Well, let's have a look. It's Boccherini's tomb.
How did it get here? He was born in Lucca, of course,
Though he lived in Madrid. You may remember
The Madrid Guard on record.

But that wasn't the first thing of his I'd heard.
It was rather late in my life before I'd even heard his name;
And the place and time were rather strange.
Gödöllő, the school gymnasium. There were a hundred of us.
Or more. And a little rotten straw.
The only place you could go out to was the yard,
Where the snow was deep. We could wash in it,
But then (do you remember? it was a cold winter) it froze,

And they urinated all over it... but, you recall, once
You got in and bribed the guard and took me out to wash.
You can imagine what we were like after two weeks. But I
Wasn't the only poet in the gymnasium.
Tom Fool was there, too, who not long before
Had been writing Fascist articles, but since his luck had worsened,
All he talked about was who should hang.
And there was another, who later celebrated the hefty little leader
In such artful poems; but at times he was a real
Poet—you had to admit that—and he was also
A good mate in trouble and behaved wonderfully well—
Threatening to boot the contaminated Jews
Who sang one of the German soldier songs inside.
But they weren't the ones who consoled me; it was a red-haired printer
Who put up with all that happened, always gay and sarcastic.
It was he who whistled the Boccherini minuet all day,
That mocking ironical pizzicato minuet,
Which made fun of everything including
The minuet itself. When we were inoculated
Against typhoid and the Medical Officer remarked
That we were all pretty dirty, even then
He hissed it in my ear; and whenever I was really downcast,
He began to hum it especially for me, and that
Restored my courage and I laughed again.
Then, as you know, I soon got out of there;
I've always been something of an exception. He went up to the front,
From which he managed to return, God knows how;
He joined the Party, but I haven't heard anything about him for a long
                                                            time;
I'm not even sure he didn't emigrate on one occasion or another.

But now here in the dark church I remember him
And in thought bend my knees not to Francis,
The gentle, poor, super-poet, the saint,
But to the mocking minuet, Boccherini's pizzicatos.
And to Andor Rottman (now I can safely put down his name;
He turned it into Hungarian later, to what I've forgotten.)
And to C. who lived there, near the Gödöllő Gymnasium,
Something I didn't know, not knowing him at the time,
But later, when things became even worse for me, he hid me at his place,

And to A., who also saved my life
Without having been asked to, rewarded only by my disapproval,
And to K., the unlaurelled outstanding poet whom
I sent to you on a secret mission, and who, entering,
Clicked his heels: "L. K., Secretary to the Minister,"
That's how he introduced himself to the Commander
Of the Desemitizing Unit, who was armed to the teeth;
Not to mention a number of women, whose names
I shall not put down, since they would not like to appear together on this
                                                                    page,
In other words, to everyone in that dark church who then
Helped guard my sanity.

                                        (William Jay Smith)

SAINT MÉDARD

On all sides a palpitating gray;
The silver slowness of the Danube
Is turned leaden by the flattening shadow of the storm.
Nothing but birds that zigzag
With nervous grayness. Nothing but our hearts.
The designs of the steppes and the ocean
Clash once again above us:
By disturbing the depth of the continent
And engendering showers,
Masses of cold air from the Atlantic
Ease our hot summer.
Above the clouds, air masses,
Envoys of the steppes and the ocean,
Turn around, competing for position.
And by the time the moon twice gets rid of the shadow of the earth
It will have been walked upon by man.
And what will that change? Nothing whatsoever.
Or perhaps next year it will be easier for me to travel
To Szentendre by suburban train.
Or rather... Why should I go on? Your brains,
Your audacity, and your technique

Will exit from the solar system
Sooner than your wisdom from the mousetrap
Which it continues to circle.
                         On the opposite bank
The shapeless frame of the new Intercontinental
Hides the cold and burned-out gaps of the city.
And when it is erected, fresh and splendid,
As a token of peaceful co-existence,
Symbol of life in the vulgar and beautiful beyond,
What will the wind bear to Buda, a waltz or
The world-wildcat music of the electric guitar
Amplified a year from now
On the night of Saint Médard?
And what kind of tawdry beautiful-beyond blend of light
Will be projected on the dark water of the backward Danube
And who will watch it leaning from his window toward Pest?
I'm not even curious.
                         From the dusky
Excited grayness only the new bridge,
The pale silver of our will, flashes
Mysteriously the image of the bridge, the bridge. The wind of
Saint Médard shivers on the leaden-colored river,
Announcing rain, deeper grayness,
And to some a leaden-colored river.
And then it passes, as usual. But if
The private forecast comes true, for whom
Will the sun shine in the coming months?
I am no longer curious. I am not.

                                        (William Jay Smith)

NAGYSZOMBAT, 1704

On that clear, dry, cold Christmas Eve
Count Sigbert Heister's army, sent to conquer the country,
Drew toward Nagyszombat
In four columns, the fifth, the center one, being the supply column.

It was escorted on either side by two brigades led by Ebeczky
And Ocskay, who had been drinking heavily.
Bercsényi had ordered them there to harass the enemy
But they did not move to do anything. Why?
It has never been possible to decide what they did or did not do.

Still more incomprehensible were the peasants
Who had but one possession left: their souls
And with them, the masters whom they hated so much
That it seemed that they wanted only
To take revenge for their lost freedom.
This was, however, the best season for fighting
Because harvesting was over
And armed peasants like footsoldiers followed
The flags in the hope of booty.
And who were their officers?
The ringleaders of the village.

            In this whole affair,
The blind were, in any case, leading the blind.
And it was from them that I expected advice,
These losers of battles.
My lord counselors! And what advice they gave me!
And how much! Saying one thing and then
The exact opposite. Their only excuse was
Ignorance. They did not even know of the millpond
And paid no heed to the brook, the Tirnava.
I rode along the field but could see
Nothing in the sudden blizzard.
Eszterházy did not follow my stratagem:
On the left wing he placed his troops in a single line
And most of them did not take any part in the battle.
My right wing was led
By Bercsényi, eloquent in counsel,
Hesitant in action,
And indecisive in dubious cases.
Now he sent his messenger to me
To say that we should allow the enemy to pull away.
I sent back word that without a second's hesitation
He should attack the flank of Heister's army

Since we did not come here to crack hazelnuts.
But it was too late: by the time my message arrived
My right wing had been overtaken by Heister.
On the day after Christmas at one p.m.
The cannon boomed and their booming thinned the clouds,
And the enemy confronted us, already on this side of the brook.
However, Ebeczky attacked their flank
In the way that only Hungarians, at their best, can.
But unfortunately they also got hold of the supply column;
The carts attracted the soldiers who began to plunder,
And it never occurred to the non-commissioned officers to restrain
                                                            them.

Seeing this, the two German squadrons that had changed sides
Outflanked and routed the brigade.
I moved up, giving orders to my riflemen
To follow me. But the noblemen, on orders from
Ádám Vay, out of love for me,
Seized my horse. But none of them took charge of the riflemen
To put an end to the confusion.

Thus the greatest battle of the war came to an end,
The first battle I had led.

Then Bercsényi and I collected the runaways.
He knew the Hungarian genius:
It is enough to assemble them in army corps;
They take heart, as if no one
Had ever defeated them.

And I also had to continue as long as I could:
To deserve this incomprehensible trust
Once my destiny had been divinely decided.

                                        (William Jay Smith)

Author's note: This poem might well be called some kind of collage: except for the last three lines,
not a word is by me. I took it all from Rákóczi's Mémoires, written in 1716 in exile in France, five years
after the defeat of the struggle for independence that he had led, when he was about to set out for his
even more painful exile in Turkey that was to last for almost twenty years, until his death there in 1735.

The poem takes its theme from Rákóczi's own description of the first major battle of the war—lost like most battles fought according to the rules of conventional warfare. (Austria was able, however, to suppress armed resistance by Hungary only after another eight years.) What I did largely was to rearrange Rákóczi's words and adapt a few sentences from other parts of the *Mémoires*, mainly from a passage in which he, overcoming his own social conditioning with sovereign magnanimity, describes with sharp wit the social classes in the Hungary of his day.

The words of the poem are, however, also my own. Rákóczi did not write his *Mémoires* in Hungarian, but in French. He did so in part with a diplomatic purpose in mind: to attract the world's attention to the Hungarian cause before embarking on his Turkish enterprise. On the other hand, Habsburg power politics had separated him from his mother when he was still a small boy and had sent him, born into the highest Hungarian aristocracy, to be educated in Bohemia, where he could hear no Hungarian spoken, in order to wipe out all national feeling in him. He was a grown man when Count Bercsényi taught him to speak the language, which never became a natural medium of expression for him. He wrote his autobiography, *Confessiones*, in Latin. I translated his *Mémoires* into Hungarian twenty-eight years ago. It seemed a far cry from poetry. But, then, my poetic sensibility has always been attracted by the elegance and shy poetry apparent in Rákóczi's actions, manners, ways of thinking, and in his style. The Hungarian words of his *Mémoires* are therefore more or less my own.

The words of the last three lines cannot be found in the *Mémoires*, at least not in the same direct form. In them I summarized what for me constitutes his most personal message. He was a hero who had no intention whatsoever of becoming a hero. Or of becoming a leader or rebel either. At the start he did not even want to be a Hungarian. But on those rare occasions when I myself feel something like pride in being a Hungarian, Rákóczi plays an unforgettable part in this by having, despite everything, become one.

LÁSZLÓ KÁLNOKY
(1912–)

DE PROFUNDIS

No towers tremble now at the blast of my sighs,
the red stream of my blood makes no roaring through the
                                                        lands.

No giants with stone-axes and
huge hands all thumbs slash
my likeness in rock.
Love's Christmas-tree
stuck once with colored candles of desire
has glided into unknown far-back childhood,
and any tears that fall for me are falling
not on fresh body but on mummy-cloth.

Where have all the young women gone
who spirited off in such sweet oil
the rosy salmon-slices of my heart
and shut up in a pin-box
my feelings twisted on a spool?
Where have those girls gone
who stepped out on their starry trajectory
shining down on my dim and always dusky sky?

When I soak my lonely looks
in the green veins of neon signs,
when I flounder on
like a lumpish-headed diver
deep in seas of the past, I feel

my shadow quietly flaking off
from my heels and vanishing
in reverse. I feel
fate has stopped waiting for me
neighing, stamping, bridled.

More and more impossible
the lavatory-brush moustaches
below noses like carrot-stubs,
the flatfish faces swimming on TV
and the ears that sail away.
More and more I panic at
the rattling detritus in the skull.
More and more I linger musing
over letters spelt in ashes.
If no one overhears me,
more and more I let it out—
the crippled cedar's shocked and whistling cry.

(Edwin Morgan)

DESPAIR

The candles inhale their own flame.
The derelict bunch of flowers hangs
its yellow shadow from the vase. Scrabbling
can be heard in the wall, not long before an arm-
bone, shin-bone shatters the paper.
The not yet run-down clock stops impotent.

Birds rush to escape the gale.
Blue screeching rasps at icy gables.
The tramp throws his pack on the highway,
his feet fumble, he slumps in the snow to die.
Cries are forced out howling for no one to hear
from the rib-cage of this world wandering through space.

The sleepless man sits up in bed.
His loneliness seeps down a lined bleak face.
A new indignity, a stab of pain.
Not young now, and his flesh hangs heavy.
In lungs and heart the ruinous army gathers.
His eye strains for a face he does not find.

(Edwin Morgan)

INSTEAD OF AN AUTOBIOGRAPHY

Waning daylight all round.
From unread lines of a book
the squeezed sunset rebuke.

The pin-pricks of self-mockery
disguised on the face
by fly-specks caking the mirror.

Will time slow down
to mend the scribblings
of ragged compasses?

Vain shifts:
giving stone statues wigs
or laving dead men's mouths with wine
after the fashion.

The man who has his own measure
walks past others' weights and scales,
he knows too well
he is like some loose-walled ruinous stronghold
whose keepers have died out
neglecting to strike the flag.

(Edwin Morgan)

GYÖRGY RÓNAY
(1913-)

THE TEACHING STAFF DISBANDED

Strange, what I thought last night, waking
after the first, short sleep, when one is jolted
by silence, with no more buses running
down in the street. Between one sleep and the next,
in this waiting that lasts five or ten minutes—
or less, it could be, only a matter of seconds—
I thought: they've gone. I have no more teachers.
That frightened me. For a moment, before
sleep came again to dissolve it all,
I felt forsaken. Why, I can't say.
The classroom was large, just larger
than the old, familiar one. I sat there alone,
on the old hard bench, my textbooks
and exercise books all neat on the desk.
The morning break is over, I look at the green door
and wait, as the silence hardens, for someone to come.
Nobody comes. The lesson's been cancelled,
with not so much as a stand-in provided.
Then it seems that the bell has rung; and again
I sit on the bench and wait, in a silence
that's hardened now. No one comes. Four periods, five,
and at last the knowledge breaks through:
I'm waiting in vain. There are no teachers
and none will arrive. There may have been
a notice even, saying the staff was disbanded,
and as usual I simply forgot
to look at the board. So I may as well face it,
what sooner or later I have to do:
disenroll from the school and leave as they left.

(Michael Hamburger)

SÁNDOR WEÖRES
(1913–)

ANTITHIN

At last it has leaked out—thin men are the cause of everything.
They wait in ambush on streetcorners and if an old woman comes by,
they don't even greet her. They are more concerned with exchanging their
straw hats for lottery tickets, and with naturalizing crocodiles in
the waters of Europe, so that even there there should be no safety.
They always begin their fishy deals in their beds at dawn, and
afterwards go to the street. Some work in offices, others ostensibly
are waiters or locksmiths—they all disguise themselves. But their
true trade is thinness. At last it has leaked out—thin men are, etc.

(Richard Lourie)

THE LOST PARASOL

I think there is much more in even the smallest creation of God,
should it only be an ant, than wise men think.
ST TERESA OF AVILA

Where metalled road invades light thinning air,
some twenty steps more and a steep gorge yawns
with its jagged crest, and the sky is rounder there,
   it is like the world's end;
nearer: bushy glade in flower,
farther: space, rough mountain folk;
   a young man called his lover
   to go up in the cool of daybreak,
  they took their rest in the grass, they lay down;
the girl has left her red parasol behind.

Wood shades sunshade. Quietness all round.
What can be there, with no one to be seen?
Time pours out its measureless froth and
    the near and the far still unopened
    and midday comes and evening comes,
no midday there, no evening, eternal floods
that swim in the wind, the fog, the light, the world
and this tangle moves off into endlessness
like a gigantic shimmering silk cocoon,
skirted by wells of flame and craters of soot.

Dawn, a pearl-grey ferry, was drifting
    on its bright herd of clouds,
from the valley the first cow-bell came ringing
and the couple walked forward, head by head;
    now their souvenir clings to the shadows,
red silk, the leaves, the green light on it, filtering,
    metal frame, bone handle, button:
    separate thing from the order of men,
    it came home intact, the parasol,
its neighbors rockface and breeze, its land cold soil.

In a sun-rocked cradle which is as massive
as the very first creation itself
    the little one lies, light instrument
on the blue-grey mossy timber of a cliff,
around it the stray whistling, the eternal murmuring
of the forest, vast Turkey-oak, slim hornbeam,
briar-thickets, a thousand sloe-bushes quivering,
noble tranquil ranks of created things,
    and among them only the parasol flares out:
jaunty far-off visitor whose clothes still shout.

Languidly, as if long established there,
    its new home clasps it about:
the rocks hug their squat stonecrops,
above it the curly heliotropes
    cat's-tail veronica,

wild pinks push through cage of thistles,
dragon-fly broods on secret convolvulus,
dries his gauze wings, totters out:
so life goes on here, never otherwise—
a chink in the leaves, a flash of blue-smiling skies.

The sea-lunged forest breathes at it
   like yesterday, like long ago,
mild smell of the soft nest of a girl.
   Shy green woodpecker and russet
frisky squirrel refused to sit on it,
who knows what it hides: man left it;
but a nosy hedgehog comes up to the ledge,
the prickly loafer, low of leg,
like a steam puffer patrols round the rock;
puts heart in the woodpecker tapping at his trunk.

The sun stretches out its muscular rays:
you would expect the bell of heaven to crack.
Broad world—so many small worlds find their place
in you! Through the closed parasol's hills and valleys
an oblong speck moves: an ant that drags
the headless abdomen of a locust with rapt
persistence and effort: up to the bare heights,
down to the folds, holding the load tight,
and turning back at the very end of the way,
floundering up again with the body. Who knows why?

This finger-long journey is not shorter or sillier
than Everything, and its aim is just as hidden.
Look: through the branches you can see the hillside,
there a falcon, a spot on the clear sky,
hangs in the air like a bird of stone:
predator, hanging over from history.
Here, wolf and brown bear were once at home,
crystalline lynx lay in ambush for the innocent.
God wetted a finger, turned a page
and the world had a very different image.

A sky-splitting single-sloped precipice,
its lap a lemon-yellow corrie of sand,
far off a rosy panorama of mist,
curly hills in a ragged mauve cloud-band;
above, the couple stood; below, the sun-wheel stirred;
in the dawn-flames, so interdependent
they stood, afraid, at the very edge of fate;
boulders rolled from beneath their feet
     they were quarrelling, tearing their hearts,
each of them deaf before the other starts.

In the tangled thicket of their young blood
the luminous world skulks off, sinks;
     shame like a rose-branch cut
          the boy to the quick:
beyond entreaty, ready to throw himself down to...
His white shirt gestured against the blue,
     at the shrubby scarp with its bindweed
          he lurched forward, forward
growing smaller and more-distant—and his frightened girl
runs after him through briars, her knee's blood is a pearl.

     Tall sedges lean over the gorge
          and like a gemmed porch of the depths below
an army of tiny shining shields of weeds
     and a thick dark couch of green
cling round the bark of a stump that points nowhere, here their frenzy lost its rage:
they twined together, to ask why, to cry,
like the horned moon the white flash of a thigh;
a hooded boletus at their feet
fattened its spore-crammed belly, not bothering to mate.

     The hilltop sends down
          wind tasting of stone
     to crochet sudden air-lace;
     and the lost parasol
     shivers and half lives;

in the endlessly intricate forest, in the deep maze
   of its undergrowth, a breeze
lurks, but takes off at the sharp rock-fall,
pouring over that solitary wall
and across the ravine, flying light to the dale.

   Zigzag mane of the thicket
      wavers and swirls,
     the forest depths are sighing,
a thousand tiny leaves, like birds' tails, flicker
    and glint in the light like scales;
drawn up from a breeze-wakened copse
yeasty, spicy fragrances are flying;
   a snapped thorn-branch stirs, drops,
     catches on the soft fabric:
on the tent-like parasol the first tear is pricked.

   No one is sorry—
right above it an oriole is calling,
   inside it a bow-legged spider scurries
   round and round the scarlet corrie
and makes off: under the metal-arched ribs
a lizard twists in search of his siesta,
   he guzzles the oven-heat and like a jester
propped on both hands peeps out from the midst;
later some mice come running in and out
and the shaft has a gaudy tit perking about.

In the vault of summer skies, diamond-blue,
an ice-white lace-mist moves in a smile;
over the plain, at the foothills of heaven,
there are dark woolpacks hanging heavy
and truant cloud-lines in crumbling style;
Apollo, body stripped, striding through,
   runs young, strong, and fresh,
hot oil steams on the earth's rough flesh;
in air that rocks both valley and peak,
in empty immensities—a red spot of silk.

The girl of the neglected parasol
is just as small, lost in the broad world,
a tiny insect dropped in a sea-wide flood;
    no one to talk to at all,
wrapping her own soul round her fear,
        she curls up in a curtained room,
    and hears a whipped dog whining there
as if there was no misery anywhere,
no other wound to ache in earth or heaven;
or does he howl for all the pain of men?

    Hanging on the sky's arch
        at the lower bank
            the dusk
            is hazy.
    The first? How many before? On the lazy
    ridge no grass or insect measures it,
    neither cuckoo nor cuckoo-spit,
the twilights turn for ever, as created.
At the rock's edge, with forever's speed
the sleek silk vanishes into foaming shade.

Night's victory, yesterday's goodbye:
huge galley in the bay of earth and sky,
floating catafalque of dead Osiris;
scarlet embers fall into saffron high-tide,
peacock of air bends his fan from the heights,
shimmering feathers are roses and night-stocks;
an organ of gold installed in space
opens up all its pipes and lips,
pencils of light-rays spring from the rifts
and stroke the hills while darkness fills their cliffs.

    On the foamy crest of foliage
        light and shade come knotted together
        like the body's pain and pleasure.
Fading now, from its covert, the cuckoo's message,
        and the motley unison

of piping, chattering, chirping, splashing
        prankishness and passion.
    The evening light, that turns dreams on,
    bends through the cool slow-surging trees,
gleams in the silvery homespun of twittering beaks.

    Each smallest voice is poured
        delicately into the quiet;
    the nightingale among thorns, like
        a plucked metal string
        casts a few notes into the wind,
    then uncoils one ringing thread
        floating and spinning,
        then flicks it like a veil, languid,
    then bunches it rippling, potent but light,
and it fades: into a bed carved out of quiet.

    Then western sky is drained
    of the late dusk's arching marble veins,
    and the lit-up, burnt-out body of the sky
        leaves a steep column of smoke,
    pierced through by stars as sharp as steel:
    pearl-crest of Boötes between waving trees,
    Cygnus a cross drifting lazily by,
    Cassiopeia with its double dagger, the rope
    of the faintly glimmering Milky Way
loosely folding dead black space away.

    The valley, a deep arena, rests,
    crisscrossed by shadows of slashed buttresses;
        in the cirque a buxom Venus dances,
    approaches, spins round, offers riches,
    dances naked, white as snow, touches
    her feet upon the dew-drenched hills,
    soft-bodied, plump, with shining curls,
    the slippery form is merged in darkness,
    avid monsters stare her through and through;
in a swoon she waves goodbye and the curtain snaps to.

Like rows of houses in an earthquake:
great tangle of trees at the wood's edge
　　stagger and shake;
a green shoot flies up into the whirlwind,
a grindstone shrieking comes from rocky ledge,
　　the wilderness tosses and groans;
　　on the cloud-capped hilltop a thin
　　lighting burns, crackles, cracks,
then the long crisped fires streaming like flax
split above the cliff, a lion's growl at their backs.

　　The storm flickers through the twigs,
　　its thousand necks turn and twist,
　　it wrestles with the stumbling forest,
　　a writhing timber in its fist,
　　leathery roots clutch hard,
　　lightning tingles in the bark,
　　hundreds of birds crouch and start
　　in nests that shake them to the heart,
　　the burning, clammy monster rages still,
the sky, bowed low, seethes around the hill.

　　Torn-off leaves whirl anywhere,
　　roots of a gouged beech prod the air;
　　the parasol has been swept off the rock,
　　into a bramble-bush, beside a tree-trunk,
　　　the downpour slaps its silk,
　　it is all smudged now, frayed, and the ribs show.
　　It is indifferent to its fate—as the hilltop holds
　　its head without complaint in thunderbolts,
　　　and with the sky huddles low,
and fixed by sticky clouds watches the daybreak glow.

　　The parasol has a new home:
　　the secret world in fallen leaves,
　　cool dark earth and mouldering grove,
　　pallid trailers, roots in graves,
　　horrors endless, puffy, ropy, cold,

centipede country, maggot metropolis;
    the days swing round like catapults,
casting the full sun over it, the old
weltering moon; and the parasol sprawls
like a flaking corpse, though it never lived at all.

Autumn rustles: stuffs dead leaves in it;
    winter gallops: it is all snow;
    the thaw sets it free again:
        earth-brown, washed-out now.
    A sprouting acorn pushes,
        and through the slack, loose
        fabric a tiny flag
        thrusts the fibres back:
green, tender tassel steers to the weathervanes;
a few more years and a tree will shade the remains.

The parasol has changed: it has left human hands;
the girl has changed too: she is the woman of a man;
once, the red sail and the steerer ran
    lightly together, roving free,
while hosts of drunkenly foaming plum-trees
tempted the wasps to stir noisily
    and deep in the girl's heart the bumble-bees
began to swarm and buzz mischievously;
    since then, this wild army has been busy,
building a fortress in her woman's body.

Both man and woman have forgotten it now,
though it was the first witness of their linked fates:
Lombard silk and red Rhine dye,
long-travelled Indian ivory,
Pittsburgh iron, Brazilian wood, how
    many handcarts have trundled its parts,
    they have gone by rails, they have gone in boats;
    a world to make it! son of a thousand hands!
    yet no curio: old-world frippery;
lost: no joy in that, yet no great misery.

Branching veins draw it into the dark,
  light-unvisited mud weighs it down,
it is mere rags, dying in dribs and drabs,
it has stopped serving exotic demands
and like a bird escaping its cage-door
  takes up its great home:
the dissolving soil, the swirl of space, the rays
draw it all ways confused, astray,
old shoreless floods map its new phase:
this is creation's first emergent day.

Neither sun, moon, nor watch
can measure creation's second and third days:
the father of vegetation keeps his watch
over it, pumpkin-head, Saturn, dark face
with grey eyebrows hanging to his chin.
  Pulsing life-fluid filters in:
powdered cloth, rotten wood, rusted iron
dissolve and disappear in tangle and thorn,
and sucked up slowly by each hair-vein
it seethes alive again in the humming vortex of green.

Its handle is visible through the leaf-mould.
A brown moth settles there, perches awhile.
  By midnight it has laid
hundreds of eggs, a mass of tiny balls
placed in smooth strips, finely embroidered.
And like a biblical ancestress
she opens her wings, floats victorious,
queen fulfilled in happiness,
  not caring that dawn brings death:
God in the sky drew up my trembling crest!

The parasol no longer exists: bit by bit
  it set off into the open world,
  all changed, part after part;
even the eyes of Argus might find no trace,
  swivelling across the light,
  sliding down to the shade;

only a single feeble fibre remains,
poised on the top of a bramble-prickle,
it is mere fluff, next to invisible;
flies up from the thorn-prick, jumps into the saddle

of a storm! Air-pockets toss it lily-thin,
    the mountains shift below
in stampede, buffalo trampling buffalo;
fog-blanket opens on dark forest paths,
brooks twinkling down in the shy straths,
sharp drop of the crag wall, a mine,
toy trains of tubs moving along the rails,
scattered homesteads, a town with its smoke-trails,
and overhead, the great bleak acres of silence
and below, the hill from which the tuft went flying.

Upwards, still higher up it floats:
the moon hangs close like a white fruit,
the earth is a round, tilted, blotchy shroud
    framed by blackness and void.
        Bathed in airy juices,
the fluff swings heavy like a full leather bottle,
    descends to the ground, settles:
on a green plain, in drizzly mists,
it hovers lightly among the acacias
and probes a calf's ear as its resting-place.

A thunderstorm crashes, carries it off,
flies with it raggedly over moor and bog,
like a spool it turns, winding the fog,
    and when it is all spun onto a distaff:
low blue sea and high blue sky are combers,
    two sun discs gaze at each other
    and between the two blue shells
        a ghostly sail
        sways, tranquil,
uncaring whether it sways in air or swell.

The vapor-tulip throws back its head,
a glass-green other-wordly meadow glistens,
at the horizon a purple thorn gathers;
darkness surrounds the far-off island;
a little ray like a woman's glance flickers,
caresses its fugitive lover, glitters
as it flutters onto its drowsy son,
while a smile dawns eternity on man,
its arches bend and march on their way
between watery shores, Theatrum Gloriae Dei.

* * *

The red silk parasol was my song,
    sung for my only one;
this true love is the clearest spring,
    I have smoothed its mirror with my breath,
I have seen the two of us, the secret is known;
    we shall moulder into one after death.
Now I expend my life exultantly
like the oriole in the tree:
till it falls down on the old forest floor,
singing with such full throat its heart must burst and soar.

(Edwin Morgan)

LE JOURNAL

a mare ran into the yard
a cedar caught her sight
virginal phenomena paired
"its image is my spirited spirit"

O to sing in Horsish
bitted and bridled by the Muse
the saddle receiving Orpheus
ode psalm hymn in my jaws

Chung-kuo Hellas France Mizraim
would marvel at my hoofs of porcelain
my white lamp my socks prim
beyond the lasts of our understanding

a spherical breviary would come
up gratis sogar
I'd need no honorarium
only heavenly fire

I'd lift into the light of the sun
I'd fall into the dew of the moon
with sweet fruit pouring in
the hieroglyphics of my skeleton

anthropoid heaven-dwellers by the score
would be houyhnhnmized in my horsehood
and Xenophons' belief be proved
if I sang to my horsely score

the apehead is an evil pitcher
heavenly sparks prance there
and sink back to cinders in matter
as soon as they are music and picture

on the plain the bacchanalia
on the peaks King Zeus in the abyss
Aphrodite Pelagia
coral-reef in purple darkness

Helen's brothers in the skies
far flame no spit can sting
your groin-spasm in heavenly fires
you've as much domestique orang

your hand creates no more
than a fold on Diotima's robe
and she smooths it on her breast
to shine where it was pressed

thinking about the authority
of Attica of Italia
a stoa of babblers actually
serenade for Garufalia

one morning I get up early
look stomachly footly handly
my loving Garufalia
is in love with Garufalia

I gaze at you O Garufalia
mirror-wall of my being
I sniff my own snout finally
self reconciles everything

but lifelike side by side
shepherd shouts sheep graze
man and worm forage
on woman horse and other gods

orang komm her look around
no mango palm liana sandalwood
your country dreams in other images
concrete bulks steel stretches

on the shore of the city's man-din
the field's girl-body lies
with stripped hills the victim
of shuddering technologies

Danube gets the gull's droppings
the swallows shit on the porches
a Hittite king goes jigging
under Lajos Kossuth's portrait

balsam for all the inhabitants
to make the limb sweet as a violet
mummies shut in mastabas
you're a Hittite don't deny it

the Hittite the Hittite
a strange race is the Hittite
it's believed by every Hittite
everybody else is Hittite

an odd bird is the gull
it's believed by every gull
that whenever he meets a gull
it is never really a gull

let your dreams revolve your potential
it grows light over the city
the dustman starts up early
his nag no Pegasus after all

in the fading whirlpool of stars
his dagger-point stabs flying paper
while Debrecen wakens on the shores
of the Ganges where palm-trees waver

Sárika goes in her sarong
by the Déri Museum for a stroll
musk-smells drift along
by the six-footed Golden Bull

endless dreams of the plains
painted on mirage-soft seas
Aurengzebe's mosque raised
above Hindu temple-cornices

waves from Debrecen's Great Wood
flood a sleek barber's shop
snails octopuses are whirled up
mirrors lose their drowsy mood

attentive assistants in white
stand in water to their brows
customers in the muddy pit
foam infusoria on their scowls

patch on patch the sea grows
Golgotha is drenched Csokonai
hangs on a giant cross
Tóth and Gulyás by his side*

oh I need no foolscap to write
for if I should shed my skin
the same dumb witness would rise
from the hieroglyphics of my skeleton

what I don't know let me say
what I do know let me hide
and when tomorrow flies and I stay
I am asked and my skeleton replies

what I don't think let me declare
and what I do think let me conceal
shut up the truth the fake is shrill
the rest must be clawed from its lair

in chinks between lines of verse
angels and prophets cluster
the paper's whitest space
worth more than any letter

creation never bettered a stroll
blessed trackless periplum
but the pyramid's no joke at all
clinging to each minute-long millennium

the sewer clogs you with weed
to keep you here in the world
Homo Esothericus and your fellows
droves of Homo Bestialis

the sisterhood of Narcissa
recommend a solitary love-in
and the goat-breeders's synod
adopts the puny faun

* Csokonai, Tóth, Gulyás: Hungarian poets born in Debrecen.

Hellene eye and Hebrew sight
have their lines crossed in such a state
that hell-egg and heaven-fruit
make pining-apple omelette

orang geh weg give no sign
you are a useless oracle
all this is natural miracle
says Franz Kafka the divine

already both sides of our moustache
hold little bubbles in a net
and there is a rout of goldfish
from jaws now wide and wet

the whole aquarium wakes
to a throbbing panicky stir
the old cupboard shakes
and even the thermometer

but the dingy family faces
look blankly down from the walls
winking no come-ye-alls
either to us or the fishes

marvel rather at the charger
it knows indescribable things
its smile in its soul is larger
than any its lips could bring

its harness and saddle are alien
yet it bears them if laid on
all it shuns is the muddy fountain
and the fallow field is its domain

what it accomplishes the many tasks
are not for it to meditate
by the time it has its questions asked
its hide squeaks on our feet.

(Edwin Morgan)

MONKEYLAND

Oh for far-off monkeyland,
ripe monkeybread on baobabs,
and the wind strums out monkeytunes
from monkeywindow monkeybars.

Monkeyheroes rise and fight
in monkeyfield and monkeysquare,
and monkeysanatoriums
have monkeypatients crying there.

Monkeygirl monkeytaught
masters monkeyalphabet.
evil monkey pounds his thrawn
feet in monkeyprison yet.

Monkeymill in nearly made,
miles of monkeymayonnaise,
winningly unwinnable
winning monkeymind wins praise.

Monkeying on monkeypole
harangues the crowd in monkeytongue,
monkeyheaven comes to some,
monkeyhell for those undone.

Macaque, gorilla, chimpanzee,
baboon, orangutan, each beast
reads his monkeynewssheet at
the end of each twilight repast.

With monkeysupper memories
the monkeyouthouse rumbles, hums,
monkeyswaddies start to march,
right turn, left turn, shoulder arms—

monkeymilitary fright
reflected in each monkeyface,
with monkeygun in monkeyfist
the monkeys' world the world we face.

(*Edwin Morgan*)

QUEEN TATAVANE

O my winged ancestors!
Green branch and dry twig you gave me
for my two empires, to plant one and to lash one.
I am small as a weasel, pure as the eastern Moon,
light-ankled as a gazelle, but not poised for flight—
my heart lies open to you, to every silent suggestion.

The Elephantstar took my fifteenth year,
the Dragonstar brought this, the sixteenth.
I am allowed three husbands by ancestral decree
and seven lovers beneath the holy jasmine-leaves.

Not for me to escape with girl-friends to the fields,
for happy laughter, goats to milk, fresh milk to drink,
instead I sit on the throne in your light year after year,
an ebony idol with the world's weight on my neck.

Negro caravans, Arab ships are my traffic and merchandise,
I pay well, though I see most as polecats and monkeys,
but even the sky rains on unchosen ground, seeds burst unchosen.
I survey the naked hosts lost in their prison,
all of them I love as if they were my children,
punishing them with the rod and if need be by the sword,
and though my heart should bleed my looks are frozen.

Wake up, my fathers and mothers! Leave the ash-filled urn,
help me while the mists crawl;
your dark little daughter pleads with you as the last queen,
waiting among the garlands of the cedar-hall.

My seat among stone lions, the man's throne empty at my side,
my brow is glowing ruby-wreathed like the dawn-clouds,
my purple-tinted fingers, my drowsy almond eyes
shine like a god's as they strike down and raise;
what you found sweet and bitter I come to, I taste.

Orange veils on my shoulders, fireflower wreaths on my dark hair,
the reedpipe cries, the eunuchs drone, the altar's set.
Come Bulak-Amba my starry bull-browed ancestor!
Come Aure-Ange my lovely holy milk-rich ancestress!

Mango, areca, piled on the altar,
the year's brimming rice, brown coconut, white copra,
all round, red flower thrown on red flower,
sweet sandalwood fumes float up into the air.

Great man-spirit with no name: eat!
Great woman-spirit with no name: eat!
Huge emptiness in the silence behind the drumbeat: eat!

I call you, my father over the foam,
my old begetter, Batan-Kenam,
you are coming in your sun-chariot, four-elephant-drawn,
through the head-waving rattlesnakes of five cosmic storms,
my soldier, ageless, coral-garlanded,
blue-shirted arms,
lance of sky's shark-bone, turtle shield,
cut-off locks of the seven dancer-stars shimmer at your belt,
your elephants lumber and stamp, tiger-herds are felled,
and you rest on your elbow at the world's end in the lee of
                              the loud blue mountain—
I salute you my glittering visitor, my far-off father!

I am wrapped in my veil, I am hidden,
the welcoming hostess is timid,
I hand out half-peeled oranges on a gold dish:
look at me here, I am your own flesh,
you know I am supple and clawed like a forest cat,
you pause if you see my dark green shining eyes,

my white-hot teeth-embers,
behind, my skeleton is lace-fine, a dragon-fly:
see your one-day-old woman! one smile is all she would wish!

I summon you Aruvatene, my mother!
I call you. I am your daughter. Do you love her?
Your little one, will you be her protector?
Look, Nightqueen, at your tiny drop of dew:
the sparkling skin, the swelling breast!
You thick-starred heavenly palm-tree, I dance for you.

Blow the pipe, roll the drum,
my dance-wind skims about you, let it come!
my silver ankle-jangle chatters—from you it came!
my orange shawl flies out—you gave it my name!

But if your beautiful face goes ashy as mist
I give you my blood to drink from your ancient chalice,
turn back, I leave you in peace,
eat, drink in silence.

Come too, Andede, good grandmother,
you are as old as the wind
that snuffles in the oven-cinders.
I shall never be so old,
fugitive with blowing flowers.

Andede, good grandmother,
you are as wrinkled as the stone
that snaps off from the mountain.
I shall never be so wrinkled,
I am the rock-escaping fountain.

Andede, good grandmother,
you smile like a yellow desert place
grinding its bones, toothless sand-cascades
skirting the cosmic border.
That is not my smile,
I am the lady of two empires,
sword and bread on my lap together

under the trickle of my tears.
Andede, good grandmother,
you champ and smack like the green dragon
that swallows up the wildest moor.
But I can never be satisfied,
two nations fight to eat from my hand
and bread forever lusts after sword.

Andede, good grandmother,
perpetually decaying, never destroyed,
you are puny but sinewy like a root in the earth,
I am the mother of everybody,
I would take them all on my lap,
I would let them all eat and sup,
but when I even raise my hand, I die.

Great man-spirit, with no name: eat!
Great woman-spirit with no name: eat!
Huge emptiness in the silence behind the drumbeat: eat!

Come forward, now, great, ancient, unforgotten,
every sky-dome-breasted queen,
every lightning-dashing king!
I know that your good
is our only food,
but if misery surges again,
here I am—my blame alone,
I your shadow, your orphan,
prostrate under your cane,
beg for that bastinadoing!

For heaven's sake help me then!
Oh I am the virgin peahen
who instead of living eggs
found redhot stones between her legs
and with anxious wings spread wide
broods to hatch a void.
Pain of two nations is fire under me,
who will ever hatch the happiness of the world?

                                        (Edwin Morgan)

LANDSCAPE WITH MOUNTAIN

In the valley: ever-rumple of brook,
And the ever-rustle of bird-voices.

Above: silence hangs
Where the rocks reign. Rock-face;
God-face.

Higher still and very high, assuredly nobody sings.
At the very top: grindstone-screech,
Icy crackling headpiece.

(Peter Redgrove)

INTERNUS

Growing Old

My brain's gutterings unwind,
its light—that poverty of mind—
keeps drawing in its radius,
keeps glowing in still dimmer space;
with God's help, I shall hardly see
how far off the cell-wall may be.

Self-Portrait with Dog

The man I was is dying, his gasps are faint:
the heart is like a stone that stops the throat.
The life-spark, to get back its breath, leaps out
at long last from the miserable body
into a dog, to find tranquillity.
I lay my head down on my master's foot.
I don't feel his pain, I don't remember. I don't.

Dissolving Presence

It's not my self that interests me,
only that my death, so certain,
saves me from unwanted clowning,
though a tramped-on worm can hurt me.
Is dying going into nothing?
No more despair, no more desire.
But afterlife may be no plaything?
I can endure from fire to fire.
Life and death don't interest me,
I only need that harmony
which matter cannot ever bear
or reason take into its sphere.

Double-Faced

My self: though this perpetual guest
is hardly boring company,
he's a tick to bite my privacy,
without him I'd have quiet and rest.
Because he's attentive to my demon
and shapes its early hints in words
I put up with his earthy being
till evening ends, not afterwards.

Out of the Inner Infinity

From inward infinities I still look out
now and again, seeing through my face
clouds or the winking lights of stars in space.
My eyesight fails, that leaves me like the rest,
the outside world has shut my gates, I'm left
where there is no earth left, but only sky;
and no event, no grace and no surprise,
no surface, nothing seen, no nebulas,
only reality at peace and luminous,
boundless and measureless and nameless,
a love that's still desireless and still changeless.

The panic world is baffled at my gate:
"Madman! Egotist! Traitor!" its words beat.
But wait: I have a bakehouse in my head,
you'll feed someday on this still uncooled bread.

The Muddy Drink is Going Down and the Bottom of the Glass Shows Through

After death shall I still exist?
No handcuffs then upon my wrist,
I have dissolved identity,
why wish it in eternity?
Being or nonbeing: nakedness
suits undying presences.

I never thought it could be so:
my body gasps for its last breath,
yet still and easy is my soul.
My life is wantless and unwanted,
a beggar going on undaunted,
even by my death unhaunted,
with losses and with gains untaunted.
Fate is too kind! I had best not
die this way, like a dying god,
a smiling victory well flaunted;
I should be pulled up by the root
with a cowardly last shout
and get the real end of a man,
not judged for what I solely am.

Nocturne

Bored with my being, unutterably,
boxed in male bones perpetually,
I'm given no rest from his presence,
he and I are old bedfellows,
I can feel his warmth, his sweat,
from his hair-roots to his feet,
feel the twistings of his bowels,

his man's-stump and his milkless nipples,
the wheezing of his lung-bellows,
his heartbeats on uneasy pedals,
his gnawing and his stabbing pains,
his lusts that break the lagging reins,
his times of hunger and of thirst,
his filled-and-emptied bag of dust,
and what he feels and thinks within
I feel and think, unmoved, with him.
In beastly body-warmth I lie
stuck to a drumming rancid sty.
His daytime braying makes me sick
like his dead snoring, I can't stick
his senses' narrow window-glass,
the wooden O of his mind, a mass
of memories, symbols parroted
hand in hand and madly led.
I'm sick of dandling, pampering him,
of wiping the tarry rump of him,
of taking in his hungry cares,
of making his head utter prayers;
I've been his patient unpaid slave,
caring nothing for what I gave.
Not executioner, but guard,
I hold him close, but killing's barred:
he will die someday just the same,
die in peace or die in pain.
Each cell and seed he has, in its fervor
would go on fucking and gorging forever,
and the pitiful keen-kindled mind
forever have new knowledge to find,
but clenched in vice of flesh, I stiffen
in cramps of an enclosing coffin.
His life and stir are my own death,
and I fly on his final breath
into the love of God, fly back
till I'm a stitch in nothing's sack
and need no longer share my soul
or body with my self at all,

being unbounded plenitude,
the latency not understood
who taking all things into him
pours his wealth from a stintless brim.

(*Edwin Morgan*)

VARIATIONS ON THE THEMES
OF LITTLE BOYS

1
When I'm six I'll marry Ibby
And drive a big Mercedes—Ibby
Won't get in it—she can't come
'Cause she'll have to stay at home

2
CHARLIE IS A FOOL
JONIE IS A FOOL
    NOT ME—IM REEL COOL
    I got brains evry place—
    LOOKIT—even up my ass

3
    Squads, right
    Squads, left
I lead the squad—Hup! Ha!
We're going to bury my Grandma!

4
Watch my Daddy build a house:
First the chimney puffing smoke
Next beneath it comes the roof
Then the windows front and back
Can't see through them they're so black
But you can see through the walls
Because they are not there at all
Now the walls are on their way

And one by one the rooms around
When the house gets to the ground
My Daddy cries, "Hip, Hip, Hooray!"

5

Tommy, running through the yard,
Catches Suzy, beats her hard—
Out of her beats the bejesus—
Then cuts her up in little pieces,
Strings her innards heart and liver
From one fence over to another.
Suzy's thinking: "This won't do
I will not let go of you.
Reassemble me, you fool,
Or you'll go to Reform School!"

6

On the house the sun shines bright
But in the sky there hangs night
And so Good Morning and Good Night

7

Peter and Pussy (begging your pardon)
Do nasty things in kindergarden;
Look at the pigs!
The other children stand and stare.
Teacher Abby says, "Look there—
Ugh, what pigs!"
Flashes her pointed pen,
Waves it in rage; Abby then
Writes: "Dear parents—dissipated lot—
Look what nasty kids you've got!
Can't you give us something better?"
Debauched parents then reply:
"Dear Abby: We sure try.
Now we marry, now divorce—
Makes all kinds of kids, of course."

(William Jay Smith)

THE SEVENTH GARDEN

Never another garden where the clock
has stopped among the lilies, without hands.
   Time is counted there
no more than shade and starlight hemmed by leaves.
Does he to whom the Angel beckons linger
   still, revisiting
that place of sun whose diary is told
with a bell of stone, oblivion
turning on the marble of the columns?

Even turning face to face, they stand
with backs to us, all whispering afar
   in the garden. Days
to come are left behind if, fallible
and pale, they dare not brave the sun's bright blade.
   Tomorrows will return
if our kerchief should be left in them,
caught on the railings of the copper day
shredded gladly by the spikes of sun.

Drowsy the garden, yet pure sorrow's here,
though who'd not weep for happiness if tears
   could well from dew-washed statues
such as we are... How can I help desiring
you who scorched me? Figure slim as flame,
   lead me from this place
of silence, let me follow after, clutching
at your green sparks, beloved, like an infant
at a loose thread on a mother's dress!

(Daniel Hoffman)

ELAN

Glides along midnight, holding up her lamp
in a light loose cloud, cut apart by light,
dances off on surf, russet-velvet clad,
veiled in purple air, seashore cutting in
below the mountain edge which the water bites,
     runs off through the pines, to the clearing comes—
from where do you rise so the wind of the sea
never ripples your cloak, nor your shadow pass
on the ribs of the reef where the breakers break
nor your shadow touch the conical peaks
that align the shore nor the desert space
bear the print of your shape yet the clumsiest hut
is a place of love when you come there; where do
you go to, heavenly one? What do you intend?
What do you plan with our brushwood fire
whose flaming teeth never reach your steps
floating off above the wasps of fire, and the flaming
roses, leaving embers, cinders, cold, flying ash
only sorrow, desire, and black greed—O
naked reality of heaven, to what home do you call me?
     passes to midnight, now into the clouds,
     now beyond the clouds, topped with heaven's bowl,
     now her space uncut, and herself not hid,
     with no sleep her eyes and her heart no lid,
     with her grace unwilled and her heat untold
     with her words unsaid and her name unharmed
unblessed her desire to aid—not until
iron chains no more keep the bull's head down
and rats and snails guard the treasure trove
and children are fed on the blood of pigs
will the great goddess give up being cruel

                    (William Jay Smith)

ZOLTÁN JÉKELY
(*1913–*)

THE ELEGY OF A BRONZE AGE MAN

Visit to a Museum

I

Time has been when I longed for this safety—
when the walls of our hut at midnight shook
to the shaggy brown beast-backs rubbed there,
the teeth and horns whetted, sharpened
there on the stakes... I was a brat on a dog, riding:
and even at that age my friends disappeared,
bear paw, eagle claw seized them, hauled them,
their shouts of pain hammered and hammered the rocks.
Time has been when I longed for this peace—
when savage invaders at midnight shot
their flaming arrows at our hearth and
their voices barked out claims for us to die...
I was a brat huddling in my mother's bed in the dark,
my mother's lap with the sheepskin over it.

Thank you for coming after me into death,
now we can be at rest together in the earth.
Only here is there peace, in your open lap;
the moment now is a moment for ever.

They know why man and wife are laid in one grave.
There is no clash in our bones now.
Our heart let it flutter out, the mad bat,
Terror,
our belly let it slide out, the black snake,
Hunger,
our mind let it fluster out, the blind owl,

Anxiety.
Jealousy, vanity, envy, all all left behind,
frantic insects from the log rolled into the river.

No need now to meet each day and match it!
No need to kill to miss being killed!
No need to fear others might possess you.
I have you here in the good dark earth:
the earth is warm!
And here are my good weapons: the spear,
the bow, nine arrows, the good quiver,
my knife, my drinking-cup and the dear
little flute also—and all this is for ever.

2
I always liked to trace the bones
that lay under the shape of your flesh.
How often I pressed your jaws, stole
glances at your hips—often! Yes,
under the passing flesh I felt
and followed what can never melt.

Don't think it is a compromise
to lie together in this place!
The smile that glints on your white teeth
is brighter than a living breath.
Look at your jewels, set and worn
as you had wished and I had sworn.
You needn't be afraid of thieves
coming in unkempt alien droves;
round your breast is the embrace
of twelve thorny flowers in bronze,
on your arm-bone a bracelet weighs,
two shining pearls are in your ears—
beautiful on flesh, on fur,
but now their beauty is most pure.

3
The day we dropped here under ground
our names were no more to be found.
We neither felt inferior
to others, nor wanted to be better.

You are you, I am I,
in the grave's long night we lie.
No one calls my name at all
now, not even you can call.
What was my name? I've forgotten it.
I know I got many blows for it,
a hundred times I wanted a name
more splendid, more colorful, more grim.

Or else I wished I'd been a bear
and shaken my great chops, or had the fear
of the quick wolf in my own teeth:
I wanted the vulture's wingspread, the keen
hawk's sight—
but most of all the raven's three hundred years of life.

All these desires were to remain in a
limbo by the calm cycles
of the millennia.

4
I don't deny the joy would be immense
to know who walks above our tombs!
And why do we never end wondering
where the world is wandering?—
Even now I find I want
a net to cast, a fish to net!
To throw a ball on the green grass,
play catch with bones on a big rock,
kindle a fire to hear it crack—
oh, living has such happiness!

5
What a betrayal you'd give me now
if I thought you regretted following me here!—
but even so I would haunt your steps!
Not for a moment would you be
at rest.

I would embitter your drink and your food!
I would insinuate myself into your kisses:
with you they would not find happiness.

My things that you still kept would be round you,
gathered like breathing demons at your ear,
you would hear creaks, treacherous slitherings
come between you and every pleasure.

Bloody, in spurts of bestial pain,
the embryos would be dragged from your womb;
tortured by daily fiends you'd trail
daylight through a living tomb.

Sleep on therefore quietly in this earth
till your bones and my bones tangle into one.

                              (Edwin Morgan)

LÁSZLÓ BENJÁMIN
(1915–)

POEM BY AN UNKNOWN POET FROM
THE MID-TWENTIETH CENTURY

They ranged themselves in facing lines
—switches would soon be thrust in their hands—
and we were braced to run the gauntlet
down through that pure and heartless band.

It is to induce salvation in us
that ethics swishes from both sides;
and if not by fear and humiliation,
we're bent by chronic belly-gripes.

Endless vigilance, the very virtues
thumped into my long-hunted spine
cheated me of my power to act,
that many-splendored only-mine.

Between four-dimensioned hell and
two-dimensioned heaven, intention
is no more than a scurrying shadow,
reality a fading apparition.

The world is both a game and a role,
and anyone shouldering its truths should
turn himself to a harlequin
when sets become discarded wood.

Let him play for a life and death,
play (he thinks) the man of action.
If being true's a sin, we must
pretend right through to self-deception.

The double line remains unmoved.
A man's face begins to change.
And he forgets his memory,
bricks up all his thoughts, makes strange

his decent ordinary speech
clattering like a jester's rattle:
to alienate false friends, to fool
the informer, he must do his Hamlet.

And the words from the deep!—from those born
to be industrious, born to console:
yet even they, reaching the peak,
wore holy claptrap for the cold.

I gave the age the best I had,
it made me in return the gift
of an individual's death—
and this I think should make us quits.

Since I, if wanted to outwit
its pretty schizophrenic teasings,
should really have been Caesar, not
this faded epigone of Jesus.

Marches blare out in my ears,
armies mobilize, my name
is being called. What name is it?
Is my name truly still the same?

I know the world needs every man
to lift its burden by one shoulder.
But tell this to the one who bore
my name, tell it to that stranger.

(*Edwin Morgan*)

CAVE DRAWINGS

1

A fire in a worldwide darkness.
The old folks' stories.
Through the words and the bones, over the stones,
blackhearted shadows flicker,
negatives of flames, night's
unpredictable monster-cubs,
ravening phantoms. The terrors
of childhood. The dead.
Fear lives in my skull,
in my stomach. By day it lives there,
in my dreams it lives there, I fight it,
fight death coming at me from all quarters.
Fear makes me think.
I waylay the shadows curling across the rocks,
out of the twilight, my fear carves them,
I bind them in unflickering stone.
Copies, imitations? No, but transmuted!
For these are the bold spirits, the foxy hunters,
the fertile mothers, the masters
and guardians and renewers,
the ones that shine out of the dark,
not prisoners but keepers of time.
From the rock-wall they survey their bones.

2

Under my feet the stone,
paved world of men,
hordes, petrol-stench.
Modern times!

A spade's depth under the stone
the earth's worms are swarming,
the upholders of order, the doers of justice.
And sunk in deeper, the junk:
the buckles and the bones.

The ferns, the steamy jungles,
gardens of Semiramis, wonders of the world
all pressed in plant-collectors' wallets,
millennia in slivers,
laminated history.
Nothing but the hopes of those who were shut out
of the promised land—salvation—age of gold—
agnostic heaven: nothing but the future.

It's all one!—the knuckles sketch a gesture.
No use!—the jaw shards clatter.
The future began when
silent death fumbled over us,
rolled our bones in earth.
We are advertisements for hopelessness,
agitators for drift:
Remember death!

3
I do remember death,
and I commemorate the dead.
While I am here, I carve the images
of life, the words of life, in the stones of the city,
in the memory of the living.
As for that clutter of bones in the ground,
that toothless skull,
everything I shall come to—
it is not that future I am concerned with.
In case they should be buried with me, my plans
I want changed to everyday things.
In the present tense.
My burdens are for no other shoulders!
For good order, for good hunting,
for ourselves and for the unborn
I have sought out friendly hands,
called to kindred passions,
pulled hatred on my head:
and for something more than fear of the dark.

                                        (*Edwin Morgan*)

GÁBOR DEVECSERI
(*1917–1971*)

THE WORLD AWOKE ME

The world awoke me; its flood freeing
My wits from dream, starting up memory,
Puffing my past into a globe of being:
"I shall be myself soon; soon I shall be me."

(*Robert Graves*)

THE BATH IN PYLOS

Sweet Polycaste, Nestor's youngest daughter
Here washed Telemachus, as was most fit.
Well oiled and scraped, she drew him from the water
To don bright garments—custom called for it.

Heroic youths invited to this hall
Knew that the youngest daughter of its king
Would soon dart forward—what more natural?—
And give them, within reason, anything.

The grime that from his limbs she scoured for us
Has gone, by diligent procumbent women
Long ago wiped away. Telemachus
Himself is dust. Yet the bath she put *him* in
Richly proclaims the blessings of survival
Antiquity rephrased and without rival.

(*Robert Graves*)

HIS LIFE

His life is a mere
  Day's happening:
He feels no fear
  For the evening;

He has always done
  What he had to do,
While light of the Sun
  Fell sharp and new.

(Robert Graves)

ODYSSEUS IN PHAEACIA

Whom might this shipwrecked man most wish to meet
  As here he crawls ashore in full undress,
And whose kind patronage would most assist him?—
  Say, for example, that of a Princess?

And should he trouble much about her lineage—
  So long, that is, as she will not withhold
Garments and food; shows magnanimity
  And dutiful concern; and is not bold,

Nor curious? Let the princess point the way
  To her home town (if not too hard to reach),
Meanwhile letting him gently lie and rest
  Under the olive shade beyond this beach,

This hospitable beach of kindly pebbles;
  And since his life has once again been saved,
Why not begin afresh? What a fine notion!
  Though at the spring he dutifully laved

His hair crusted with brine, matted with weed,
    His face, his shoulders, yet "Escape from Death"
Rings in his proud heart unrestrainedly—
    A godlike vaunt while still he can draw breath

And still repeat his story: "Here stand I
    Who plunge undaunted into every sea
Where Death's own creatures vainly lay their ambush
    For this immortal and infinite me."

("Princess, I thank you for your splendid kindness
    But I am indestructible—look here!
Once more I go where the loud mocking seas
    Multiply dangers that I scorn to fear.")

(Robert Graves)

WOMEN AND MASKS

Women and masks: an old familiar story.
Life slowly drains away and we are left
As masks of what we were. The living past
Rightly respects all countenances offered
As visible sacrifices to the gods
And clamps them fast even upon live faces.
Let face be mask then, or let mask be face—
Mankind can take its ease, may assume godhead.
Thus God from time to time descends in power
Graciously, not to a theologian's hell
But to our human hell enlaced with heaven.

Let us wear masks once worn in the swift circlings
And constant clamor of a holy dance
Performed always in prayer, in the ecstasy
Of love-hate murder—today's children always
Feeling, recording, never understanding.

Yet this old woman understands, it seems,
At least the unimportance of half-knowledge,
Her face already become mask, her teeth
Wide-gapped as though to scare us, her calm face
Patterned with wrinkles in unchanging grooves
That outlive years, decades and centuries.
Hers is a mask remains exemplary
For countless generations. Who may wear it?
She only, having fashioned it herself.
So long as memory lasts us, it was hers.

Behind it she assembles her rapt goodness,
Her gentle worth already overflooding
The mask, her prison, shaming its fierce, holy
Terror: for through its gaping sockets always
Peer out a pair of young and lovely eyes.

                                        (Robert Graves)

IMRE CSANÁDI
(1920-   )

SILENT PRAYER OF PEASANTS

Lord, it's very hard to get
your politics, try as we may.
Bad times—you can see it yet.
That world war that came our way,
crisis and such we had to shoulder—
you know it seemed at times we'd rather
snuff it than go on. Made us bolder
in rapping your saints, you too, father.

What would your reaction be right now
if you were in the room with us, to watch
the showers that have been pouring down
like nemesis, our whole summer awash?

Look at our hay rotting in clumps,
our meadow utterly rained away
in floodwater. The cow lows at us:
what will she chew in winter? clay?

Frogs are croaking through our wheatfields,
reeds and waterplants make merry...
And what's the future of this story?
We don't know what tomorrow yields!

But you are not our only Lord—
we're in the slobbery ravenous jaws
of other lords that never pause

in their "more! more! you can afford
taxes! taxes!"—They ask, they get;
add fret and fever to fever and fret.

Your Four Horsemen gallop and neigh.
The four corners of heaven shake.
Night-watchmen drive dogs mad, and take
the call-up papers for next day.

(1941)   *(Edwin Morgan)*

HOLIDAY-AFTERNOON RHAPSODY

Trombone blurts plumply,
taut-bellied drum mutters,
laid-on Entertainment gasps
in self-complacent rapture.

Otherwise dumbness,
furnace heat, clotted deafness.

In scrawny shade of acacias,
listlessly shouldering their cart-rail manger,
steers munch, brandish tails,
whisk the stinging flies away.

Co-tenants with the dungheap,
in lard-melting sun
sheep stand on splayed stick legs,
stinking internees
of a pen like the palm of a hand.
Their squalid fleece drips down in threads.
They bleat vacuously, to themselves,
the torment, the Asiatic one.

Half-feathered chickens take a scorching dust-bath.

The church's clishmaclaver
filters from hollow echoing centuries
into spaces of the swept street
and sweetens into devotion.
Geese too are aware of it,
waddling home with tilted heads,
gaggling for admittance.
Goslings make music of their
girlish, wheedling gossip.

They make the local promenade complete.

The good holiday dinner
stretches fancy townee braces
over jacketless shirt, not a town fashion now—
the young farmer walks his family
down the middle of the high street:
adjusting to his changing world.

His little son is quite sports-mad:
look at the great kick he gives
the pigshit-mound with his best red sandals—

Ha-a-Ha-a-a—
from the wide-open windows
with their geraniums
and their nameless
weeds and squills
the world's radio-waves
blare a hideous aria.

Like bloodless appurtenances
old fossils bake on doorway benches
in bright white linen pantaloons
and tight black broadcloth waistcoats.

They gurgle as their pipes draw strongly,
spit periodically from the corner of their mouths,
are querulous—it's become a habit—about this world.
Soon they will get their quittance of it,

like last season's dry stalks,
papery thistles with rustling heads,
as winter yields
to newer green.

A handbag-swinging slip of a girl sets them mumbling,
that dress, should go with city pavements,
her movement, her freedom, hers or hers—
guessing: *whose brat would that one be?*
A villager?
An incomer?
For these days there are so many strangers,
God only knows and what is it to him.

Wearing alien masks
the young stream past,
stream past without a greeting—
stepping rudely
over good old customs,
traditions inherited
and held as holy.

Lonely old folk can't but blink at it all,
even their teeth chatter.
It's like: that little bench they're on,
the street, the village, the fields were off
in an earthquake—slipping, slipping,
vanishing with the landmarks,
vanishing with the fences,
vanishing with ancestral memories and pious biblical
                                                    maxims.

Where should they huddle?
What should they hold on to?
Not a chimney left,
not a boundary-stone,
not one solid fence-post—all are moving!
All break and waver like a boat's mast on water!
All are driven, all are drowning!—

So they clutch their pipes
desperately, their
little bits and pieces,
what's left of their lives,
of their old fathers' mouldering beliefs—

And trombone blurts plumply,
taut-bellied drum mutters.

Furnace heat, clotted deafness.

(Edwin Morgan)

CONFESSION OF FAITH

I have no case to bring against Socialism,
I believe in it and I want to believe in it,
as a whelp of it I have as good a claim
as some who had the foresight or the wit

to riddle into it like maggots into cheese,
and now look down on me, well-fed, askance,
taunting me with my inexpertise
in passing up the feast, missing my chance.

I love to hear Hungary hum like a top:
there's better health and talk, more bread in the shop.
And worries too—smiles broaden, sometimes stop.

No absence of dismay for mouth or mind—
I have no case to bring. It can't be blind,
some day it too will bless me in the crop.

(Edwin Morgan)

SMALL CRAFTSMAN

An "obscure craftsman" but my own man!
I'd rather be that with integrity
than puff my cheeks and jabber like a titan
in a pseudo-thunderstorm
of parody.

(*Edwin Morgan*)

GYÖRGY SOMLYÓ
(1920–   )

TALE ABOUT A FLOWER

I pace back and forth in my room, rest my knee on the
    chair before my desk, turn a book's pages, light up
    a butt, sip a drink, looking for words . . .

The large pink peony rests unmoving in the vase.

I seize my coat, rush out to take care of some business
    of mine, something I think is important, come home . . .

The peony is where it was, turned toward me, its large
    head of petals gazing at me.

It eyes me unceasingly, never tiring of me. Completely
    unfolded, a wide-open eye, huge as the rose window
    of Notre Dame.

How shall I express myself?

The peony desires no self-expression. It is wholly
    itself, without effort or art. That is what makes
    it so lovely.

It is pure sensibility. When I walk near it, the slightest
    vibration of my steps on the floor can set it a-tremble.

Am I enamored of vegetable life, of the consolations of
    the unconscious, the nonhuman?

No, I long only to be, as naturally as the peony.

It's not that I'd be a flower, but a man in the way that
    the flower is a flower . . .

The great pink peony.

(Daniel Hoffman)

TALE OF THE DOUBLE HELIX

Son of my mother
          father of my son
I was born
          I was begotten
I was reared
          I was reared
I took over
          and handed over
I buried
          and will be buried
I slowly achieve
          what is achievable
on the crystal chain
          or basic bonds
of the single life
          made from two
It is Time
          makes me unique
with every rank
          and binds me fast
with every valence
          But these my cells
have no idea
          caged in themselves
how far the cells
          through them ascend

on and on
                    the dark steps
of the spiral stairs
                    or Jacob's ladder
in the desoxiribo-
                    nucleic acid
sky-dome
                    or skull-hole

                                        (Daniel Hoffman)

TALE ABOUT A/AN...

The only contentment for our bodies
                    on the inhospitable earth
is the pure effort
                    which earns its reward
maximum rest
          after
                    maximum performance
is the only grace
          there
                    where there is nothing but judgment
where he stumbles
          in the dust
                    who was taken from dust
in vain he spreads over it a
          barrel-roofed
          dust-free
          mudless
          glutinous
                    covering
and under him the glide
                    of steel, rubber, or inflatable cushion
in vain he'd push off in the ponderous
                    distance of weightlessness
Illusions dearly bought
                    of the solid and the straight

of the measurable and the limitable

                         the integratable by velocity

while

   . blood

    water

    digestion

    secretions of lymph

    mucus

    hormones

            continue

in us incalculably to wind their ways

                      toward their destinies

Our Father which art in our bodies, Revealed be thy name (which after
so many divine revelations and so many millennia of profane speech and
comprehension exercises remains still unuttered) nomen tuum nomen
tuum nomen tuum for Thou art the Way, the Truth, the Life just as
Thine is the Kingdom, and the Power, and the Glory as well as all the
Names and everything Unnameable that has been given Thee by man's
centuries of despair and elation in our nerves as in our words for since our
conception we have lived in Thy kingdom and Thy Will till our death
panemnostrumquotidianumdanobishodie so that we needn't get it in the
daily humiliating barter deals of Sin and Forgiveness and lead us not
into Neurosis but deliver us from the daily catastrophes of vegetative
life and consciousness in the Name of the Holy Trinity and Holy
Unity of Organs Nerves Thoughts Now and Forever Amen

                                           (Daniel Hoffman)

SÁNDOR RÁKOS
(1921–)

PHEASANT

The brow of night is stricken and turns frosty.
The dawn is breaking, as the cock-crow scatters,
some idle blades untangled are still drowsy—
and noises strengthen, waking shadow clusters.

Round seven o'clock the landscape fills with people.
Down at the meadow the task is haymaking.
One reaper wades in mist up to his middle:
like someone's ghost, with no one's legs, he's walking.

A pheasant sparkles in the tattered bushes.
Drops from a branch lightly, then flies away.
Wings take the summer as surely as feathers,
only the memory follows that way.

(Alan Dixon)

INTERROGATION

behind the door
they are plotting our lives
we don't even know the questions
we try to pass off answers
memorized beforehand
anxiety
beads our faces

solitude of minus 273°
maybe our turn will come soon
before the granite
slabs of waiting
topple
and crush us

(Daniel Hoffman)

CREATURE

He muscled in on my turf
trampled the grass in my lair
baited traps under trees
waited for me in a high blind in the branches
the first day I stayed clear of him
kept my distance the second and the third
not that I was afraid but
he disgusted me
for three days longer I kept out of his way
but at last
on the seventh day
I just got sick and tired of his filthy
treachery
waiting in ambush
and with the sun's rising
I stepped from the leaves' disguise
into the clearing
for an instant our eyes met
his eyes and mine
then my revulsion
while his finger
tightened on the trigger
transfixed him
between the movement
and the blast
—in that glimpse
was my life

(Daniel Hoffman)

JÁNOS PILINSZKY
(1921–)

UNDER THE WINTER SKY

Over my head the stars
jostle their icy flames.
A sky without mercy.
I lean my back to the wall.

Sadness trickles searching
past my orphaned lips.
What happened to my mother's milk?
I smudge my coat.

I am like the stone—
no matter what comes, let it come.
I shall be so obedient and good
I shall lie down full length.

I shall not deceive myself any longer.
There is nobody to help me.
Suffering cannot redeem me.
No god will protect me.

Nothing could be simpler than this
or more horrible.
The biblical monsters
start slowly towards me.

(1943)   *(Ted Hughes)*

SIN

You are still a child but already your limbs
almost deliberately dazzle
in the dawning
system of curves.
And, like a secret smile,
if not your hip, your shoulder
forgets you, and betrays you.
I see you from head to heel.

I look at you, till I can no longer bear it.
One move
and my life starts to slip softly
like a crumbling sand-pit.
You are still fragile—escape
before it reaches you!
Your head topples with a nod.
It was hit by the first blow.

The collapsing years
mine towards you, greedily.
Like starved sticks
the immense forest comes to life.
My nights! The shivering
mob of my nights.
They pounce on you bodily—
a morsel of bread.

They snap your young wrist
they crush your back
they are seeking the happiness they never
found with me.
The lost child,
blinding youth!
And they throw you away empty
like a gutted sack.

Is this what you are saving for me?
I watch you, detached, numb.
Where is the shoulder that flared
the hint of its splendor?
My hands hang, confused,
in empty air.
Would it be you that was killed?
Would I be the one who killed her?

(Ted Hughes)

PASSION OF RAVENSBRÜCK

He steps out from the others.
He stands in the square silence.
The prison garb, the convict's skull
blink like a projection.

He is horribly alone.
His pores are visible.
Everything about him is so gigantic,
everything is so tiny.

And this is all.
                    The rest—
the rest was simply
that he forgot to cry out
before he collapsed.

(Ted Hughes)

THE DESERT OF LOVE

A bridge, and a hot concrete road—
the day is emptying its pockets,
laying out, one by one, all its possessions.
You are quite alone in the catatonic twilight.

A landscape like the bed of a wrinkled pit,
with glowing scars, a darkness which dazzles.
Dusk thickens. I stand numb with brightness
blinded by the sun. This summer will not leave me.

Summer. And the flashing heat.
The chickens stand, like burning cherubs,
in the boarded-up, splintered cages.
I know their wings do not even tremble.

Do you still remember? First there was the wind.
And then the earth. Then the cage.
Flames, dung. And now and again
a few wing-flutters, a few empty reflexes.

And thirst. I asked for water—
Even today I hear that feverish gulping,
and helplessly, like a stone, bear
and quench the mirages.

Years are passing. And years. And hope
is like a tin-cup toppled into the straw.

                                        (Ted Hughes)

APOCRYPHA

I
Everything will be forsaken then

The silence of the heavens will be set apart
and forever apart
the broken-down fields of the finished world,
and apart
the silence of dog-kennels.
In the air a fleeing host of birds.
And we shall see the rising sun
dumb as a demented eye-pupil
and calm as a watching beast.

But keeping vigil in banishment
because that night
I cannot sleep I toss
as the tree with its thousand leaves
and at dead of night I speak as the tree:
Do you know the drifting of the years
the years over the crumpled fields?
Do you understand the wrinkle
of transience? Do you comprehend
my care-gnarled hands? Do you know
the name of orphanage? Do you know
what pain treads the unlifting darkness
with cleft hooves, with webbed feet?
The night, the cold, the pit. Do you know
the convict's head twisted askew?
Do you know the caked troughs, the tortures
of the abyss?

The sun rose. Sticks of trees blackening
in the infra-red of the wrathful sky.

So I depart. Facing devastation
a man is walking, without a word.
He has nothing. He has his shadow.
And his stick. And his prison garb.

2

And this is why I learned to walk! For these
belated bitter steps.

Evening will come, and night will petrify
above me with its mud. Beneath closed eyelids
I do not cease to guard this procession
these fevered shrubs, their tiny twigs.
Once Paradise stood here.
In half-sleep, the renewal of pain:
to hear its gigantic trees.

Home—I wanted finally to get home—
to arrive as he in the Bible arrived.
My ghastly shadow in the courtyard.
Crushed silence, aged parents in the house.
And already they are coming, they are calling me,
my poor ones, and already crying,
and embracing me, stumbling—
the ancient order opens to readmit me.
I lean out on the windy stars.

If only for this once I could speak with you
whom I loved so much. Year after year
yet I never tired of saying over
what a small child sobs
into the gap between the palings,
the almost choking hope
that I come back and find you.
Your nearness throbs in my throat.
I am agitated as a wild beast.

I do not speak your words,
the human speech. There are birds alive
who flee now heart-broken
under the sky, under the fiery sky.
Forlorn poles stuck in a glowing field,
and immovably burning cages.

I do not understand the human speech,
and I do not speak your language.
My voice is more homeless than the word!
I have no words.
                    Its horrible burden
tumbles down through the air—
a tower's body emits sounds.

You are nowhere. How empty the world is.
A garden chair, and a deck chair left outside.
Among sharp stones my clangorous shadow.
I am tired. I jut out from the earth.

3
God sees that I stand in the sun.
He sees my shadow on stone and on fence.
He sees my shadow standing
without a breath in the airless press.

By then I am already like the stone;
a dead fold, a drawing of a thousand grooves,
a good handful of rubble
is by then the creature's face.

And instead of tears, the wrinkles on the faces
trickling, the empty ditch trickles down.

                                            (Ted Hughes)

POSTSCRIPT

For Pierre Emmanuel

Do you still remember? On the faces.
Do you still remember? The ditch, vacant.
Do you still remember? Down it trickles.
Do you still remember? In the sun, I'm waiting.

You are reading the *Paris Journal*.
It's been winter since then, nights of winter.
You are laying the table in my sight,
you are making the bed in the moonlight.

You are undressing with silent breath
in the desolate house, in the blackness.
You let down your shirt, your clothes.
Like a blank gravestone your back rests.

Image of strength in unhappiness.
Is anybody here?
                        Waking dreams:
there is no answer as I cross
through the drowned mirrored rooms.

Is that my face then, is it that face?
The light, the silence, the sentence shatter
as my face, this stone comes flying
towards me from the snow-white mirror!

And the horsemen there! The horsemen there!
I'm hurt by the lamplight, troubled by the twilight.
Water drips in a thin trickle
down the imperturbable china.

It's closed doors I'm knocking on.
Your room breathes darkness: coal-dust sleeping.
In the cold the walls tremble.
I smudge the wall with all my weeping.

Help me roof-tops heavy with snow!
It's night-time. Let whatever is lonely
blaze brightly before the sun of *nada*
appears. Let it blaze on vainly.

I lean my head against the wall.
Handfuls of snow from all around me
are held out, mercy is held out, handed
by a dead town to a dead townsman.

I loved you! A single shout, a sigh,
a flying cloud is scurrying, vanishing.
And the horsemen clumping bluntly, cantering
up with the draggled dawn, are entering.

                                        (Edwin Morgan)

FABLE

Detail from "KZ-Oratorio"

Once upon a time
there was a lonely wolf
lonelier than the angels.

He happened to come to a village.
He fell in love with the first house he saw.

Already he loved its walls,
the caresses of its bricklayers.
But the windows stopped him.

In the room sat people.
Apart from God nobody ever
found them so beautiful
as this childlike beast.

So at night he went into the house.
He stopped in the middle of the room
and never moved from there any more.

He stood all through the night, with wide eyes
and on into the morning when he was beaten to death.

(Ted Hughes)

AS I WAS

As I was at the start
so, all along, I have remained.
The way I began, so I will go on to the end.
Like the convict who, returning
to his village, goes on being silent.
Speechless he sits in front of his glass of wine.

(Ted Hughes)

CELEBRATION OF THE NADIR

In the blood-stained warmth of sties
who dares read?
And who dares
in the splintering field of the setting sun

when sky is at its high tide
and earth at its ebb
set out, anywhere?

Who dares
stand still with closed eyes
at that lowest point
there where
there's always a flick of the hand,
a roof,
a lovely face, or just
the hand, a nod, a movement of the hand?

Who can
with a calm heart sink slowly down
into that dream that overflows childhood's
pain and lifts
the whole sea to his face in a handful of water?

(William Jay Smith)

I SHALL BE WATCHING

I shall be watching how the water trickles—
branching in faltering delicate paths—
the inscriptions of agony
and chance, their long outlines
on dead stones, living faces—

I shall be watching them before
I gain oblivion.

(William Jay Smith)

JÁNOS PILINSZKY

METRONOME

Measure time
but not our time,
the motionless present of splinters,
the angles of the drawbridge,
the white winter of our execution,
the silence of paths and clearings,
in the setting of the fragmented jewel
the promise of God the Father.

(William Jay Smith)

EXHORTATION

Not the respiration. The gasping.
Not the wedding table. The falling
scraps, the chill, the shadows.
Not the gesture. Not the hysteria.
The silence of the hook is what you must note.

Remember
what your city, the everlasting city
has not forgotten.
With its towers, its roofs,
its living and dead populace.

Then you may make known,
perhaps, even in your day,
what is alone
worthy the annunciation,

Scribe

then perhaps you will not have passed in vain.

(Ted Hughes)

EVERY BREATH

Every breath wounds me,
every heart-beat knocks me down.
Odd that the sea is immortal
although its every wave is doom.

How does God govern his eternal
presence, in the forever
perishing field of creation?

Like the resigned life of grasses,
the heart-beats of mortals,
in the end that is what glory must be—
the grave happiness of God.

(William Jay Smith)

THE REST IS GRACE

Terror and dream
were my father and mother.
And a corridor was the
country opening out.

So I lived. How shall I die?
What will my end be like?

The earth betrays me in its embrace;
the rest is grace.

(William Jay Smith)

JÁNOS PILINSZKY
MEETINGS

How many kinds of meetings, Lord
being together, being separated—farewell.
Wave meeting wave, flower parting from flower,
in the windless calm, in wind,
moving, unmoving,
how many different transfigurations,
how many interchanges
of the perishable and the imperishable!

(William Jay Smith)

CATTLE BRAND

1
There is no cattle brand
I don't deserve.

It will be good for me to cross
the white-washed threshold of death.

Everything we have deserved is good.

2
With a nail driven into the world's palm,
pale as death,
I flow with blood.

(William Jay Smith)

ALL THAT IS NEEDED

However wide creation is,
it is more cramped than a sty.
From here to there. Stone, wood, house.
I do this and that. Come early, am late.

And yet at times someone enters
And suddenly what is expands.
All that's needed is the sight of a face, a presence,
and the wallpaper begins to bleed.

All that is needed, yes, is a hand
stirring the coffee, or
withdrawing from an introduction.
That's all that is needed for us to forget the place,
the dismal row of windows, yes,
when returning at night to our room—
for us to accept the unacceptable.

(William Jay Smith)

ÁGNES NEMES NAGY
(1922–   )

STATUES

Bitter the sea's taste, bitter when
I tumbled down the gorge of stone
a pebble spinning down the spiral steps
that droned behind me like a conch's shell,
memory's drone between the walls
in a deserted house—
I clattered
shrapnel fragments rattling in a skull

    Then out on the beach I rolled
    among the statues

On a plinth
a tortoise-egg covered with skin
my skull was baking in the sun
my helmet a white bubble on the sand
and in soiled uniform I lay
my shoulder to the rock

    —Whose slab is this?
    Who hacks
    this uncaring shape
    with terrible passion from a hill of slate?

Sheet metal covers me, sheet metal
dented boxes
reflecting pieces of the light,
  wrecked airplane shines like this

but the survivors move inside it...
a little blood's there on my watchband,
I lie spreadeagled on the stone,
a splotch of life's refuse

What a stubborn thing to do
Stubborn
to throw yourself into the stone

Salt and sand and the stone slab
like a cave scooped in the sky
this relative eternity
this halflight of the minerals
—Who carved this
from a slate mountain,
who carved your living throat?

The water roars, roars, its bed is Earth,
its bitterness is in a dish of stone.

(Daniel Hoffman)

I CARRIED STATUES

To the ship I carried statues,
Vast and nameless were their faces.
To the ship I carried statues
Island-bound for destined places.
Straight-hewn nose and sculpted ear
Huge, set perpendicular,
But no other markings found.
To the ship I carried statues,
And so was drowned.

(Daniel Hoffman)

ÁGNES NEMES NAGY

BETWEEN

The air's enveloping capacious sleeves.
The air on which the bird disports,
which ornithology supports,
wing on the ragged edge of arguments,
foliage bearing astonished reports
a minute of the sky takes, leaves,
the trees of the tremulous mist, spiralling
their longing to the upper branches,
each minute breathing twenty times
the huskiest angels of the frost.

And here below, the weight. Upon this plain
vast chunks of mountain tremulously moan;
rocks, ridges of rock, peaks, though they lie
are able to kneel upon one knee;
sculpture, geology combine;
the valley, a distraction of a minute,
is displaced by blocks, the restless volumes
muscling an outline on the chalky bone,
identity crumpled into stone.

          Between the sky and ground.

Loud dislocations of the rocks.
As the translucent ores within sun's heat
almost metallize, if glowing stone
is stamped on by an animal, its claw
spitting out smoke, above the rocks, rise, soar
the twisting ribbons from the kindling hooves,
and then the night in desolation,
the night as it extinguishes, reaches in
to the spine, intrinsic rock, the glacial night,
and as the ligaments, joints, stone blocks
wrinkle and fissure, cleaved to racks
of aggravated endlessness
in a splitting ungovernable trance,

habitually in black and white
the forging hammerings of the lightning strike—

Between the day and night.

The devastations, lacerations,
the visions, the drouth, the privations,
the disproportionate resurrections,
the verticals intolerably taut
between the lower stretchers and the high—

Meridians. Conditions.
Between. Stone. Ruts of tanks.
Scribbled reeds across the desert margin, black,
two lines, in the sky, on the lake,
on two blackboards, a system, a coding,
accents of stars, reed lettering—

Between the sky and sky.

(Alan Dixon)

DEFEND IT

Defend it, call it a thing of worth,
worth all the effort, call it best,
worth climbing, putting it to the test,
the high benevolence, the strife,
the hidden edge on the lagging knife,
the brave death at its stealthiest,
say, say that it was worth the love
of mind traversing a dark recess
flashing its streaky beam to prove
it worth the gasping, the distress
of breath withheld, the postulates
of intellect, the dumb word's gist,
the abstract nouns, distinction, the chest
stiffening as the heart digests

its flame in cloud gravid with snow,
internal cloud, snow biting, to last
in a city where the flames must grow,
say it was worth it to our time,
while on two shoulders not to cease
and on two wrists and on two feet
irrevocable injuries teem
and burst apart, infliction's waste,
continuous blood, a blackened stream—

                                    (Alan Dixon)

A COMPARISON

One who rows a storm at the inception,
quadriceps aching to the uttermost,
who strains to push away that rock, the footboard,
whose right hand loses, all of a sudden,
substance and effort as the oar bends backward
appropriated from a fractured handle,
whose liberated body then
convulses—
can gather my meaning.

                                    (Alan Dixon)

THE SHAPELESSNESS

The shapelessness, the endlessness.
I almost fall before I cut away
my statement from the timelessness.
With sand I wall a bucketful of sea
against a waste of nothingness.
Perpetual indifference should be
intolerable to consciousness.

                                    (Alan Dixon)

ISTVÁN KORMOS
(1923--   )

I AM BEING DRAGGED BY RED DOLPHINS

dragged along by scarlet dolphins through a sea of soot in darkness
thrown on the shore I find that shore the shore where my collapsing heart is
blindness couldn't stop me going my dream-built house of you still lingers
but your gate is open-knife-gate light through your window sending signals
and hands hands hands hands hands send me off and don't reprieve me
soundless voice I should release you soundless voice I ought to leave you
you are not the one to return tugged back far into your childhood
wings of my imploring words flutter wasted on your forehead
cannot-be-lights in your glances speak of what cannot be spoken
that you'll not be that I'll not be agonized the laughter's broken
still-born son our future goes floating through the sooty oceans
scarlet horses that once dragged me are devoured now by the dolphins
a solitary dog is barking calling my name but not my being
the sky over my bowed head glitters like saltpetre freezing
the cell of loneliness is here I the son of gods am silent
Paris Marlotte Normandy vanish under my Atlantis

(Edwin Morgan)

THE LAMENT OF ORPHEUS

I began to play my music and the raven stopped in mid-flight
the foal fell on its knees wildly shaking its neck-bell
the waters lost their anger sun moon ran to me in joy
the outcast figtree wept out its pleasure in grainy pearls
somewhere the gods were frowning listening with folded arms

they drove Eurydice from their feet to follow me and laughed harshly
my ears were full of crying my heart full of iron nails
my eyes full of tears of salt I said no to my twitching fist
I didn't turn! it's a lie! I swear by my mangled music!

(Edwin Morgan)

VOYAGE

Ulysses' flying window dodges
lightswords of troutmoons and doughnutsuns
seas like saharas under ships like camels
lightning housewalls rusthairy woods
his name police names scored out dashed down
well no one runs to his gate to welcome him
poloneck sweater cigarettes in his pocket
sits on some stone lights up sulphur spark
a shout ripples out brims him to the eyes
he ought to stand but only waves says balls

(Edwin Morgan)

AFTER US

After us there will be truer men.
The great knights-hospitallers of mendacity,
the cap-and-bells of lurking lip-service,
the incurable epileptics of system and dogma,
the sleazy sleeve-twitching ace-of-spadesmen,
and the crows too that ravage our crops,
and at last the foxes, will all disappear.
If you come, Golden Age, we shall have gone.
You must bring clear-browed boys with you!
You must bring merry-limbed girls with you!
They will give each word its naked meaning,
and put all things to rights—after us.

(Edwin Morgan)

LAJOS KASSÁK

Károly Koffán

Zsuzsa Koncz   Lőrinc Szabó, jr.

MILÁN FÜST   LŐRINC SZABÓ

GYULA ILLYÉS

ZOLTÁN ZELK   ANNA HAJNAL

Layle Silbert   Gábor Komáromi

AMY KÁROLYI   ISTVÁN VAS

Demeter Balla   Demeter Balla

LÁSZLÓ KÁLNOKY   GYÖRGY RÓNAY

Layle Silbert

SÁNDOR WEÖRES

Demeter Balla

ZOLTÁN JÉKELY

János Reismann

LÁSZLÓ BENJÁMIN

GÁBOR DEVECSERI

János Reismann

Demeter Balla

IMRE CSANÁDI

Demeter Balla

GYÖRGY SOMLYÓ

Ella Wellesz   Károly Koffán

SÁNDOR RÁKOS   JÁNOS PILINSZKY

Layle Silbert

ÁGNES NEMES NAGY

Demeter Balla

ISTVÁN KORMOS

János Reismann

MIHÁLY VÁCI

János Reismann

LÁSZLÓ NAGY

János Reismann

ISTVÁN SIMON

JÓZSEF TORNAI

FERENC JUHÁSZ

MARGIT SZÉCSI

GÁBOR GÖRGEY

Demeter Balla   Demeter Balla

GÁBOR GARAI   SÁNDOR CSOÓRI

Demeter Balla

ISTVÁN EÖRSI

Demeter Balla

ÁGNES GERGELY

Demeter Balla

Demeter Balla

MIHÁLY LADÁNYI

Demeter Balla

MÁRTON KALÁSZ

Demeter Balla

OTTÓ ORBÁN

László Kaszás

JUDIT TÓTH

József Hapák

ISTVÁN CSUKÁS

Demeter Balla

ISTVÁN ÁGH

Demeter Balla

DEZSŐ TANDORI

MIKLÓS VERESS

Demeter Balla

Demeter Balla

GYÖRGY PETRI

György Gara

SZABOLCS VÁRADY

DEEP SEA

Deep-sea darkness, deep-sea silence.
Drowned objects: table, chair, tumbler,
ink-water in the tumbler, white shirt
thrown on the floor, and pearly letters
'Attila József' studding my wall, somewhere
a weasel-legged second hand,
the room's four corners plunged in pitch,
can you be there—

I welter with my sleepless bed:
island drifting between coral teeth;
face held in palms; palms, if you were sand
you could soak up the drops of my wakefulness.

If you saw me now! absence-imprisoned!
Birds would mount from your tight eyelids
fluttering onto the walls of pain,
splitting my darkness with their beaks
and splitting my silence with their wings.
Then your forehead would gleam,
bringing back memories of my boyhood,
St. Stephen's day with its rocket-stars flashing
green, white, red, yellow, your ten fingers
gliding along my temples like light,
your sweet breath on the skin of my face.

You would send up three bubbles
of laughter-silver to burst on the wall,
out of the first a drowsy foal,
out of the second some hay, and the third a crib,
and silvery bubbles would float up again
and out of them Three Kings; they come
here to my bed, Caspar, Melchior, Balthazar,
they chant, they bang down their great staff.
After them it is you, willow-wand-waisted,
you step from your shoes, bend over me,
your two knees shine, electric fish,
swim apart in the deep-sea darkness,

recharge its warmth; the forest of your hair
shakes loose, splays over me,
you let its raw fires pour out,
your heart's carillon peals.
Drowned objects: table, chair, tumbler,
ink-water in the tumbler, white shirt
thrown on the floor, and pearly letters
of Attila's name studding my wall, my borrowed
watch with its weasel-legged second hand,
the room's four corners plunged in pitch
come vaguely into view as your hand moves.

But now, this deep-sea silence is everything.
This deep-sea darkness is everywhere.
Salt sweat, snap of shoulder-bones.
A window scrubbed by rain and wind.

(Edwin Morgan)

MIHÁLY VÁCI
(1924–1970)

BEFORE I DIE

Before I die, to suffocation's level
    I must inhale this bitter carnation;
before I die, we'll stand and drink together
    a strong coffee to feed our attention.
Before I die, many will telephone me:
    friends, acquaintances I've forgotten,
whose handshakes I know, whose letters will be
    safe in my life's collection.
Before I die, I'll journey to say farewell
    to submissive villages,
and see for the last time beribboned wind
    like the shaking of manes.
Before I die, I shall open my window
    to the sky, my soul shall be lifted,
carried away with commands of wild geese to the spring,
    which they, the harsh-voiced, have announced.
Before I die!—but until then I'll keep holding
    onto determination's torment—I live!
as if my life is surely reaching its end
    in all the last hour must give.
For me each hour is the only one,
    and each new action;
I feel that each kiss I'm sharing
    bears, though brief, no repetition.
I look on sky, on earth, on women,
    into eyes, and to the stars
with the sullen look of one saying good-bye,
    who, sure he is dying, waves.

I am a man condemned, with his final wish,
    taking his last wine and breath,
knowing the last hour's last minute;
    I do not take them from my mouth.

(Alan Dixon)

THE MOST-AGE

See how we produce
with the most modern technology
for the most varied purposes
our most identical products,
in the most varied assortments—but within these
keeping a most eagle eye
on the most similar measurements
most understandably, surely, for within each group
the most minute variation
would cause the most massive confusion, this alone
must be most clearly
most understandable, must it not.

Following the most international interests
the most individual requirements
must be the most universally satisfied. Today
the most individual is what
is the most ubiquitous, and
the most original is what
is the most such-like as
the most absolutely
non-like. Everyone
would most preferably be like what today
mostly everyone is. The
most individual individual is
the most similar to everyone and the one
we can most readily be similar to. The
most original is what
most can

most readily attain. Today the
most dissident is the one who's
the most readily acceptable. The
most dissenting, to whom
most people
most readily
give assent in most things. The
most revolutionary, whatever
can be played with most safely
with the most innocuous aim
with the most meaninglessness
for the most people.
Today the
most
is the
mere.

This perhaps is
the most understandable
even for the most few
and the most futile too, is it not.

(Edwin Morgan)

LÁSZLÓ NAGY
(1925–   )

FROSTS ARE COMING

Hard frosts march together—
white rage, a ruthless guard
snapping down the shoulder
like pretzel in their tread.

Where to live without you?
That makes fibres shiver.
Your nearness a refuge
dawn's slow fires discover.

I can't bear the sight of
that winter-cold platter.
Take it! Feed me with love
now my shadow wears thinner.

Let me put the roof on
our love's burning-tower;
unfasten the skirt on
your hip's gold and lustre.

(Alan Dixon)

THE COALMEN

In the outer suburbs the coalmen race their carts,
they forget the decorum proper to men of trade,
"G'D' yup" they roar, and hoofs strike sparks from the dark,
"G'D' yup," and the jolting cart-lamps leap and fade.

The carts are coaches! Their drunken, heroic burdens,
rolling and grabbing-hold in a splendor of black,
billow wraith-blooms of rum on the jangling air—
dangling to watch the wheels, or lolling back

in a dog-tired daze, beyond the constellations,
with nothing above but the depths, the empty spaces;
they obey no law, they're numb to the tumbling hailstones
pocking like birdshot at their coal-grimed faces.

Steam flies, foam flicks!—the mighty, drenched dray-horses,
sniffing the stables, bolt for their fodder and sleep;
but that Palace is far from lust for the dusty lads,
who will find sharp draughts, dead fires, and walls that weep.

No wives await them, no girls that are game for fun
will wiggle wide hips and giggle behind the beams;
saltpetre will limn their lecherous lips all night,
the ammoniac stink of horses will plague their dreams.

Cold comfort for those who must lose the kind Kingdom of Booze,
—for such is their fate: even booze will be taken away.
So remember the lads on the carts; their rough-hewn hearts
deserve more than the coal-ash burned on a winter's day.

(Tony Connor)

THE BLISS OF SUNDAY

Many worship you, Sunday, throw into you feverishly
six days and themselves: you the seventh, you the free.
In crowds we flock to you, you our good shaman who
need no consulting-room yet heal us sweet and sure.
Our stifling rose-grove lungs groan for you to arrive,
dark stars of soot have burst in them like butterflies.
We come to you with heart tremors and chilled kidneys,
high blood-pressure, toxins, rages, stitches.
Scare off these goblins, rout the microbe-gangsters,

organize peevish organs into peace with a mum's stare.
We come for our quietness to melt our raw nerves,
your dear cool hand to pillow half-crazed heads.
You are the best go-between, the brightest-minded,
you are the violin where dance and kiss are kindled.
You are also the goal, the nearest: the island where
fabulous clangor strikes from the loved workshops of pleasure...
The blue wheezing night-ship creaks against you—
what breaking radiance, what ruby hullabaloo!
The red gangway of dawn is lowered—but it's still
only the silent old folks who step ashore: the song, the din
lie sleeping in laborers' hearts, dead done like them;
wrestlers with iron and air stay to draw out their dreams.
Grannies trot about like toys, may they know long days!
They mutter anxiously, set the kettle on the gas,
the milk bubbles up, hop-pop, it's almost over,
the malt-coffee's boiling, fizz-frothing, golden,
the bread-cubes dance as they redden in the fat,
to drop their fragrance on the brown soup steaming in the pot.
A rainbow throbs on the vapory mist and falls on the heart,
it urges me to get up and wash, I whistle in good part.
The lather puffs out my face, the razor walks round
to show how sometimes suffering pares you down.
Oh, let fate keep that strange razor from your cheek:
you grow pale and thin, the stubble cringes, bunches up thick.
My ancient pair of shoes has filched the morning star—
nylon socks on the line, two tiny shining sacks
flutter, and under fine soles will steal a fine day again,
the ironed shirt winks mother-of-pearl, teases your brain.
Clean shirt: your clean world, this is the bliss you want,
pray for it if the branch of your good smile is cut.
Mirrors, soften your truth for kindly vanity,
let them look and still say: I'm pretty, I'm happy.
If her face twisted up, oh, what would become of her!
Let the women dance, hawk-brown hair or starling-black or
blonde exploding with hydrogen peroxide
or long-dead Titian's dream of a redhead.
I love them all when I look through the window and admire
their earnest iron will—imprisoned in humming driers,
with tropical heat floating on the waves of their hair

and alpine-brilliant ice-white mirrors everywhere.
She drives me crazy, the girl who stands in the snow
against the wall in her lunchbreak to be burned by the glow;
eyes closed, tempting a sky of ice to tan her slowly,
she spellbinds sun-rays into kisses, ultraviolet only...
White-gold-handed Sunday, you scoop out small boys
with their bullet heads from bed like well-shelled peas,
they roll and tumble like mad, bump heads together,
they are pothooks like the letters in a jotter.
Bees drone in swarms, bells clang their songs at me,
the rushing windstream sets imagination free.
My villages, yellow, white, watchers along the road-dust,
I see you tip your roof-caps to disaster.
To number your names is music; Vid, Nagyalásony, Doba,
Egeralja, Káld and Berzseny, Kispirit, Csögle, Boba.
A universe you were, now you are its mica-flash,
frighteningly huge this life, frightening to confess.
I was a millet-seed in you, now you are that seed,
the memory pushes out a tear and it mists all that scene.
Then memories peal like bells and ringing years leave sleep,
the boy I was is here, the pond-murmur, the day-dream.
No desire to be Peter Pan but no desire to die,
the flash on the fine silver poplar-leaves his reverie.
The student I was is here, splitting skies are above,
Sunday, the bombs lash your light into blood,
butterflies panic and flap in his hair, his head
nettle-stung like his mind life-stung, he lies on his side.
Well, I throw down a horse-rug under the silent stars,
I throw my troubles open to the mercies of flowers.
You bud-bright peonies, cover me in pity,
tight baby bombs, blow up into flowers on my heart.
And let my whole being be irradiated with new colors, new rays,
let the frescoes of horror and tribulation be wiped away,
the terror-born figures smeared teeming on my soul's wall
be banished with Neros and popes, fell Crescent and yataghan, all
needles in fingernails, Haynau's icy pupils, heads awry
in living-death mid-nodding agony.
And blood-soaked earth, soot-sky lit by a skull,
let burning phantoms of sea and air go dead and dull.
What am I that I should endure what makes my flesh creep?

I can wait—no moments of magic waken that bad sleep.
Many pleasures move me, yet cannot break the spell,
bringing only strength to defy, to bear a great shame well.
You who sink down on the horse-rug beside me, Hope
my edelweiss-eyed angel, you know I am no fool, I grip
you, whirl you about like a green branch, Jacob
was not more diligent in flooring God's angel.
Yet stay by me, don't cry; I have to stamp on the monsters;
whisper to me that the road I go is not monstrous.
I am desperate fighting for beauty, I want to know the sun
dazzling, the singing green-gold forests, bright winds that stun
the leaves, tall flower-stems shaking tiny dewdrop earrings,
petals and veins like girls in love, trembling even in breathing.
Being shouts out: no no! It doesn't want to be dead yet.
The wasp drones off at a tangent, spins out the moment.
Highest, deepest teats are sucked by emerald heads:
cherry and morello, emerald aching for red.
The golden oriole calls out its glorious Sunday,
and father brushes chaff from his hat, walks away
to see the world: silver-blue sea of rye,
copper-ruddy carrots, maize standing straight and high.
Blind love wraps the crop-gazer as he pads on his way,
a hundred disappointments dissolve in his love of this day,
sweet-pea in his hat, even that makes him rich,
he flicks his boots with a flame-red willow-switch.
Oh, all those paunches to be taut as drums, the draught animal
champs and stuffs itself with grass after six days' toil,
the belly of the hill, the boneyard broods in hunger,
full now of nothing but sunlight and acacia-flower.
The blessed meadow, it wants happiness,
goodbye now to memories of pain and sharp distress.
The telegraph wire chirps half-asleep, no news or orders
whizz over it, the post-office girl writes a letter:
Come, I'm dying for you—and the wonder seizes her heart:
she is clasped from behind with a kiss by her soldier at last.
Bicycles, look: modern reindeers, lilac, yellow,
the wheels purr feverishly with a student and his girl to the valley,
motorbikes roar by, meteor lapping meteor,
zhee, zhoo, a woman's hair streams in comet-eaten air.
To vanish in the green night of the woods is marvelously good,

twin spheres of wild cherry suit the ear grown red.
For blood, like soul, goes thirsty for a storm,
a hot and forcing wind springs up, beats down the stems
of rose and lily thrown in each other's arms, love's way
is blessed, love's bed is blessed, and you, the day.
Sunday, you are here, we see the feast-day of the workworn,
the bent backs straighten in your majestic dawn.
Children at a mother's apron: they play on your barn floor
after the bucking tractor-seat and shouldered sacks galore.
The miner looks up at the sky, his crows'-feet glisten,
the grimy machinist marvels at a blackbird: listen!
The navvy who has pushed his squealing barrow countrywide
is at home, admires and makes much of his darling child.
The blacksmith's in fine fettle, the postman drops
the tiredness of a hundred storeys down, laughs and can't stop.
The seamstress heals her heartache with gleams of pleasures,
a myriad tiny daggers glint on heart-shaped cushions.
The workshops are empty, the stitched jacket on the dummy
holds up in one arm the pain and point of creativity.
The blue dynamo squats stiff, cut off from savage energy,
the belt wilts, the transmission is silent and weary.
Nothing and nobody runs, the turning lathe is asleep,
a rainbow strip of peeled steel in its teeth.
Dour mouths of iron vices gape, the quietness is a sea,
rasps doze like fish, scales glimmering fitfully.
Beer froths in the brewery, matures, hums a wild dream,
horses' harness flashes its moons on pegs, they lean
to the manger, those magic beer-horses, rank with hops,
and stamp in happiness with tumbling bells of hoofs.
I swim past riveting images, I see the blood-spattered
abattoir and angels walking in white there, scattering
jasmine-flowers—my heart gambols and foals
something fantastic-impossible from what is truly-real;
the poleaxe forgets to degrade and lay low the gloomy bull,
or crack the star on the horse's trembling skull.
Blood for six days, but see the shrieks fly on the blade,
renew your smile, parables of blood.
You kill yourself too, to be reborn from death,
you are a Sunday phoenix, to drink and break bread.
Oh how often you have to die for one small Sunday,

how often for one far-off thought-out joy!
The victim, the dead, was always you, humanity,
no workshop, no workshop of delight this earth and sky.
Thunder? Uncouth belching, that's how they live up there,
hiding forever behind the law of the unsated banqueter.
What I sing again and again is not those loose-mouthed brutes
with their jovial riot, but all men's modest delights.
Oh it is frustratingly minute, no home for my heart,
Sunday: doused spark, dust of an imagined star.
Imagined ravishing star, that's where I'd be,
with gaiety ineradicable—oh never to see
that distant beauty!—entrance me, draw my heart out
of the dust, save me from Psalmus Hungaricus and jeremiad.
You are the goal, it is there life lies indivisible,
nothing else makes me cry out haunting the butcher's table.
It is for this that vision and holy rage are sizzling in me,
the melancholy temple of my sight falls down to make it be.
I have been gentle, it is time I was an activist,
even if you get it from hell you need joy, it is tonic, it
is rations for the voyage, how else bear the bloodstained
relay-race, without it you jackknife, stagger, sprain.
Come now, come now, set up the feast, unwind,
slice the fish, cast its scale-coins to the whistling wind,
close your eyes and wring the panting pigeon's neck,
laugh with the pot of horseflesh-soup all sweet with mignonette,
stew potted head, shred radish, and if there's nothing else
pluck at the sky, fry the red kestrel's eggs.
Eat from a striped cloth or on the grass, but sit
as an august great power, in the smile of space you are bright.
You should know that only you can kill pain and original sin,
only you have the right to feast; rifle the larder and bread-bin,
you may eat, there is no curse, drink too; drinking,
recharge your soul at the tumbled shadows of living.
Sunday today, Sunday, the sun is a frantic sultan,
his swordblade splits the earth, tears fences down.
How to hide from its fury, it extorts sharp sweat-tribute,
a dream of plunging in snow to escape the churning heat.
Softly rounded hips strip off at the water's edge,
they put on wavy green-cool skirts for dancing. Foliage
opens and beckons so fresh and cave-like below,

shades of the beer-garden come to life, beer foams
as tap-copper turns, jugs clink weighty and cold,
hats and caps are cocked jaunty on every head.
The ice-cream freezes, its tent floats like another heaven,
the cones are tucked up in towers, high and even,
towers to be annihilated by an army of children—
at last rebuilt no more as cold winds freshen.
The summer is a breast-pierced bull on the frost-pinched sand,
the leaves are blood-drenched, the gossamers fly around.
The hawthorn shivers, shakes its blood-red pearls,
and don't think it's the sunset-embers of the flames that fell.
The fevered stags begin to butt each other's brows,
they bell, the steam fans out like storm-blown boughs.
The setting sun paints fire on the windows of the city,
Sunday, your tempo quickens, drives us crazy for beauty.
Hundreds of thousands throng the streets, din fills the air,
they march with their furled flags of desire and power.
And the funfair bangs out, its daft delights come cheap,
a dream-orbit round the earth—we bucket and leap,
and shame on us, we monopolize the toys of our sons,
the scarlet-feathered whistle-cock crows smartly in our hands,
paper-trumpets blare—vermilion-nosed horses
carrousel their sexy-seated women-riders forward...
The earth whirls with time and sky like a star-wheel,
this is beyond play, it roars round your head, you reel.
Insane fragrances invade you, the wine fizzes,
meteors plunge and plunge, hearts take their bruises.
The instincts flower, fear of mortality bids
revelry and bids it quick, sit in the midst of it!
Whisper and sigh: you, thin violins, weep it out,
and you, lumpish drums, take joy and beat it about.
Roll drums, cry violins, we must have a dance,
the spurs of your music make me rear and prance.
You can see through this intoxication everywhere,
your feet itch to trample king, president, emperor,
your sly fate too, which covers you with wing and claw
and lifts you up only to dash you like a griffin's prey.
You drink deep, clink your glass, you need this spirit, this fever,
this is for loosening your tongue and see how it sobs, how it reasons!
Your fingers spread into the skies, watch-towers of your truth,

would that no tomorrow saw them shaken and ruined!
I sing and sing of the great joy of the many, now
darkness is theirs, furrowed by the star-plough.
The crop of dreams is murmuring, the ear of corn is harder,
men cut it now, the reaping-song strange pearly laughter.
Strange cables these, the cemetery telephones,
from the wisdom of death some send messages:
leave no stalk of delight uncut, someday you will be sorry,
enjoy yourselves my daughter, little son, little grandson, my orphans!
Huger the hunger, the thirst, wilder the music,
it rings and wrestles with the dear dead message.
Light-power, teeming current charges the muscle-springs
prone to dance, the bones with their live ball-bearings.
He who kisses today tastes lava, he himself breaks
into flame and his whispered words are crested flames.
A spark-shower hits the icefield, between damnation and salvation
even the border can be on fire, now the mind is in its passion.
Night: life in space, its obscure laws welling,
bodies: saturns rolling in their erotic rings...
Here comes the end of our star-being, the end is here, goodnight!
The heart is orphaned, Sunday's flowers—gone in what flight!
Cooled stones, snow-drifted stubble, alien wind-song,
snow-curtain dances—and man sleeps deep and long.
Sky, like mind, must want again to lighten,
and soon on the unhidden breasts a dawn whitens.
The world that was all glow and flame's now white, my dear.
Wake up, wake up, it's morning, the winter is here.

(1954)   (Edwin Morgan)

FAIR IN FROSTY MAY

My dreams foam cherry blossom—
but where are the pots of beer?
My heart's set fair for a feast,
and only crows appear.
Wild cherry leaves are trembling,
flushing to eerie oxblood;
the sky is whimpering to itself,

crows dance in the small wood.
Where are the lively lads?
The first was seduced by slide-rules;
his noughts are newborn babies
crying behind cot rails.
The second, with pump and ladders,
rides the red siren's shriek;
the third humps ships' cargoes—
I hear his poor spine crack!
The fourth is dead: he froze
in a camp amid deep snow;
they tossed his shell-hard ears
into the grave too.
Ah, where are the fairs of old!
My friends, I see what waits:—
our stripped bones whitening
while youngsters clink our pots.

(*Tony Connor*)

THE FERRYMAN

After the blaze out of the darkness
has died, who will hear the cricket
singing? Who will light the ice on

the tree? Who will divide his body
into the spectrum? Who will kiss the
buds into life with his tears? Who

will absolve the insanity in the cracks
of the sky? O, after the blaze
out of the darkness has died, who

will annihilate the buzzard circling? And who
will carry the little white cat of
your body, Love, across the black river,

ever flowing, safely into the fresh kingdom?

(*George MacBeth*)

LÁSZLÓ NAGY

PRAYER TO THE WHITE LADY

Creature of flame, out of
the sun's bow I call you:
moment of crystal for the throwing-knife,
  lighten my darkness, I
need you now.

O, lady of the small larks,
keeper of the instruments
in the zenith, last room of the king,
  lighten my darkness, I
need you now.

Palm in the rain of sorrow,
fire under glaze, lifting
the twin domes of your body above me,
  lighten my darkness, I
need you now.

Mistress of Victory, flame
of the gathering storm, brightening
into the jails of my eyes,
  lighten my darkness, I
need you now.

Nurse of the war-wounded, yours is
the house of the Jew and the Negro:
draught of the bee's kiss, mysterious honey,
  lighten my darkness, I
need you now.

Lady, oblivious of blood and money,
belly-dancer of hunger, echo
and resonance of the millennium,
  lighten my darkness, I
need you now.

O, my dear one, tempered
   by the beam of the laser, torn
by the stone body of the gorgon, the man-child,
    lighten my darkness, I
need you now.

Always your tall house was open to me,
glittering with expectation: O, godlike
above the bronze cauldron of your beauty,
    lighten my darkness, I
need you now.

In the beginning I felt your body lap me,
drowning into the saraband of love:
killer of the black crows that haunt me,
    lighten my darkness, I
need you now.

Now, on the brink of the vacuum, at the edge
where the million tendrils of nothingness
are erupting, even out of my own mind,
    lighten my darkness, I
need you now.

Lady of pain, sharer of this affliction,
sufferer under the same electric coil:
now, as I reach for the dark pill and the needle,
    lighten my darkness, I
need you now.

Only in you will the house of my body glisten
gold in all its chimneys and veins:
only in you will the white pigeons flicker,
    lighten my darkness, I
need you now.

                              (George MacBeth)

SQUARED BY WALLS

Couldn't you have died,
or at least bled,
instead of pacing the floor
stunned with despair?
You kept clear of trouble;
bullets, armored track, emblazoned
girls' screams. Nor for you broken
wheels, scattering rooftiles',
grim gangs of working lads,
and soot-brindled petals.
You did not spill one drop
of blood, and when it stopped,
you had only gone grey and mad.

In usual winter weather
you stand here; no other
but yourself, and wide awake,
squared by walls that echo
a cough like raking
gunfire. It's not merely
your flesh that's cold;
mind and heart are frozen—crowned
by knives of ice.
You are ashamed of your melting phrases;
as if you had lost the right
to think of spring
and lilacs—the lung-like trees blossoming.
What agony for a Lord of Life!
Yet, deep in the secret places
of your being, furtive with guilt,
you are breathing on the frosted pane,
that you may look out at the world again.

(Tony Connor)

WITHOUT MERCY

You lay down under a blasting light,
a flower at your elbow,
over your inward head
my love's wild flags flew.

I sit alone in the luminous dark
of a room with closed shutters;
the scabby slats break—
drunken sunshine enters.

Raspberry twilight in a rose-glass;
fragrance of the clipped rose
drifting upward to enquire
my summer scope and size.

In place of your waving-goodbye hand
vacant air vibrates;
memory is an enormous
butterfly on your bedsheets.

Splaying sparks, the summer's grindstone
is honing my dulled heart.
Let recognition wake you
under a blasting light.

Young blood soon tires of sacred love—
return to me, undress:
let's wrestle our lives away,
majestic and merciless.

                                        (Tony Connor)

LÁSZLÓ NAGY

THE BREAK-UP

Madness, I shall betray you. In all my poems
you were the one I steered by, your light
led me through the black summer. Today

the wind plants its flying sticks
into the filigree of my window. I am full of holes
like a sieve. Neither foetus nor avocado crawls

in the blazing dream of my head.
The sentry-box is empty. Your poor soldier
has withered into his own tissues.

Look for me in the kitchen. No, I am not
in the trash-can. Are you my enemy
with your gold eyes? Here are the papers

I used to be so vigilant with, observe
the ashes of my eyes. I used to burn
(do you remember?) images, images, for you.

Now I have gone. Into another country
you would have to follow me. And there is thunder
and lightning at its ivory gate. Look, I am there.

That's me in the moist saw-dust amongst the wasps
under the gay look of the pin-ups.
Look, I'm not even wearing my jacket.
     I'm drinking again.

        (George MacBeth)

THE PEACOCK WOMAN

Last night I dreamed of storms. Through all my skin
The moon drew on the tides. O, how those floods
Crashed on my ribs. In ice I froze and screamed,
Hearing my death in glass. And then I woke

To sun through windows, and the stir of Spring.
Beside me lay my queen in all her pride.
Along the shallow green, her glory shone
As eyes of gold. In wowen flames she moved,
My peacock, and the winter night was day.

It happens always. In the night I die
Back to the towers, and the sheets of foam,
The cold sea breaking on far shores. And then
I wake beside her, and the waters fall
Into my future: I am well again.
She flirts in safety with that other self
I fear to touch. Her feathers brush the dew
From my taut lips. Then, I can speak again,
Rich in her praises like a field of corn.

My darling, in your eyes I see the sun
Rising in glory. Over you the sky
Arches its bow of blue. Through winter snow
I wade to greet you, and it melts in joy
All round my feet. The hills are lush with gold,
The poppies bloom in blood-red. Everywhere,
The sea has sunk away to fields of green,
And I am in your arms, your wings of flame,
Beyond all dreams, in safety in your eyes.

(George MacBeth)

LOVE OF THE SCORCHING WIND

To Margit

Wind, O you wind who storms my blood
sigh of she-lion, sudden southerly
clash, you coppery-breasted brilliance
you buffet my eyes, you dance, you kiss; it's a distemper,
the green hill of my youth is yours forever,
I look back to where it is furrowed from your fire-passage,

guerilla wind, you stretched horizontal scream
sawing ribbon-silkily at my shoulder, fiddlestick
my veins' vibrator, playing my bones' membranes,
what orbiting star ordered you against me
to so fever-flood me, with restlessness fill me,
glaze my eyes with the wild lace of lightning, your voice
for which angry star does it pass sentence: "There is no mercy,
there'll be no mercy"?—but serves me right, serves me right,
I chose to begin my life in your corrupting superstition!
Here you are circling around my throat, chasing a tail,
phosphorescing with cyanide and arsenic fury, you've haltered me forever,
ah, my throat's your axis, you blurred disc aglow,
my wide collar of drought, plate spinning of hallucination—
full-blown with sacrifice you run amok in howling
intimidation for my raped early treasures, you bring wild-tasting
bunches of green love and kisses, my daybreak squeals in you,
so too the lamb of innocence, my chaste verse, gold hair,
my exorbitant foam, the sugared chain of my sins,
and in the middle my fool head—I'm singing for you,
whirlpool of whirlpools, wreath of Babylon sand stifling me,
you scorching, you yellow gypsy wind—you gypsy!

Stop now or slacken, I'd like to see my treasures!
All my happy years kick in a bundled foetal membrane,
I untie it with my mouth's strength, I sniff it nervously—
as a tired animal its litter—my jaw drops at my memories.
Blood and eyes are remembering faery light's leap,
the court of torments where lives a certain little king
at the world's centre in the sour-cherry tree, and wind
blows through it, a bell alive in passion's green-red tree—
that bell is I, both love and alarm
are booming in me, but no one hears, no one can see me—
look over here, dark girl! Only her necklace
throws flashing copper-coin suns in my face, she won't raise
her eyes from the cornflowers, though all the sanguine troop's asleep,
radiant the dreams of cowbell-hammerers, copper-kettle men,
they lie in the field all beard and hair, black nails in the grass,
the women dreaming too on their backs with bared breasts gaping,
springy hillocks where curly-haired babes are slithering
in milk and sugary spittle—oh, is there a God?

Look at me, dark girl! Only her helmet-pointed breasts are looking,
she binds herself with a cornflower wreath, with azure chains,
though the gypsy king in the tumbril snores bible-darkly
the tower of judgement's leaning, his unharnessed donkeys
and iron-shod hares are musing in the golden barley;
but blessings on the Moses neck over the tumbril's backboard,
let his keg-shaped head dangle, let the sun come between his snoring lips,
let the wind play over his thousand showing teeth, his hair
that touches the grass, and his wine-soured bubbling spit!

Come here, dark girl! She's standing, she's turning towards me,
small copper-oven hips tense and from between her thighs
—like a golden caption from a saint's ecstatic lips—
a miraculous bright ribbon issues. Don't be scared! I close my eyes.
Your wreath's nice. You're lovely. And like the wind, scorching.
My balls and everything burn like mad, my teeth are chattering for you,
I'll kneel for you, I'll use bad words—oh, this afternoon is but
damnation in disguise, a death's-head's feathered bonnet!
Do you hear this row? Old bags and know-nothing virgins
rattle off a litany to Mary in the silk-snowed grove of flags.
Its noise makes me sweat; banners, tinkling little bells,
hateful bells coming to me through the cornfields;
you'll die you villain, snaps the priest, and the swords
sprout enormous and some swelling Hungarian kings ride
erect over me—oh, their curses befoul even my dreams!
Dark girl, you have left me. Your wreath's a dear blue-scaled snake
here on my numb asleep arm shivering as it dilates,
the long-haired tribe advances in the white dust down the highway,
and the scorching wind lets fall your song upon my sorrow.
Sitting on the yellow ramparts restless with desire for you
I hum awhile smoking myself into a stupor because of you;
by the time my fingers and lips ripen to gold you arrive,
I laugh and cry, what a fright! your poor little head's bald,
and you throw the bound sheaf of your hair at my feet bawling.
Who sheared my faery girl? Death—the song's "old man death"
because she stole a small hand-mirror—"that bloody old death,"
caught by his dog, held by his son, that's how death sheared her.
I'll die if you cry: look, here's a little fleecy cloud
to drink your tears, from a smacking kiss your hair will grow again,
as for that old man with his son and dog, I'll castrate the lot

and add salt and red pepper seasoning; he won't shear any more faeries.
I sprinkle your dead hair upon the wind, there's a bird
to bear each strand into the blue air where they'll all sing sweetly
and a heaven of birdsnests will rejoice at your gleaming hair.
Lion-maned faery, my blood's corridors are clanging from you
when the town's green belt begins to droop in the heat,
when towers everywhere sigh away color and turn pale,
the tar-paper shanty roof gyrates like a leaf, and
emaciated horses are panting diamond-studded with flies
at the time of the wind when starred enamel flakes off
grass-overgrown thrown away pots and laths come away from fences,
at the time of wind and flame when a stray glimmer is enough
to pierce the violin to the heart and God's yo-yoing balls the larks
flying up and down shriek through superheated gullets,
and when I've fallen on my back and crickets chirr in my hair
and a blade of grass smokes between my teeth and catches fire,
for fire is waiting for fire and should not wait in vain:
then in a yellow skirt you step over my head, you delight, you mourning!
At the Grand Hotel B., I confess to the old waiter:
The wind of Balchik, grandpa, the Bulgarian Balchik
eats my blood, dries up my bones, but there's no mercy
nothing, neither refrigerator nor North Star protects,
and here is her letter of fire: If you are brave, you can come again!
Her message flickers with a yellow flame in my darkened room,
my eyes in vain contend with the blackmail of visions;
the last green crown is burning over the sandpit,
love consumes it at the stake of our two selves,
icons flush with fever, from the trees a glowing caravan
and a hundred Persian stallions from Dobrudzha run roaring
into the Black Sea to cool off—oh, what of me?
Before the gun-barrel gaze of the airport customs man I confess:
Yes, I took out with me a rose but brought only its ashes home.
I've arrived—what a place! What martial stone men,
a cold wind from every bored hole in their stone heads:
turning you to stone, turning you to stone, turning you to...
No! I shall not turn to stone, you stone faces; too bad, stones
for the scorching wind is my religion, I'm shouting for her through my tears,
with my fiery knife I'll fight against your frost, you moguls of stone.
Your smile sears me, come with me Streaky Haired Girl,
our singing shall be the scream of blood against stone,

I shall be good at suffering—fate killed the idyll,
but the scorching wind will walk me over the waters of horror
and razoring rocks even, for she marked me for herself long ago.
It's a miracle that the lightning of your teeth
and dancing streaky hair can fit into this tiny rented room—
my suffocating delight! You are like the wind, scorching!
The best man whom we selected turned prematurely to stone,
your bridesmaid's lace dress is nothing but limestone,
we are marrying in your rose-embroidered blouse and my only shirt humbly,
it's nineteen fifty-two, our wedding banquet's a plate of sour black cherries
and breadcrusts our landlady set up on her kitchen cupboard to dry.
Your lips and eyebrows are writhing into my white shirt: first sickness
and your womb's fruit ripens at the golden trumpet call!

Wind, o you scorching wind guarding my grave,
you faithful bitch of mine—my faithful wolf rather,
who can the star be that created you to sit here at my head,
who sent you that I should have even here no rest?
Though no shred of my flesh remains, only bones, lonely
poor bones, thick hair and uncrumblable crown!
Wind, conjuring wonder wind, ushering prophesy,
it's you who will whisper, murmur, howl: Resurrection's here!
You are first to stand up, you kill off the damp
and the dark frost, you start digging the earth, you fiery
gypsy wind, you'd scratch up carrion even;
wind, you wild angel blowing your own soul into me
you set my crown on and drive me into Eden swords-flashingly
up the green grassy hill to meet every night with her
under the huge moon, she whom you've chosen for me,
so that the world should be stunned at each sunrise
to see blackened places on the glistening hillside:
Look there, where again Love was lying all last night!

(Kenneth McRobbie)

ISTVÁN SIMON
(1926–1975)

RHAPSODY ON TIME

1

O transitory season, lightningless,
perhaps no winter ever saw your back;
at autumn's end the border-marches cracked,
obliterated where pigs root and press.

A nervous countryside; a sea of grass
with periscopes that pop up, veer and tack:
the gopher weaves and sniffs, drops quickly back,
the snail retracts his horns as shadows pass.

Only the weird hill junipers sink claws
into the earth and grasp it as a child
will grasp its mother's lap, by right, by fate,

saying, you too should keep your useless tears,
but seize and saddle, bit and bridle wild
time that accelerates at such fearful rate.

2

Such fearful rate! but I don't understand
what we can measure headlong life against,
for I have had the same pace, the same thrust,
since I am no longer mother-wakened.

Yet any time my automatic hand
switches the light off, I can hear from darkest
endless night: "Oil's not for you to waste!"—
and I'm at home, that moment, in my mind.

And now again, half-choked in tears and laughter,
we start to count how many puffs I take
to blow the lamp out from my bed; and after,

I sense the warm delight achievements make,
and watch the childlike family having fun—
one movement of the hand, and this is done.

3
A gentle rain has drifted down tonight;
through it I can still feel that tomorrow
I may be able to give honor to
the old field hazels, goatee-bearded, bright

with blossom: for they've been set alight
since last year, and I only listen through
the rain-voice to dead soldiers in their sorrow,
marching into one forgetful night.

But when? All's one. I remember the day
I sky-gazed in Thebes, at the royal tombs:
cloudless, like five millenniums away—

an image or experience to blow
the mind with a new metaphor for time:
a mousetrap that snaps man in iron jaw.

4
I stood that same season on no-man's-land,
like a boat on a sandbank, gone to ground;
for that one moment, currents that swirled me round
left me, I had no law but my own hand.

On a bleak steading, under a maple-tree,
I leaned my elbow into my rifle, made
myself a living helmeted cross, the dead
were fifty million earthmen under me.

I almost wept at that strange threshold where
I flung my haversack; what is that door,
thrown flat into the mud, I stammered there,

does it mean this was the last escape of war,
or did it let in endless peace?—I swear
I've asked and asked, but no one can answer.

5
There was a time when time, stretched over space,
struck down at each of us and gave us all
musical instruments; we didn't know
it was a job of work that set the pace.

The droll and double-tongued bassoon, for instance,
fell to the lot of the poor hoarse cuckoo,
who made us shudder when we heard his cry,
hidden, announce the years we'd left to us.

Cuckoo, cuckoo... Catch him, Uncle Pista,
they used to tease my father with their pleas.
He said, if I could see him I would seize him.

Ruthless trap, your teeth are fallen away,
and no one now cries at another, they
fly from Earth to Moon through silences.

6
O transitory season, lightningless,
perhaps no winter ever saw your back;
the meadow deeps already show the track
of gopher periscopes bobbing through the grass.

Haven't the tree-rings made a great advance?—
one chatters to the sleepy snail. Don't slack!
And the snail gets to grips with the birch bark,
wiping his dandy glistening moustache.

And while the weird hill junipers sink claws
into the earth and grasp it as a child
will grasp its mother's lap, by right, by fate,

the snail says, don't forget to check your watch,
to see if I can count the rings—by miles?
I hardly feel time passing, at my rate.

(Edwin Morgan)

JÓZSEF TORNAI
(1927-   )

YOU MUST HAND OVER

You must hand over your love
when they take her
you must hand over
from head to foot
together with her breath
the color of her skin
her glance
her buried thoughts
together with the way she dresses and undresses
with her flickers of joy
her caresses
together with her caressed body
her longing to be elsewhere
her opening up at night
together with her weariness
her huge Egyptian eyes
her kohl-tipped lashes
together with her whispers
with the exultation of her loins
together with her disappointments
the wave-play of her passion
together with her Asian-seeming face
together with her known
and measured existence
you must hand over

(William Jay Smith)

WE SAY THIS PRAYER

You opened up like a plum,
more than a plum,
you opened up like a wave,
more than a wave,
you opened up like a book,
more than a book,
you opened up like a wound,
like wood split along the grain,
like dry, cracked soil,
you opened up as I did,
I opened up as you did,
and the stag swooped in:
on one antler there were tanks mired in the swamp,
on the other the eyes of burning cities,
on one antler an infant tied by string,
on the other a toad, machine-gun tucked between webbed feet,
on one antler a church, the nave caved in,
on the other a linden-tree in a rainstorm,
on one antler a moonlit boat,
on the other crosses of rye,
crosses of windows, of wood,
on one antler the sun-disk of your face,
on the other the sun-disk of my face,
and we say this prayer
for all time:
do not let our hearts be torn out,
sun god,
do not drown us in darkness:
we dance only once
here on the grass,
only once before you
can we be stone, water, flame,
birdwoman and birdman.

(*William Jay Smith*)

JÓZSEF TORNAI

TO DIE FOR SOMETHING

If one could only die for something,
all at once, bloodily, for certain,
not like this, year by year,
tooth by tooth, so that
already I am bored, bored to death
by death.

(William Jay Smith)

MR. T. S. ELIOT COOKING PASTA

That crackle is well worth hearing.
He breaks in two the macaroni tubes
so as to make them fit the pot,
then casts them with both hands into the water
above the white electric range.
The water bubbles, seethes, the *pasta*
sinks to the bottom of the pot.
Mr. Eliot casts a glance
through the wide kitchen window toward the park:
it is raining there, and water
pours down the trunks of trees in substantial quantity,
tousling the lawn into a poison-green
Sargasso Sea.
Which reminds him of the pot.
Just so much contemplation has sufficed
for the rising of the *pasta*
to the water's surface.
He fishes out the bouncing ropes
with a colander, American-made,
and runs cold water on them from the tap.
"One is obliged to do so, otherwise
they will stick together." So Mr. Eliot writes
to a friend, later that evening.
"Still, the most gripping moment

comes when the macaroni
are broken in two with a dry crackle:
in that, somehow,
one recognizes oneself."

(Richard Wilbur)

FERENC JUHÁSZ
(1928–)

GOLD

The woman touches her bun
of thinning hair. She laughs,
and drops a spoon and a hunk of bread
in their reaching, grubby hands.
Like roses divining water
the circle of thin red necks
leans over the steaming plates;
red noses bloom in the savoury mist.

The stars of their eyes shine
like ten worlds lost in their own light.
In the soup, slowly circling
swim golden onion rings.

(David Wevill)

SILVER

The traveler stands in the freezing cold
surrounded by drowsy old men.
His moustache is ice, his eyelashes
inhuman half-moons of silver.
He stands watching the horses,
the snow dusting under their hooves
like a cloud of millions of comets
misting the milky star-roads.

His ears are silver, the hair is silver.
The horses twitch their manes and tails.
Silver the velvet nostrils, the steaming flanks.

(David Wevill)

POWER OF THE FLOWERS

O Rose and Hyacinth, Honeysuckle and Peony,
half-awake you sway in moonlight's lakes of mercury,
you moon peeling upon islands of lights, fugitive slim Poppy,
face bloodied with rest, sleep oozes in you mysteriously,
like mothers standing at open windows, their bellies swollen,
becoming aware of teeth and eyeballs forming within them,
crying softly as they sway, dew on the dragging soreness,
a bright salt-fall in the moonlight upon weighted white breasts,
so you, trembling tall flowers, stand here in silence,
while the sphere of space powders your heads with yellow phosphorus.
In the steaming mooncake's white glimmer there dreams a Narcissus
like a thought on its long stem, in evening's stunned dusk,
you concepts, flowering out of slow speculation's soils,
love's embraces, shadowed kisses upon close bedside walls,
dear thoughts, wrung from a first metallic wince of worry,
sweet-smelling womb by wings enfolded flutteringly,
are you also to be found upon other planets circling by
and back again into unfathomable distance, upon star-larvae
in their meadows bathed by chrome sprays, cells steaming, your breath
clouding under foreign moons, with sticky armpits, because our earth
is but one among the Milky Way's thinning forests of blood-vessels
                                                    stretching
far out, do you sense the spine's vertebral keel of blind being,
and if a new bone should form, roadside sad wanderers, in time's
                                                    conical tail,
will you appear there too, who, arriving last, have yet not traveled at all?
Do you exist there, in some blissful place where no man nor beast is
                                                    heard,
in some newly exploded or for a million years formless desert,
among red glues which the cooling striated matter secretes,

your fragrance singing among the columnar scaly pre-human beasts?
Are you trembling, as the rough pine-forests sough with choking
                                        wind-snot, why
should you not shiver at the beaked shrieks from the feathered bird's
                                        eye-covering sky,
fairy eyes, angel hands, tiny calf-mouths, ears of babies,
Moonflower, Hyacinth, Evening Primrose, Sweet Scabious?
Time's ears register sounds from space, on drawn threads of tin
silvered cups pick up voices and vibrate under the moon,
you are beyond understanding, miracles shrivelling and renascent,
Sweet Violets, boneless bodied, green-spined dreams with brains
                                        of scent,
bells of silence, one-legged secrets, lungs laid bare,
red kidney tissue, mute voices, who outlive time there,
yet you may not speak of those things which are your living secrets
through pollen-hoarse cords transformed into plant-glands in your
                                        throats.
Are you to live only here, doomed to earth, to life exiled,
sentenced to beauty, with roots through this soil's tissue nailed,
to live only here, nowhere else, upon no other star nor planet,
with these waters swollen, dropsical, and with viscous fluids matted,
inhaling fire from a sun that sets system to atoms of the Milky Way,
like gold images your clustered stamens' facets catch its flames
                                        gloriously,
under only this rainbow-scarfed and flowerless moon,
like thoughts nowhere else to be found, nowhere else to be born?
O Rose and Hyacinth, Convolvulus and Celandine,
honey-thick flowers flowing over moonlit fields, releasing fine
scents in the slowly fuming lakes of air, why do
I feel my heart aching so, when I listen to you?
A homeland is what you are to me, no other earth I know
but this one, sour, white alkaline, nourishing black loam,
I cannot know whether your petals open ribbed baskets upon other
foreign planets; are such flowers there, Cornflower, Wisteria,
Musk Rose, Horned Poppy, Autumn Snowflake, Verbena,
Rock Rose, Convolvulus, Wild Fire Iris, Magnolia?
I cannot know, faithful ones, whether you are found in other soils,
do you light up beside hot waters, ignite where the sun's surface boils,
or faithfully only here push up leaves, wordless petals, stalks,

again and again, this earth's loyal children, cuddling her plains, her
                                    gentle hillocks?
Tiny mauve umbrellas, mute-tongued bells, soft dreaming towers of
                                    bloom,
from boughs hang blown flower-skulls, wax-petalled jugs with
                               inscriptions of perfume,
stars of dust, treelets of mica, smooth veined petal-eyeballs,
foam-ribbed green candles, bloody beadings, straining projectiles,
along the roadsides you swallow dustclouds whitening the ditches,
there you burn on, in the grinding roar and through the silences,
as granite sifts over stone-breaking machinery's gears and grooves,
your outlines blur beneath fine dusts speeding from tires and hooves,
only the dew washes your faces, and the day's light rains
moisten ragged sun-dried foliage, hair-patterned veins,
through steam, sparks, soot, you push up along the railway-cutting,
on cinder-rivered trackbeds between sleepers and rails on tiptoe
                               standing,
out on lakes of pitch and oil you swim, blue swans, heron-like plants,
yellow-headed, ochre-skulled, patiently surfacing at last,
firmly braced, metal-foliaged, pliable-skeletoned, whom courage stays,
when a slow freight-train rumbles by the milk-boned flesh tugs and
                               sways,
O virgins, breaking forth into the light, from the sharp black froth
                               of slag-heaps,
nymphs of the garbage, who can know anything of your joy's secrets?
You break out between the rags, the splintered glass, through rusted
                               pots,
you are cradled, as if by floes, upon oceans of filth like white
                               sailboats,
in crannies of newsprint, among pondweed-tangled metal shavings,
                               wires turning brown,
you grow like living coral, starry-fleshed chandeliers, in an Eden
                               sea-garden,
you live on like insouciant immortals, or those resigned to being
                               mortal,
thorny stemmed or star-strewing beauties, a flower-cup's fleshy handle
pushing up through dead cats' fragmenting rank liquefying flesh,
breaking through death upon his rotting throne of phosphorescence,
studded with pale-blue shells, the wrecked galleons of mouse skeletons

and gill-petals agitate the light, flames spinning from green fins,
you light up with the candles in cemeteries down overgrown side roads
like small yellow nightlights set over the meadow-abandoned dead,
beside soldiers' snail-house wax ears, blue wounded hearts of Uhlans,
from grandfathers' beards, upon shallow graves, sprouting from stillborn
                                                    babes' white palms,
like green wax-candles you light up in the red deer's hoofmark
who bares small teeth like round corncob-rows to strip young bark,
even on the dunghill among the pigs' feet, chicken skulls, and frayed
                                                                hooves,
on black iron bough-work, and fishscale-shingled sagging hutch roofs,
in the dragonfly-nosed wrecked airplanes' instrument-panels' earth-caked
                                                                  dials,
in oily rubber-smelling membrane wings, where scorched aluminum
                                                                 curls,
your phosphorus-green growth encrusts pearled keels of green-slimy
                                                          sunken ships,
from the whitefish killed by pressure you creep forth from crumbling
                                                             fin-tips,
on islands of rotting fish-heads, cannon-shells, on doom-bombs' fins,
burning among brass cartridge-cases' lead-cored copper-sheated organs,
your red lamps light up, and your white faces blink on again,
under the hairy flapping horse-carcass, where the light streams in
you stain the watery taut veins, and split the long bones' dry
pillars with white tortures, you ignite as you leap at the sky,
you ascend, like the revolving evening star, wet with tears, solitary,
you ascend, you shine resplendent in unutterable purity,
you ascend, green spirits, on green wings that beat up from the dust,
you ascend, your white glory unfolding, with radiant acceptance,
you ascend, skulls splitting, the black and yellow brains laid bare,
you ascend, from opened heads grow hearts of peace and also anger.
O Rose and Hyacinth, Narcissus and Fire-Tail,
sinless ones, that our hearts are less kind I know well,
such robust and mighty ones, who are brought forth in silence,
you know how to die without a word, lovers of meek yet heroic stance,
so many sins we carry, desire, selfishness, self-delusion,
saddened by suffering, indifferent through vanity, felled by resignation,
for we are but human, the substance we share is the same,
birth is a cry, and death a cry, and life a cry of pain.
The animals yelp also, panting they spill out their young in lairs,

to hatch her speckled eggs the small robin flushes with fevers,
the woman wails, screams, curses, heaving herself up like froth
before the bloodied brown infant's crown squeezes from her sheath,
and the child too is hurt, by the more than beautiful fearful combat,
pain turns it blue as a fish, screeching in slime, in blood, in fat,
in my last throes my body with dense cold pearls is studded,
I lie hardening into an idol of obsidian upon my bed,
but you flowers, who are pregnant with time, yet lack tongue
and protective skin, nerves of the earth, what makes you so strong?
You come suddenly as love, and pass like sorrow from where once you
stood,
simple-minded almost, intuition brims your chalices of solitude,
upon the thin brows of poor grazing lands, in the reaper's apron
you nod for the last time in the light, slim-legged, as he passes on,
blue veins start out of your calves, wings sprout at earth level, snake-
clawed
dreaming there and dreaming on, knotty-backed, bloated treefrog leaved,
tongues clubrooted, tongues purple, tongues in pollen-floured mouths,
tongues like tridents,
flowers beheaded, six pendant petals like wry earlobes, a torso's desire
speaking from bell-trumpets,
upon the quaking bog's clayey skin, where waterlogged feathergrass
grows green,
in the loose slides of shale upon hillsides, where grey falls of scree
careen,
on the fine soils' creamy surface, where dry wrack withers between
extruded roots,
on the wilted, grey-tufted alkaline earths, on the long limbs of exposed
salts,
you brood on the slow brooks' spongy banks, green-scaled goldenheaded
river nymphs,
and on the sour mountain pasture, the long ridged prairie's lips,
you are the earth's vocal cords, bulbs of honeyed salivas, with spinal
columns of fish,
soft teeth of living tissue for the neck's nape, bladders for ears, foreheads
growing fins,
in the tangles of underbrush, underneath rotting treetrunks and toadstools,
upon pale circles of limestone rubble, covered with shell eggs of frail
snails,
you silent fairy-named flowers close-knotted to my heart,

Christ's Glove, Baby's Breath, Blue-Eyed Mary, Sweet Violet.
Here you flame up in me, mute souls of my earth, joy and sorrow,
Snowball Rose, White Wings Rose, Christmas Rose, Meadow Rue,
your roots pass around my heart, into my broken soil you enter,
for I am this Earth that reared you, I your mother, your prisoner,
nor would I be myself without you, I who sent you out to live,
bald wastelands would poison me, but you live on because in you I
                                                     believe.
I would stare blindly into the void, if metals and minerals covered
                                                     my surface,
if barren colored dusts coated my face, what would be my purpose?
Here glimmer the star-like head, green stalk, blue window of your
                                                     body,
Lady's Mantle, Crimson Flag, Pearl Bush, Blue Rosemary,
here you dwell in me, Snowdrop, Winter's Sexton, Autumn Snowflake,
Sweet Cornflower, Marsh Marigold, Fire Thorn, and Tamarisk.
O you dispellers of sorrow, magic-named wordless breathing wonders:
Love Lies Bleeding, Love-in-a-Mist, Orange Heliopsis, Everlasting
                                                     Flowers,
Bishop's Hat, Lords and Ladies, Black-Eyed Susan, Blue-Eyed Mary,
Golden Rod, Blue-Eyed Grass, Yellow Gorse, Blue Holly,
Bears' Ears Primula, Leopard's Bane, Peasant's Eye Narcissus, Hound's
                                                     Tongue,
Horned Poppy, Opium Poppy, Iceland Poppy, Wallflower Fire King.
And all of you whom I have not called upon, whom I do not name,
                                                     mate
upon my summits, on my high pasture, in my lowlands you vibrate,
striking root overnight, breaking time's close-mouth rock with quiet
                                                     insistence,
bringing with you sweetly sorrowful yet joyous scent of pristine
                                                     existence,
you, born in the settling still-warm muds, after the first blow of creation,
little sisters of the metals, and salts' daughters born in cosmic copulation,
you starry breasts of radiance, bird-form constellations, spiral nebulae
                                                     of the snails,
voracious progeny at the nipples of the elements, who sink down slow
                                                     black nails,
you green calves suckling at the teats of phosphorus, copper, boron,
                                                     sulphur, iron,
salts' ganglions, kin to volcanoes, feathers ruffling along beds of silicon,

you dreams of nitrogen, whose kiss burned off the last particles of metal
                                   when you left the womb of gold,
procreations of flame, embryos of creative mists, messages such as
                                     shifting rainbows hold,
you materialize from vapors dense as hot aluminum, you are the germinal
                                        desires
of blue rainfalls, the incubated spinal cells of the sun's centre fires,
green slimes, membranous goiters, heart-hatted necks, grand-children
                                      of conflagrations,
growing out of the blood-colored, the yellow, the blue-black bottle-green
                                    rocks, your relations,
you slight womanish brothers of the thundering oceans, primeval mothers
                                    of greasy whale herds,
infant twins of crabs, of long-necked ocean-cleaving finned things and
                                    wading tall birds,
sisters to fishes and dragons, lizards' great-grandfathers,
cousins of snakes, birds' forebears, insects' elder brothers!
You are the future of the fires of metals, iron semen seethes in your
                                    hormones,
mothers of oils, coal's genitalia, redeeming heralds of bones,
you flowers have travelled through measureless time and space
on frail green-shod feet, rooted always in one and the same place!
O flowers, nothing is unknown to you, flowers of my land,
through your cells there is howling still the primeval wind,
it roars through the inner rooms of protons and neutrons,
proclaiming the blessedness of birth in their starry constellations,
it blows across the frontiers of fire and procreation, through the scented
                                    silence,
and your milliard heads sigh together, touching in bliss, in loneliness,
gold godheads are blown forth from your wombs, creatures of fine meal,
and your open love was covered by a flowing yellow veil,
flowers, who have lived through the past, what know you of me,
what do you know of my heart, why it lives so avidly,
why proud faith is beautiful, why I find pain in the rain showers,
why my consciousness puts forth heavy-scented, undyingly fair flowers?
Flowers, timeless ones, yet easily broken as I have seen,
with narrowing leaves for shoulders, hips of gelatine,
gland-browed, lips growing from larynx, and tenderness in your thorns,
my flowers, fragile dreams, pliant-ribbed, spear leafed ones,

my flowers, black tongued, gold collared, milk within you for blood
                                        circulating,
my flowers, bald lunged, tallow skulled, from a corpse's armpit
                                        growing,
my flowers, flat your close hair, your adam's apples with shell ribbing,
mealy vocal cords from the open-wound larynx like clappers hanging,
my flowers, watery fleshed, with milk at the waist sagging,
what shall man do, when he is left to himself, and his dreaming?
My flowers, I call on you conquering ones, and say that man must still
                                        dream on,
you must never fall, for only thus will he be able to remain human!
Live on, you green instincts, unfold into the young air
your resplendent lip-cups, on wide-arching pillars of green hair,
like parachutes opening out into each other in series
slung from the male body, their chain falling across space,
so you float across the million years' plain, opening and re-opening,
on and on, umbel, stalk, tuber eternally opening, eternally floating.
You have heard the seething of a tremendous sea which never knew
                                        jellyfish, crab, nor stingray,
and have seen the towering jets of whales disporting in the moonlit
                                        bland bay,
and how the yellow-finned, pole-necked, mouse-toothed Plesiosaurians,
the swimming mammal lizards, kissed the purple sea-anemones in the
                                        oceans,
seen the stranded rose-headed squids upon the sands drying out to glass,
how soft red bellies of the cactus-armored reptiles touch in gentle
                                        dalliance,
back and forth swinging between shell-covered thighs, the soft-veined
                                        onion-clapper
in the blue furry nest, and glass-brittle melonballs in the lined sac move
                                        and quiver.
You saw the armored Gigantosaurus' bloody battles,
the rending jaws of chrome green, thorn-crested reptiles,
how the Tri-Corn pushed his bone pike far into the breast of the
                                        Lizard King,
whose yellow-purple lung-clots and fats welled out with the flood
                                        of blood mingling,
the swish of the first birds on squealing wings, the awkward
roaring also of turtle-sized beetles you heard,

you felt the procreating storms of love-symbol marked moths of great
size,
you saw the painful slow trek of the turtles, heard their death sighs,
you felt the wind of man's flashing metal arrow,
you saw the pursed sweet smile of the Avar baby, and long ago
the Huns' rushing cloud of horse, huge-chested whirlwind of a thousand
nostrils,
in your dew the Thracian virgin washed her blood-gummed nipples,
a love-sick Latin maiden gazed up from where she lay at the axes
of your petals,
and you set upon the gypsy's nose, when he bent over you, a yellow
pimple,
you heard the bellowing of bullocks when from the dust-cloud they
raised
the Magyars swooped, harrassed behind, longing for the beeches' shade,
in that wanderers' apocalypse, the battle-axes, death rattles,
wailings, and spears, are preserved in your parts with the great lost
battles,
iron flowers of silence, glass-tongued flowering clubs, grasses like wires,
you have preserved the possible conceiving of curses, kisses, prairie-fires,
and the dust-veiled dirge of every ragged devout procession
that carries the green-stone form nailed onto wood, the Second Person,
you hold the wilted suffering of all guilty rebels,
the mail-clad stallions' grey-green lips of rheumy piles,
beneath the passing shadowed roar of the bomber each of you trembles,
collapsing stone-woods, burning blood bubble-sprays stain your petals,
you have heard the soft addresses of stern poets,
life-giving mothers' ecstatic screams, cursing of prophets,
flowers, crucibles of scent, in the moonlight here trembling,
shining like money, like divination, tender shadows throwing,
oh in the steaming mooncake's white glimmer, the brooding Narcissus
blooms beside sleeping saurians and blue lizards,
I hardly know whether small moths or petals, mongrel-descendants,
are flooding the little brook with quicksilver blue radiance,
under films of nickel the in-motion for eternity sleeping foliage floats,
in and out dance the tiny scintillating fishes with pulsing white
throats.
I know only this, that I am human and from instincts of seaweed,
hot primeval muds, mortal and eternal, I have risen indeed,

consciousness purified in flame, a cell arrived at man's estate;
I do not know, world, your ways, but I manage, I estimate
what is to be done with courage and as you, world, would have it done,
this you can in no way understand, Violet, Viburnum.
You can in no way understand that what is brought through me to
                                          blossom among us
is a flower that can speak, and is fairer far than the moonlight Narcissus,
its stalk grows up towards space, giving its scent to time's future,
meteoric time dusts its stamens, its petal's root will not wither,
thinking back to the first cleaving evokes pain and impurity in turn,
I carry within me the scales, dragon-crests, gills, fins, skin,
feathers, star-mists, seas, plants, fires, iron, lime, sand,
oh this, flowers in the moonlight trembling, you in no way understand!
You do not fathom it, Iris and Rue, though you outlive me,
Rose and Hyacinth, Honeysuckle and Peony.

                                    (Kenneth McRobbie)

THE BOY CHANGED INTO A STAG
CRIES OUT AT THE GATE OF SECRETS

Her own son the mother called
from afar crying,
her own son the mother called
from afar crying,
she went before the house from there calling,
her hair's full knot she loosed,
with it the dusk wove a dense quivering
veil, a precious cloak down to her ankles,
wove a stiff mantle, heavy-flaring,
a flag for the wind with ten black tassels
a shroud, the fire-stabbed blood-tainted dusk.
Her fingers she twined in the sharp tendrilled
stars, her face the moon's foam coated,
and on her own son she called shrilly
as once she called him, a small child,
she went before the house and talked to the wind,
with songbirds spoke, sending swiftly

words after the wild pairing geese,
to the shivering bullrushes,
to the potato-flower so silvery,
to the clench-balled bulls rooted so firmly,
to the well-shading fragrant sumach tree,
she spoke to the fish leaping at play,
to the mauve oil-rings afloat fleetingly:
    you birds and boughs, hear me
listen as I cry out,
    and listen, you fishes, you flowers
listen, for I speak to be heard,
    listen you glands of expanding soils
        you vibrant fins, astral-seeding parachutes,
decelerate, you humming motors of the cape
    in the depths of the atom, screw down the whining taps,
        all metal-pelvised virgins, sheep alive under cotton
    listen as I cry out,
    for I'm crying out to my son!

    Her own son the mother called
    her cry ascending in a spiral,
    within the gyre of the universe it rose,
    her limbs flashing in the light rays
    like the back of a fish slippery-scaled
    or a roadside boil of salt or crystal.
    Her own son the mother called:
come back, my own son, come back
    I call you, your own mother!
come back, my own son, come back
    I call you, your mild harbor,
come back, my own son, come back
    I call you, your cool fountain,
come back, my own son, come back
    I call you, your memory's teat,
come back, my own son, come back
    I call you, your withered tent,
come back, my own son, come back
    I call you, your almost sightless lamp.

Come back, my own son, for I'm blind in this world of sharp objects,
within yellow-green bruises my eyes are sinking, my brow contracts,
my thighs—my barked shins,
from all sides things rush at me like crazed wethers,
the gate, the post, the chair try their horns on me
doors slam upon me like drunken brawlers,
the perverse electricity shoots its current at me,
my flaking skin seeps blood—a bird's beak cracked with a stone,
     scissors swim out of reach like spider crabs all metal,
the matches are sparrows' feet, the pail swings back at me with its
                                       handle,

come back, my own son, come back
my legs no longer carry me like the young hind,
     vivid tumors pout on my feet
     gnarled tubers penetrate my purpling thighs,
on my toes grow bony structures,
     the fingers on my hands stiffen, already the flesh is shelly
scaling like slate from weathered geologic formations,
     every limb has served its time and sickens,
come back, my own son, come back,
     for I am no more as I was,
     I am gaunt with inner visions
     which flare from the stiffening hoary organs
     as on winter mornings an old cock's crowing
rings from a fence of shirts, hanging hard-frozen,
I call you, your own mother,
come back, my own son, come back,
to the unmanageable things bring a new order,
discipline the estranged objects, tame the knife,
     domesticate the comb,
for I am now but two gritty green eyes
glassy and weightless like the *libellula*
whose winged nape and dragon jaws, you know it well
     my son, hold so delicately
two crystal apples in his green-lit skull,
I am two staring eyes without a face
seeing all, now one with unearthly beings.
Come back, my own son, come back,
     with your fresh breath, set all to rights again.

In the far forest the lad heard,
at once he jerked up his head,
with his wide nostrils testing
the air, soft dewlaps pulsing
with veined ears pricked, harkening
alertly to those tones sobbing
as to a hunter's slimy tread,
or hot wisps curling from the bed
of young forest fires, when smoky
high woods start to whimper bluely.
He turned his head, no need to tell
him this was the voice he knew so well,
now by an agony he's seized,
fleece on his buttocks he perceives,
in his lean legs sees the proof
of strange marks left by each cleft hoof,
where lilies shine in forest pools
sees his low hairy-pursed buck-balls.
He pushes his way down to the lake
breasting the brittle willow brake,
rump slicked with foam, at each bound
he slops white froth on the hot ground,
his four black hooves tear out a path
through wild flowers wounded to death,
stamp a lizard into the mould
neck swollen, tail snapped, growing cold.
And when he reached the lake at last
into its moonlit surface glanced:
it holds the moon, beeches shaking,
and back at him a stag staring!
Only now thick hair does he see
covering all his slender body
hair over knees, thighs, the transverse
tasselled lips of his male purse,
his long skull had sprouted antlers
into bone leaves their bone boughs burst,
his face is furry to the chin
his nostrils are slit and slant in.
Against trees his great antlers knock,
veins knot in ropes along his neck,

madly he strains, prancing he tries
vainly to raise an answering cry,
only a stag's voice bells within
the new throat of this mother's son,
he drops a son's tears, paws the brink
to banish that lake-monster, sink
it down into the vortex sucking
fluid dark, where scintillating
little fish flash their flowery fins,
minute, bubble-eyed diamonds.
The ripples subside at last in the gloom,
but a stag still stands in the foam of that moon.

Now in his turn the boy cries back
        stretching up his belling neck,
now in his turn the boy calls back
        through his stag's throat, through the fog calling:
        mother, my mother
        I cannot go back,
        mother, my mother
        you must not lure me,
        mother, my mother
        my dear breeding nurse,
        mother, my mother
        sweet frothy fountain,
        safe arms that held me
        whose heavy breasts fed me
        my tent, shelter from frosts,
        mother, my mother
        seek not my coming,
        mother, my mother
        my frail silken stalk,
        mother, my mother
        bird with teeth of gold,
        mother, my mother,
        you must not lure me!
        If I should come home
        my horns would fell you,
        from horn to sharp horn
        I'd toss your body,

if I should come home
down I would roll you,
tread your loose veiny
breasts mangled by hooves,
I'd stab with unsheathed
horns, maul with my teeth,
tread in your womb even.
If I should come home
mother, my mother
I'd spill out your lungs
for blue flies buzzing round,
and the stars would stare down
into your flower-organs
which once did hold me,
with warmth of summer suns,
in shiny peace encased
where warmth never ceased,
as once cattle breathed
gently to warm Jesus.
Mother, my mother
do not summon me,
death would strike you down
in my shape's coming
if this son drew near.
Each branch of my antlers
is a gold filament,
each prong of my antlers
a winged candlestick,
each tine of my antlers
a catafalque candle,
each leaf of my antlers
a gold-laced altar.
Dead surely you'd fall
if you saw my grey antlers
soar into the sky
like the All Soul's Eve
candle-lit graveyard,
my head a stone tree
leafed with growing flame.

Mother, my mother
if I came near you
I would soon singe you
like straw, I would scorch
you to greasy black clay,
you'd flare like a torch
for I would roast you
to charred shreds of flesh.
Mother, my mother
do not summon me
for if I came home
I would devour you,
for if I came home
your bed I would ravage,
the flower garden
with my thousand-pronged
horns would I savage,
I'd chew through the trees
in the stag-torn groves,
drink dry the one well
in a single gulp,
if I should return
I'd fire your cottage,
and then I would run
to the old graveyard,
with my pointed soft
nose, with all four hooves
I'd root up my father,
with my teeth wrench off
his cracked coffin lid
and snuff his bones over!
Mother, my mother
do not lure me,
I cannot go back,
for if I came home
I'd bring your death surely.

In a stag's voice the lad cried,
and in these words his mother answered him:
    come back, my own son, come back
I call you, your mother.
    Come back, my own son, come back
I'll cook you brown broth, and you'll slice onion-rings in it,
they'll crunch between your teeth like quartz splinters in a giant's jaws,
I'll give you warm milk in a clean jug,
from my last keg trickle wine into heron-necked bottles,
and I know how to knead the bread with my rocky fists, I know how
                                    you like it,
bread to bake soft-bellied buns for you, sweet bread for the feasts,
    come back, my own son, come back
from the live breasts of the screeching geese for your eiderdown
                         I plucked feathers,
weeping I plucked my weeping geese, the spots stripped of feathers
                               turning
    a fierce white on their breasts, like the mouths of the dying,
I shook up your pallet in the clear sunlight, made it fresh for your rest,
the yard has been swept, the table is laid—for your coming.

O mother, my mother
    for me there's no homecoming,
do not lay out for me twisted white bread
    or sweet goat's milk in my flowered mug foaming,
and do not prepare for me a soft bed,
    for feathers ravage not the breasts of the geese,
spill your wine rather, upon my father's grave let it soak in,
    the sweet onions bind into a garland,
fry up for the little ones that froth-bellying dough.
    The warm milk would turn to vinegar at my tongue's lapping,
    into a stone turtle you'd see the white bread changing,
    your wine within my tumbler like red blood rising,
    the eiderdown would dissolve into little blue flames in silence
    and the brittle-beaked mug splinter into swordgrass.
O mother, O mother, my own good mother
    my step may not sound in the paternal house,
I must live deep in the green wood's underbrush
    no room for my tangled antlers in your shadowy

house, no room in your yard for my cemetery
     antlers; for my foliated horns are a loud world-tree
their leaves displaced by stars, their green moss by the Milky Way,
     sweet-scented herbs must I take in my mouth, only
the first-growth grasses can my spittle liquefy,
     I may no longer drink from the flowered mug you bring
only from a clean spring, only from a clean spring!

I do not understand, do not understand your strange tortured words,
                         my son
you speak like a stag, a stag's soul seems to possess you, my unfortunate
                                one.
When the turtle-dove cries, the turtle-dove cries, when the little bird
               sings, the little bird sings, my son
wherefore am I—in the whole universe am I the last lost soul left, the
                     only one?
Do you remember, do you remember your small once-young mother,
                     my son?
I do not understand, do not understand your sad tortured words, my
                     long-lost son.

Do you remember how you came running, running home to me so happy
               with your school report,
     you dissected a bull-frog, spreading out on the fence his freckled
               webbed paddle-feet,
and how you pored over the books on aircraft, how you followed
     me in to help with the washing,
     you loved Irene B., your friends were V. J.
     and H. S. the wild orchid-bearded painter,
and do you remember on Saturday nights, when your father came home
               sober, how happy you were?

O mother, my mother, do not speak of my sweetheart of old nor of my
               friend,
     like fish they fleet by in cold depths, the vermilion-chinned painter
     who knows now where he has gone his shouting way, who knows
               mother, where my youth has gone?
Mother, my mother, do not recall my father, out of his flesh sorrow has
               sprouted,

sorrow blossoms from the dark earth, do not recall my father, my
father,
from the grave he'd rise, gathering about him his yellowed bones,
from the grave stagger, hair and nails growing anew.
Oh, oh, Uncle Wilhelm came, the coffin-maker, that puppet-faced man,
he told us to take your feet and drop you neatly in the coffin,
I retched because I was afraid, I had come straight home from Pest
that day;
you also, my father, went back and forth to Pest, you were only
an office messenger, the rails twisted up,
oh, the stabbing knives in my belly then, shadows from the candle
ravined your tight cheeks.
Your new son-in-law, Laci the barber, shaved you that day, the candle
dribbling the while like a silent baby
regurgitating its glistening entrails, its long luminous nerves like
vines,
the choral society stood round you in their purple hats mourning you
at the tops of their voices,
with one finger I traced the rim of your forehead, your hair was
alive still,
I heard it grow, I saw the bristles sprout from your chin
blackened by morning; the next day your throat had sunk beneath
snake-grass stalks of hair,
its curve like a soft-furred cantaloup, the color of a yellow-haired
caterpillar upon blue cabbage skin.
Oh, and I thought your hair, your beard, would overgrow the whole room,
the yard,
the entire world, stars nestling like cells in its hiving strands.
Ah! heavy green rain started then to fall, the team of red horses before
the hearse neighed in terror,
one lashing out above your head with a lightning bolt hoof, the
other relentlessly pissing
so that his purple parts passed out with it like a hanged man's
tongue, while their coachman cursed
and the downpour washed round the huddled brassbandsmen, then
all those old friends blew with a will,
sobbing as they played, beside the globe-thistle studded chapel wall,
those old friends blew till their lips swelled blue, and the tune
spiralled out and up,

the old friends blew with cracked lips bleeding now, with eyeballs
                                                            staring,
blew for the card games and booze, the bloated, the withered and
                                          the trumped women,
played you out for the red-letter day beer-money, the tips sent
                                whirling into space after you
they blew, sobbing as they blew sadly down into the sedimentary
                                  layers of silted sadness,
music pouring from the burnished mouths, from rings of brass
                                into putrescent nothingness,
out of it streamed the petrified sweethearts, rotting women, and
                          mouldy grandfathers in the melody,
with small cottages, cradles, and rolling like onions a generation of
                          enamel-swollen, silver-bodied watches,
Easter bells and multifarious saviors came out also on wide-spreading
                                            wings of sound
that summoned up satchels, railway wheels, and soldiers brass-
                                buttoned at the salute,
the old friends played on, teeth reddening behind lips curled back
                          and swollen like blackened liver,
and yourself conducting the choir—Well done, boys, that's grand,
                                carry it on, don't stop now!—
all the time with hands clasped tight, those gold spiders with huge
                          spoke-joint knotted legs, resting on your heart,
in the cupboard your collapsed boots await the relations, white socks
                          naked on your bread-crust curling feet,
old friends that day played you out in the crashing rain, valves
                                snapping like steel Adam's apples
like fangs of antediluvian birds, teeth of the *carcharodon* looking for
                                carrion from out those brass trumpets.
O mother, my mother, do not recall my father,
let my father be, lest his eyes burst out of the reopening earth.

Her own son the mother called
      from afar crying:
come back, my own son, come back
      turn away from that stone world,
you stag of the stone woods, industrialized air, electric grids,
chemical lightnings, iron bridges, and streetcars lap up your blood,

day by day they make a hundred assaults on you, yet you never hit
                                                                   back,
it is I calling you, your own mother,
     come back, my own son, come back.

There he stood on the renewing crags of time,
stood on the ringed summit of the sublime
universe, there stood the boy at the gate of secrets,
his antler prongs were playing with the stars,
with a stag's voice down the world's lost paths
he called back to his life-giving mother:
     mother, my mother, I cannot go back,
pure gold seethes in my hundred wounds,
day by day a hundred bullets knock me from my feet
and day by day I rise again, a hundred times more complete,
day by day I die three billion times,
day by day I am born three billion times,
each branch of my antlers is a dual-based pylon,
each prong of my antlers a high-tension wire,
my eyes are ports for ocean-going merchantmen, my veins are tarry
                                                        cables, these
teeth are iron bridges, and in my heart surge the monster-infested
                                                                  seas,
each vertebra is a teeming metropolis, for a spleen I have a smoke-
                                                          puffing barge,
each of my cells is a factory, my atoms are solar systems,
sun and moon swing in my testicles, the Milky Way is my bone
                                                              marrow,
each point in space is one part of my body,
my brain's impulse is out in the curling galaxies.

Lost son of mine, come back for all that,
your *libellula*-eyed mother watches for you still.

Only to die will I return, only to die come back,
yes, I will come, will come to die,
and when I have come—but to die—my mother,
then may you lay me in the parental house,
with your marbled hands you may wash my body,

my glandulous eyelids close with a kiss.
    And then, when my flesh falls apart
and lies in its own stench, yet deep in flowers,
    then shall I feed on your blood, be your body's fruit,
then shall I be your own small son again,
and this shall give pain to you alone, mother,
    to you alone, O my mother.

(1955)   *(Kenneth McRobbie)*

CROWN OF HATRED AND LOVE

1

Oh how I hated that village, crown of thorns around my timid child's heart, at whose whimpering response to some pulsation, some birdcall from the constellations, it would bite with round tangled mouth, cruel teeth-circle, so that my larva-soft flesh bled from within towards the surface, towards the stars, and on my starwards-yearning flesh the skin flowered with freckles, like the blue graveyard dotted with All Souls' Eve candles, so that I felt my heart pouring through my limbs, bleeding like Pál Gulyás's massive-headed, mosquito-larva's translucent Christ-like staggering body, about whom once I wanted to write perhaps one of my epics' most important lines.

Oh how I hated that village, closing around me like a spined mollusc, each thorn's tip a tenacious leech's mouth, a belly beneath the hard grey shield around its malevolent hideousness like a warhorse's iron head-armor, from whose embossed orifice only the hairy muzzle's flower-whorl protrudes with whetted teeth behind spongy fur-skinned mouth's petals to sink into me, chew up my warm entrails, sip them, suck them in: this wreath of thorn-mouths woven of a thousand visored horses' heads! This living star-crown seeking refuge in stone cisterns, only its outer casing deflects the teeth, while beneath all is crumbling decay, wasting savage hungers!

Oh how I hated that village, black blinkers for my longing, absurd, clever, shining colt's wide eyes. They fastened them round my forehead to keep me from seeing as far as Sirius, that my wondering eyes should not—beyond the drifting iceflow of light-years—find answering radiance in the spring-scented fields of light from other worlds!

Oh how I hated those black blinkers, my vision's stables, set deep in my frontal bones and which I could rub aside from my eyes only by butting at the far-off star-cliffs screaming out at the terrifying kisses of ores!

Oh how I hated that village, those merciless scissors screeching open rusty hands to clip sprouting wing-feathers—slimy-sticky still like a shell-hatched chick's, clammy like the yellow wolf's-milk that covers in weeds the hillside graveyard. I hated that stony egg, straining to crack its obstinate shield, beneath which Darkness and Light were living together as in the universe; and I kept turning and turning about in the glistening embryo-fluids, with clinging pond-weedy eyelashes, nostrils stopped with viscid blood, with tongue driven back down my throat, with lungs sagging in the starved air like cellophane-straining wrapped rosebushes, so dilated by now as to fill the entire egg, faltering in its choking grip like a failing heart, for I had swollen into the pitted shell's texture, my body shrivelling, my being driven within itself by solitude's slippery concavity.

O my Village, you swamp-toad, holding fast upon the Titan-skulls of putrescent ancestors in the universe's translucent deeps, glass throat of silence, gently rhythmical cell-basket, ravenous cobweb funnel, wide-mouthed sack of pulsing fibre-animals, you submarine white spectral belly, monster mildness in the marbling bell-strokes of the moon, who subdues in its passage through you the onrushing universe, its terrific flames, feathery-crested prodigious life-mass, shy crab-droplet tears, crystalline animal-bloods.

O my Village, you flower-fragrant calf's moist cherry-muzzle thirsting for the udders of world-mists netted with rubies, why did I hate you? My morning's gold-fenced flower garden, why did I dread you? Why did I not weep for you, my childhood?

2

Frost covers the rose-trees; a few scraggy geese stand
with lead-laced wings trailing forlornly on the ground.
Octopus arms of plants wetly catch at bullfrogs.
Like dried-up jellyfish a few torn snowy rags;
long potato-stalks straggle out, limp and brown
like chicken's entrails that dried where they were thrown;
parsley alone stands out green, that frost stiffens
in porcelain feathers of color and silence.

The brown towers of burrs from hawthorn and thistle
are like tatters of mourning in a burned-out chapel,
their flower-insect eyes and cell-built cupola
like an empty wasps' nest's smoked-out architecture.
Thistles and saplings jut out from the plastered wall,
and propped there, stick-limbs knotted, helm of mossy metal,
skeleton-membrane shirted, a locust's empty shell,
image of knight's armor in dusty mother-of-pearl.

One tree still stands leaning, lightning-stallion torn,
dreaming on, while a crow caws from its glass crown.
Down from the picket-fence some rusted wreath-wires hang,
and a broken bucket lies musing on a plank.
The lilacs are creatures guided by other stars.
Hollow-toothed white hen-coops stagger with doors ajar,
just one hen left scratching about in blue manure,
picking at the bones of the cock who had her.

Proud I was, too stupid to be good, a thickhead,
not once did I listen to what my father said,
I left this house behind, with no goodbyes from me.
Slowly, humility put out leaves within me!
My heart, with birds' whirrings once inoculated,
yearned to fly away, into infinity melted,
spending itself in shame, and untrue to its nest.
Now I can only weep, here in my grief wordless.

Where is he who stayed here, and would not renounce me?
In his hot coffin he's fermenting, mould-furry!
He who poured out new wine lazily, who suffered
on his pearl-crusted face my prickly bobbing head,
scolding me so I'd weep, gazing at the smoke-palms,
to whom I would recite "The Death of György Dózsa"?
The carrion-larvaed star has drunk him up, while I
was lulled in the god's lap who always was to lie.

Where's my father now? Where? Where's my pride of those days?
I became a rainbow, and he maggoty clay.

                                        (Kenneth McRobbie)

MARGIT SZÉCSI
(1928–)

LOVE'S FOOL

It happened before my eyes:
grass sprouted miraculously,
and rancid oil on my tongue
didn't taste bitter to me.
The world of all that is not
was setting light to my hair,
in my rags just like some saint
fiercely I preached at the air.

I know now he was laughing
at me for being a fool;
O how lovely my blindness,
believing was impossible.
And you came, mud stained flower,
with such dreaming agonized,
then the sky came crashing down:
it was myself I recognized.

(*Kenneth McRobbie*)

ONLY WITH RADIANCE

When we know we are on the way out,
    our desperation is what's ugly.
Last year's bark peels from the tree
    humbly, like scabs from a body.

Roots' raging, veins, glistening, old
    trees extinguish by an act of will,
still putting out leaves to the youthful sky,
    a yellowing last smile.
O were there some sombre enough clothes,
    a transcendent uniforming,
skirts of iron to toll in place
    of me! I'll cease struggling,
I'll never again be sold on common
    self-deception, nor crawl
snake-pliant, nor wriggle after
    life running away downhill.
I'll stop... Women, women, if your shoulders
    are shapely still, chances are you're offhand
in tiny-stinged scornful maliciousness;
    this is a thing you can't understand,
old crones too: wobbly sergeant-majors
    who have already been advised
of mortality, the same revulsion stares
    out at you from my stone-cold eyes.
You without the dignity of misery,
    curlered, flabby-breasted,
you long ago saddled up with corsets,
    you arthritis-knotted, withered!
And you too whom I knew at school
    how pot-bellied and bald you've grown!
In front of the meal-ticket window
    how quietly you've settled down!
What have you now to do with me
    who wouldn't play the hand she was dealt,
who wished to win every heart
    by making others radiant!
God pelts me with little stone
    stars, friends grow more vain,
jealous cats tease of course,
    old admirers long went down the drain.
I've been left with nothing to do
    —but, thank you, I'm holding quite still,
I'm keeping an eye on my body, lest its
    dying be a public spectacle.

Is it so shameful to trudge up with nothing
 to the heights that are only death's?
Watch me: putting off all I once thought mine
 now I wear only timelessness;
away with my vertigo of shallow
 society's gossipy depths.
My sinewy brown legs are means
 of carrying on for a while yet;
then, then, fire alone the food
 my lungs' rose-bushes will get,
the heart will live only by song,
 stone-steady eyes by radiance.
I shall not play the bitch
 sniffing the pantries of the rich.
Even as I curtsied I hated them all;
 I scorned, that's why I was quiet;
everything about their culture's cheap,
 tombs with tears running wet.
I've got all I ever needed,
 now let me be free,
and though my fall is but a breath away
 I'll celebrate openly.
I am all the purer
 by what makes me ever poorer.
It's not my falling, I am sure,
 but of everything I dreamed: Life.

(Kenneth McRobbie)

THE BURNING SHIP

 Your yellow sails—a shroud,
 your vintage kegged wine rages,
 the bird catches fire above you,
 your form—torture racks,
 the foam seethes over you,

being captain ties me here,
if I leave you I'll drown,
if I stay you'll be my pyre—
how close the New World is
and how inaccessible it glitters.

(Laura Schiff)

MAN

7 o'clock, theater time, dinner time
I've made it onto the streetcar
life's mine
I bring home a nickle bunch of dead
and higher priced, a pot of condemned.

(Laura Schiff)

GÁBOR GÖRGEY
(1929–)

From INTERVIEW

1

I'm fine, thanks.
Teeth
in good shape.
Some hair, yes. I hope
it stays on, who knows.
Yes, family.
Naturally—why, don't I look
like a man who loves life?
It's brushed me, twice.
Vitality, and style.
Size 12. Yes, a little large.
I've quit, finally.
I wouldn't know.
This and that.
Here and there.
Lots.
Have a smoke? Coffee?
Any other questions, Miss?

2

Visions? Haven't any.
Shoving on step by
step through some
inimical stubborn
jungly stuff as sly
and tricky as a rogue beast,
clawing it out of the ground
down to the bone
I make what I can of it.

In childhood, once upon a time,
I had visions, lots of them,
poetic, the real thing.
But it stopped, just like that,
when I started writing poems.
Visions. What I get's the old shaft.

7
Snow? I like it, yes.
Sometimes though it seems
to sort of blend in
with the Sahara.
Discrimination's so difficult
these days, don't you think?

10
I'll tell you about that too.
I was led
to a girl's boudoir
packed with masked bandits.
I had to rescue the virgin
who gratefully gave herself to me
in that pink and white decor.
When it was over we went
for a ride, a cloud of lace floating
fragrant on the horse's rump.
Finally we rowed, I think,
on a pointillist pond.
So that's what happened
to me in the Jeu de Paume.

13
Like linens stacked
with love's fragrant lavender
in grandmother's cupboard—
in the terminal wards
old age homes
despair, loneliness
catarrhal laughter
vitamin deficiency, bedwettings,

fifty-seven varieties of cancer
lined up, neatly catalogued.
Isn't it adventurous of us
to lay our doddering folks
away so scrupulously in lavender?

16
What I admire?
Concentration of soul
giving you the strength,
for example, to burn yourself alive.
And the iron calm
of the citizen in me
listening to the 8 a.m. nowo
and cracking the second
soft-boiled egg,
so essential for his existence.

17
It's a big, fat hypothesis, of course.
But well-constructed, even
a Martian could see that.
I admit there are other
palatable hypotheses, but
I'm not about to kowtow
grovelling in the dust
with the rest of them
every time the tribe's adored totem-face
stares at me.
My backbone's no thrilling conductor
of cultural currents—
in fact I'm turned off:
because these days it's not just
connoisseurs of the primitive
but conquerors too who
ooze goodwill.

19
Were you there too? You got to see
that fabulous well, didn't you,

where tourists take the plunge
from the edge, immersing themselves,
doing the antique
abyss?
A marble phallus
broke off under me and I lost
interest in the whole trip,
but take my word for it
I was the only tourist
with that kind of luck,
and I brought home an empty soul.
That indefatigable American woman though,
what a thirst for culture she had, and
what a splash she made, ye gods!

22
Nice to hear that, Miss.
I do make a point
of shaving close, yes.
It brings in this sort
of mini-success among others.
But after razoring it clean,
deep-rubbing my wincing face—
how the lotion bites—
behind its contented grin
a bit of that endless rope of pearls
stringing out through the earth
exposes itself:
the Homo Sapiens mandible.

25
I do.
Naturally I do.
If I didn't I couldn't.
But since I can,
I have to,
and if I have to,
I certainly
can.

(Jascha Kessler)

GÁBOR GARAI
(1929–   )

A MAN IS BEATEN UP

They are beating up a man in the bar
They are banging and hanging his head with their fists
He doesn't cry out or try to protect himself
Even the blood creeps patiently over his face
They beat and beat
        a silent exhibition
broken by one voice:
        —He's probably a gipsy!
They beat and beat
        and the barman comes forward
takes a knee to jerk him outside
into the street
        A man's head smashes
against a block of hard-snow
        —Go tumble your mother!
The barman wipes his hands—easy!
The one who beat blood out of a face orders:
—Beer all round for these fellows, with a dash of rum!
The service continues without a break.

A score of other people in the room
They have nothing to do all this while?
They chat and smile together, what is it to them?

Their detachment disguises
             squalid pub-crawls
             racist fantasies
             defoliating embraces
             genocide volunteers
             jerrybuilt residences
             wandering H-bombs
             curetted foetuses
             meat-trusts ordnance-factories
             slippery so-help-me-gods
             prudent no-comment betrayals
             specious reasons interests knives
             handcuffs stocks keys

             like snakes all interlocked
             blood-money and forebodings
                       frozen hard in the ice

What if this ice should once be thawed?

                                        (Edwin Morgan)

CALCUTTA

O glowing walls of this city
weighting the earth, holding the sky
it is here the parched bodies lie.

Here in the pavement's narrow fold,
here where the wind stifles the field,
the rickshaw-puller's days are filled

with rest. No cool spell refreshes
him, only flickering palm leaves
and vision of a pot of rice.

In his dream the knock is the same,
the ten nails on his feet, the drum
he hears tomorrow in his dream.

Tomorrow's certainty will swell
and burst, and burn, it will burn while
the sun goes on enduring all.

(Daniel Hoffman)

VIGIL AT DAWN

How were the temples of the three gods built?
    No one can guess. Fragrance
of incense settles on the drooping heart.
Frogs sit motionless in pools of silence.

Spraddled on the wall, a yellow lizard—
    So vulnerable, that cool
pulsing throat. Mosquitoes on my forehead
bleed. I start up with the day's arrival.

The banyan's roots twist earthward. A hundred arms
    arise in bark of leather.
The world alights on green extended palms;
invisible spiders weave the morning's weather.

The fuzzy tongue of a red bloom hangs down;
    from paddy fields dew flies.
The haze is trembling. On the molten silence
of night's diluted gold, the bulbul cries.

(Daniel Hoffman)

GÁBOR GARAI

IN HUNGARIAN

What a language to speak!—
                    Incomprehensible to outsiders.
Those who speak like this
                    are outsiders everywhere.
Orphan, heavenly nest in a vortex of floods,
turtle-dove's leaf-braided shelter,
                    what power had you
to survive the madness of vultures
                    in brotherless loneliness?
Who brings you an olive-branch day after day?
Who entices you ashore with
                    "you'll make it dryshod"?
For you always touched land among blood-creamy rocks,
and craziness goes swirling endlessly about you
as space spins round a point
                    in the sealed circle...
Sun. Sky. Fish. Stone. Wind. Water...
                              You love me?
                                        I love you!

I take you with me like home-baked bread,
I drench you in foreign seas
and lift you clean above the wave-torn seaweed.
A miracle made flesh—my life is your medal:
your people, suppressed a hundred times—who knows how?—survived!
Look at the happier nations gawping at you—
they can't make out one word of the rigmarole.

To me, however, you are living water on the tongue:
you are my religion, and if need be, my mask,
my aerial roots,
                my guard in far-off lands,
my homeward-pointing shepherd-star.

                              (Edwin Morgan)

SÁNDOR CSOÓRI
(1930-)

GOLDEN PHEASANTS FLYING

Here they were all running, running past my heart:
the late March wind, my father's horse with his head like a burning coal,
here my friends ran by with feet dampened in dew,
ran with the great joy of the earth.

The golden pheasants flying through the forest's gate,
a wounded moon driven by the heavens' breathing
and in showers born of the rending of the clouds
the world was as beautiful as in a future Gospel.

Faces of foliage, of people, faces of waters and of girls,
you never left me forsaken in the happy chase.
We stepped over the sibylline immobility of stones
as across the forgotten dead.

And sea, once only have I seen you, but I've tasted you—
You were the summer's wine, the cooled draught of the universe,
o mystical wing which upraised me from within
above all dry sobriety and my own death.

Where are you, sea, and you, my schoolmates hiding beneath the bridge?
Where are you, ploughs of dawn with which I harrowed the sun?
Wind threading the needle's eye of Spring, revolution of the lilacs,
whose side have you joined up with, now that you've deserted me?

I stand above my village; behind me, the ancient ruin.
The woods are desolate, forlorn the meadows of boyhood.
The golden pheasant scurries among the trees, the wind is scudding too,
and I have no other joy but that I may cry out to them.

(Daniel Hoffman)

BARBARIAN PRAYER

Wrinkled, unrelaxing stone,
rock of mother-daylight, take
me back again into your womb.
Being born was the first error;
the world was what I wanted to be:
lion and tree-root in one,
loving animal and laughing snow,
consciousness of the wind, of heights
pouring their dark ink-blot down—
and here I am cloud-foundered man,
king of a solitary way,
being of a cindery star,
and what I join within myself
splits me at once, because it goes
quickly and only sharpens yearning...
Wrinkled, unrelaxing stone,
rock of mother-daylight, I
stand at the entrance to your womb.

(Edwin Morgan)

AGUE

What is this extraordinary crowding,
this seagull-torrent,
woman's screaming,
ocean-howling?

Trees collapse together
like men hit by sunstroke.
A moment ago I had a grape in my lips,
now I suck sea-ooze.
On my hand hare's blood,
frog-spawn,
silk of a night-gown are drying.
In a green coach of leaves, summer and my skull go driving.
Rain rouses me,
water stills me,
war in prospect hones the body—
Come on, I'll give even brave mouths my boot
if they hold me with their stupidity.
What is this, what is this rage, ague, change?
Poems go pounding through me like freight-trains.
Dispersed—my bones,
my vertebrae,
my brain.
My hand droops like a shot soldier
in trenches of alien beds—
Joyless fingers are busy about me,
with a blue sky they bandage me,
in the gauze of rivers they bind me,
and they carry me prone on the wind,
but where to, where?

(Edwin Morgan)

WHISPERS, FOR TWO VOICES

I was there,
yes, I was there,
a voice whispered to me between
two faded chairs: don't go away, do you hear? don't go away!
if you go it will be as if three of you were going!
as if five of you were going,
as if a hundred of you were going,

and in the glass-splintered winter
the trees will wait in vain
for your caresses,
the wheezing thrushes for your crumbs,
do you hear? you could still become the organizer of the earth,
the earth's best man—
I was there,
yes, I was there,
I even remember the pulse of the body,
the half-open door, the exposed
nerves
dangling over the threshold—
                              and then the other voice
from behind the murky wardrobe: what are you waiting for?
you will be given
nothing in exchange for quiescence,
fidelity's hibernating heart will always be surrounded by snow,
the nipples of women
could still harden under your fingers,
lips to your lips they could still
pump spring into you, but they return
to their mirrors too quickly,
to the site of their desperation,
and you, messianic buffoon: victim of their boiling blood,
will have to beg for a country
to go with the wounds of your body
while you are still able to stand,
the white shirt a wounded man's bandage.

                                        (Alan Dixon)

I WOULD RATHER RUN BACK

What a crazy saint I am,
eating insects, spending nights
among the roots,
from your weeping
and your body fleeing

into bare rooms, to deserts of rejected eyes,
and stones crawl over me like lice,
and the caterpillar-night, and familiar ants,
I journey companioned by trees
to pay my respect to the snow because it is white,
to lovers because they are in love,
but everywhere the evenings are the same,
the silences the same.
I shun the cities, they yap from the distance
like dogs,
and shun the forests because they are plundered by owls.

I would rather run back to your hair,
to your mouth,
to your creaking wardrobes,
and because you are always craving
I would feed you with myself, my illumination,
my madness, here you are, here is summer,
the blossom of acacia,
blue plum of the seas: the earth,
and I would love you
and I would love you.

(Alan Dixon)

ISTVÁN EÖRSI
(1931–   )

WHEN THINGS FALL UPWARDS

When things fall upwards, not down,
and the sun keeps its warmth to itself
hold on to the edge of the world, my dear,
        look after yourself.

If the word goes over to the enemy
and cuts the electric meters by stealth
don't move, wait there in the wolf-darkness,
        look after yourself.

Especially don't act Cleopatra,
cast the snake from your lovely breasts
o serpent-dreams o maddening apple
        look after yourself.

If your eyelids cannot cover you
if your twice ten fingers roam twenty fells
lie down in my forbidden shade and
        look after yourself.

I'd wear a rubber jacket for you
I'd sit as I did with you on a shelf
on a rail I'd sit my world only you
        look after yourself.

                                    (Edwin Morgan)

GENERATIONS

For György Lukács

You did see the forest for the trees, and now in your old age
you also see the trees for the forest, but without terror,
growing taller as you move away among stumps and logs.

Old age is nothing enviable, but we envy you nonetheless,
for we, too, grow old, but do not become contemporaries of time;
cannot mould flesh on the skeleton of ideas—
while you, from under the shadow of a winter tree,
behold both fruit and foliage naturally.

(William Jay Smith)

ÁGNES GERGELY

(1933–)

CRAZED MAN IN CONCENTRATION CAMP

All through the march, besides bag and blanket
he carried in his hands two packages of empty boxes,
and when the company halted for a couple of minutes
he laid the two packages of empty boxes neatly at each side,
being careful not to damage or break either of them,
the parcels were of
ornamental boxes
dovetailed by sizes each to each
and tied together with packing-cord,
the top box with a picture on it.
When the truck was about to start, the sergeant
shouted something in sergeant's language,
they sprang up suddenly,
and one of the boxes rolled down to the wheel,
the smallest one, the one with the picture:
"It's fallen," he said and made to go after it,
but the truck moved off
and his companions held his hands
while his hands held the two packages of boxes
and his tears trailed down his jacket.
"It's fallen," he said that evening in the queue—
and it meant nothing to him to be shot dead.

(*Edwin Morgan*)

WITH LAMP IN HAND

Men! In exchange for a good piece
Of rib, you carve, you sculpt
From our bones—you have reigned
From the saddle,
Have beaten the anvil
For centuries,

Fiddling with slide-rules.
In your alembics what haven't you boiled
And distilled
Searching for treasures,
Walking the glinting stars
Or doggedly whetting stone knives.
At last beside
Shepherd waters you've contrived
Industry: in spring
When the seeds sprout
You clip, you kill;

For you the whole
World is mould.
You hang on our loins
Aprons
Or clothe us
In your abstractions—

O, you cry with bared chest,
I'm a hero! And we,
We manage somehow
To behold you. See,
After you fall
We see, we bandage your brow—

Last night my dream beheld me
Clothed in the white apron
Of Florence Nightingale
And you, you were wounded, shot in the lung

Or was it your legs that were maimed?
Beethoven-deaf, you
In that field hospital in the Crimea

And so mercifully, with the solace
Of febrifuge from ward to ward
I went with lamp in hand
And from the first breath I knew
That you'll start it all over again
And do wonders
Anew and silly things too,
My brothers.

(Daniel Hoffman)

SIGN ON MY DOOR JAMB

In memoriam my father

I do not cherish memories
and those I have I do not safeguard.
I do not seek forgotten graveyards.
Bio-chemistry doesn't move me.

Yet at times like this towards November
as fog-damped windows seal my room
and I gasp for air and long for relief,
I sense your invisible rise
as from the waters of the mind
and odd gestures of yours re-emerge.

I sense your long and nervous fingers
arranging a thermos flask and pocket knife
with the Bible and warm underclothes
and an old can opener in the gaping
green knapsack; and under the weightless load
you can carry, I sense your back's surprise.

I sense your departure, elegant tramp, from the house:
you'd never go away, you just set out,
and look back laughing, aged thirty-eight years,
and you nod and you gesture, *I'll soon return*
(tomorrow would have been your birthday)
while your tears dribble inwards whining
and you wave—and how you wave!

Sign on my door jamb, you've remained;
the bars, the bridge, the sludgy road,
the gorging of grass, the fatal empty weakness
are only freak inventions of the mind;
for I have lied, I often see you
beneath the stifling, low November sky;
you set out with me, you breathe, and your tears
I let your tears go dribbling down my throat;
and where it had fallen, the thin
cigarette struck from your mouth
has burned on a star ever since.

(*Thomas Land*)

MÁRTON KALÁSZ

(1934–   )

LEGACY

I don't see my mother dancing—
in my thoughts she still trims vines
sprayed blue with copper sulfate
for her two bags of wheat, eight bushels rye.
I don't know if her young face
was lovely, if the other tenants
admired her dragonfly form,
or if my blond father tethered his horse only
at our cabin on the wild Whitsun ride.
I just see her in the wintry dawn
chopping cornstalks at the stove
or patching sacks in the stilled yard;
I see her at evening in the vineyard
secretly taking flowers for my dead father.
Such memories pour into me,
and whirl me round fiercely now—
my mother, whom none could help,
in the darkness of whose flesh
the cancer spread its deadly arms,
who left her son this legacy.
This is not to blame her; not one curse
ever left her lips, I know... Only, poverty
took it all from her vein-roped hands.
Half a day she walked to find me, a hand
at some far-off farm, bringing me potatoes she spared,
spending her scant savings on my studies;
and when I scanned my first lines
at the window something silvery

glowed in her eyes—joy.
And then she was gone, never to see
the first book. I could thrust no money
secretly beneath her bolster, for a dress, for salt—
her bones in the graveyard
moldered to fat silent clay; now flowers force their roots
in summer where her forehead used to be.
And I carry her legacy for good:
on my face the mark of sorrow,
in myself humility's soundless load;
until I die I shall not forget
that world of grinding poverty—
in the field we are walking
like yoked horses together forever.

(Jascha Kessler)

MIHÁLY LADÁNYI

(1934–   )

WE JUST SIT ABOUT QUIETLY

In the beer-garden with its drowsy ivy-leaves
we just sit, lapped in the clotted afternoon.

In time gone
it was far easier for us poets to die too, sir.
I mean when the revolution
still trailed round the markets looking for work.
We had nothing, but we got this one day
when we were heroes, not misfits,
when,
like those of public-square statues,
our hands were galvanized to fists.

Now,
under red sunshades, in
lemon-yellow sand, we're in the beer-mists,
and politics drifts through the conversation.
Change the conditions, and you
I've no doubt would be a proletarian,
and not, as you are, a traveling salesman
trading machinery for oranges,
Australian cigars in your mouth and
a belief that your world is absolutely natural,
your dreams handed over,
your cut of the cake as obligatory
as that of the Joneses and the fathers of the Joneses,
your flat stuffed full with technology
since that, let's face it, replaces

the ideals—
and in you, sir,
the ideal is what
I'd never feel.

I envy you your lovers, so young
and ready for anything:
working-class girls once,
with that natural grace
that makes them glow. I envy
your car,
its registration number shows
I pay your petrol anyway. Latest
model, sir, you do see how
I appreciate your exquisite taste,
and how happy I am to have met you here
in this beer-garden,
joy, joy untold.

I am a poet,
I live from the market, sir,
and I live alone in this world.

(Edwin Morgan)

LENIN

Here I am turning your words
in my hands like a crumpled cap, Lenin!
Clumsy as
an old cotter
with his weatherbeaten hat.
All the times I was taken to task in your name,
when I only wanted to talk to you!
Yet you are no god for podgy priests
to trumpet your word wherever they go,
you are no *jeune premier*
to sing in every operetta,
no greasepaint peasant in a folk melodrama!

I know
you were one
this century can never duplicate.
It hurts me that I have to hear
your sharp voice only on the gramophone!
Yet if you could come back,
back even for a single day
in the temples of our Jerusalem!
I think of this always, after all
I have no desire to see you embalmed,
I think of this always, after all
you were a man, lived in hiding on rye-bread...
I keep your words clasped
like a crumpled cap over my heart, Lenin,
I'll cheer the future with it
if I see it coming in.

(Edwin Morgan)

WHEN ALL'S SAID AND DONE

All things considered we needn't despair—I love you,
dream of you. True,
keeping precise account of every dream:
when first I was fascinated by you,
when you made me despair.
You see,
since History
was thought up by some ancestor or other
we've been unable to get along
without documentation, destined to oblivion as we are.
You see a label round the hero's neck, *Hero,*
and the hangman
with one round his neck, too.
Now and again the wording's
a little behind the times.
It's all the same to History.
It just gets on with its job,
a garbageman putting in time before retirement. Keeping his cool.

History
twists its moustache, tugs its peaked cap
over its eyes and sweeps up the bones.
It heaps together the poet's bones
with the drummer's, and when
the pile's the right size, it says:
Fine, time for a break!
   It squats.
   Spits.
   That's peace.

                              (*Kenneth McRobbie*)

INVENTORY

One balding forehead one pair of glasses
one mouth flanked by small sad lines
one neck with jumpy Adam's apple and bitter gulps
one chest no decorations but intractable red heart
one beer-belly with anxiously quaking liver
one penis with two testicles and three offspring
two legs with mud-stuffed footprints and inaccessible thresholds
and a song or two
about mud-stuffed footprints and inaccessible thresholds
a song or two
above my head
in the wind

                              (*Edwin Morgan*)

ABOUT THE HERO

The hero does everything nicely and well.
By dint of mastering epic poetry
he's learned a way of passing time
busy with heroic deeds.

It was he who ousted the coward from the textbooks.

Poor man, devoid of armor against dangers,
he can only squirm on the peak of his insignificance,
lunging and thrusting his embarrassed wooden sword
into the rumps of vindictive gods.

(Edwin Morgan)

FOR THE RECORD

Today at dawn
we had to jemmy the day's roll-shutters open,
had to break into
the tenth of November,
and had to sneak out of the drawers
eight hours of work,
eight hours of leisure,
eight hours of sleep.
(The last two drawers as good as empty.)

Afternoon
we trotted behind her
when she boarded a tramcar.
Her throat shone with a necklace
made of twenty-carat desires.
(It ought to have been snatched safely
but then we thought
it's only painted there
as our mother-tongue is on her mouth.)

Later, at the police-station of our sublets,
when the night-sergeant
fixes us with a stare,
we have to state for the record
the things we NEVER did that day.
And on counts of our gang-submission
and gang-cowardice the hellish-lonely hours
will give us this time hard labor, a night's
sleepless tossing and turning.

(Edwin Morgan)

OTTÓ ORBÁN
(1936–   )

GAIETY AND GOOD HEART

On this heavenly molehill
where a long-drawn-out war is being waged besides the local massacres
and the anonymous heroes of time squatting in the dug-outs of their days
know that a smile is only self-deception and joy is death's moratorium
for major causes are composed of minor causes
for victory is unreal in a battle where
peasants' huts are bombed with figures
for the business of living is a master sculptor and can twist a man's face
to a sheep's
and in hunger there is neither poetry nor sense of the fundamentals
on this earth where poverty is no news
and no one is fool enough to stammer or cry in deep emotion
for who has not clambered down from some cross or other
and who has not soaked his nail-stuck feet in a bowl of water
what typist has not sprung to life again after her family was sent to the ovens
and who has not forgotten her unforgettable lover's features
where everybody but everybody has shaken hands with the bereaved widow
assuring her of his sympathy gazing deep into her eyes
and has cabled ALL THE BEST on hearing of the resurrection of Lazarus
where the idea of endurance was invented to meet the torture-chamber
where there is no one who has not seen it all
and who does not have endless opportunities
and who would gladly not exchange state affairs for a fishing-rod
on the breast of this barren mother
when the stars of cosmic paralysis transfix you to the dust
and you lean on the rail and look down into the valley
you can see the hope of the age the little rickety truck
stuffed with whatever has been salvaged from the fire

sticks of furniture sacks stewpans chickens
like an unkillable bombardier-beetle
like a tin-jowled reptile flashing headlamp-eyes
and lolling out its panting petrol-tongue like a child
while in front of the flames embossed on its jolting flanks
the nickel trade-mark shines:
Gaiety and Good Heart

(Edwin Morgan)

TO BE POOR

To be poor, even just relatively poor, means that a man lacks
the brashness to decorate his speech with Christmas-tree baubles and
hold forth to the fighters of a war on the whistling wings of gorse.
To be poor is to have an irresistible wish to answer yes or no if we are
questioned. To be poor is to wade barefoot through the splintered-glass
sea of technology and hand-feed a lion equipped with every modern
convenience. To learn an upside-down ethics, to discover everything
about the concealed dungeons of a sky-bound earthscraper; to crawl
backwards along the narrowing corridors of the cavern of history
into that primordial workshop where blood and wretchedness are pounded
into Ariel-shapes of humaneness. To be poor in a world where
Romeo is a car and Juliet a cosmetic may be an embarrassing merit
but it is also a happy embarrassment, for the poor man lives
in the besieged stronghold of thought without relying on any possible
safe-conduct, and instead he gallops bareback on an earth with its mane
flying and he uses his patient anger to spur it on its way.

(Edwin Morgan)

CONCERT

As they surround the house, there is no mistaking
their expertise. No superfluous gesture. No false step.
All goes with classic simplicity as in some baroque piece
of music or in a dentist's chair. An operation, not
a manhunt. Rifles at the ready, at ease, steps right and

left, as at a dancing school. This way, please, after
you—a thrust barely noticeable yet firm between the
shoulderblades, no touch of refined cruelty. A minuet
of machines: traffic moving to perfection. Diesel-rondos,
khaki-sonatas. After formless agony an elegy of relief:
the wind rinsing the houses. Blood-clotted tufts of weeds,
sputum of mud-walls dotting a cuplike village. Standing
out like a Greek idea on the autumn anarchy the
colonnade of goose steps. A marching masterpiece.
In the Alpine purity of measure and proportion is
celebrated the practice of generations. O brushes!
O chisels! O arrested movements! No ordinary moment:
the hunter and the hunted on the same plinth of a hill.
The dénouement is more prosaic. The house as if on
second thought thrusts high its roof, then falls flat on
the ground steaming like a cow-flop. Dust circles for
a while before clearing away. One error on the map,
and earth the wiser for it.

(William Jay Smith)

REPORT ON THE POEM

From now on, the Earth. Test of Earth's gravity. Ferroconcrete sea.
Pro boxer grows old. Passions too raw for poetry
in the empty harbor, where no one wipes off tears:
 "It's time!" It is too, and the decent poet

inscribes on wood-free paper: "Age of Manhood,"
and noble emotion and restrained tears shake in his voice,
like a condom thrown in a puddle. Enough of that.
 It's the old girl's cosmetics that bore me. Let her

tame panthers on her cloudlike walks or wag her hips
in angel feathers under the stagy moon. She can hold out
her tricksy salvation, thick arias for thickheads: I know what it's worth.
 From now on, the story is more important.

The It-Happens-To-Us-All. The Only-To-Me. The Don't-Turn-Back.
The fact that won't be changed by star-soaring composition.
The fate that from unseen motives aims at a single goal
   may be smalltime, yet a matter of life and death.

From now on, the logistics-poetry of polar exploration. Foxhole letters.
In place of magic eye-and-ear enchantment: stout boots, warm clothes.
Head-clutching verse, a circus stunt,
   flight of fancy with head-in-sand.

That's how it is. Sad that our concepts of God are always man-faced.
Better to fly on wings of pity, but the interrogator comes from the
                                        interrogated.
To smoke cigarettes with spine-sized tobacco-stalks to ashes,
   anger and love, give me a light!

(Edwin Morgan)

THE APPARITION

Yes, an angel has summoned me too,
though not just like Blake or Weöres:
kindling a freemasonic burning bush in my room
or dictating lines to me over the phone.
"Come on," the voice said, "there's no one at home."
The shoddy victory among ancient furniture
was outlined sharply in the cigarette-smoke:
there we lay on the World War I family bed,
like monumental sculptures bathed in sweat.
My mouth was chapped, wine
after vodka isn't good.

The apparition kept me waiting till morning.

The wizened face and the black hair-tangles—
that's what I saw. Enough
for some nameless secret distress

opening lashless eyes in my cells
to sense the ray-scarred huntsman camouflaging his trap.
Not that I can say he told me anything,
in advance, I mean, the metaphysical messenger.
The hospital, the dying, the "Daddy Orbán,"
the pedestrian Odyssey from shilling to shilling,
the holed socks, the outgrown shoes, the "Who's going to say hello?",
in a word the whole piss- and blood-smelling novel
which Central Europe works up
from the Verona balcony-scene,
and even the guerrilla raids of more universal bad luck,
the biological mines, planted in the loam of pleasure,
detonating and detonating
in heart and stomach—all that remained hidden.
Only—the curtain went up on an ancient puppet-show,
and around us so-called destiny:
a theatrical Danube, shores scarred by industry,
a Tom Thumb country with the stolidity of a giant
darkening the sky with smoke and poverty.
How should I know whether fire scared me or deadly cold?
In some murderous medium, flashing up and down,
the butterfly-creature was in terror;
no doubt about it, already drawn to the lamp
men usually call: love.

I smoked a cigarette: modern film-hero.

But later, as the siege and the orphanage
only made a little savage of me, yet not so humorless
as to pluck a verse-harp at that crucial moment:
"O shaggy mustang, O fiery youth!"
plunging in Professor Piccard's live bathyscaphe
into the abyssal wheezing I again feel asleep.

                                        (Edwin Morgan)

THE LADIES OF BYGONE DAYS

Where with their magnetic breasts are Susanna and Martha
   and the Judys of various addresses
time has chewed to pulp Melinda and Vera and Liz my god we had
   breakfast with her bacon and eggs
Gisella what on earth was her last name gone too gone off on a Danube
   steamer
all I know about her is she was a company typist somewhere and she
   never heard of contraception till I told her and
then it was all amazement under blonde eyebrows and her Iseult-type
   blue headlights lit up
and I remember Eva too and her caveman-girlfriend the sculptress
   with her low forehead
and the gold-brown madness that looked for lasting messages among
   the trembly lacework revives
its search in their Indian laps for New World treasures
   and the Copernican theory of their hips
over the Babylonian blind the legend ALBERT HECKLER MEN'S
   TAILOR sings out and our tongues incur damnation by the urgency
   of one unpostponable kiss
and what's Tonia that wild spinster doing in Paris and where are
   the adventuresses those Aggies and Cathys and Andreas taking buses
   to with their bursting shopping-bags
they have split dispersed gone without a message all over the stubble-
   field of civilization
it makes no odds who did what the spicy details for instance whose
   husband it was dropped drunk from a New York taxi
they all live somewhere on the earth live well live poor no need to
   worry energy is conserved
where last year's snow was there's a green of this year's spring
dynasty marked for downfall youth crowned with arrogance the jacket
   taken out of pawn fitted your royal figure like a glove
ah spirit of heartrending elegies turn your noble eyes to Kertész Street
peeling plaster and whores and pensioners brought down in the world
G. T. the poet reeking of suntan-oil sported a newspaper in his breast-
   pocket for use as a flying carpet if the right moment came
and two true lovers merged into one body under a world-broad crackle
   of paper

while on the table Miguel Hernandez was dying in a gaol of laurel-
    scented terza rimas
and his flashing bones made lightning in the room and lit up the legend
    tacked to the wall A FRIEND'S FLAT IS NO BROTHEL
and apocalyptic whimpers stole out from the freedom-flavored stench
on the undying day of the faceless watches when language had still
    to invent the future tense
where the mother of two tempered by shivering fever-fits with a jug
    of milk in her hand cycles smash into a lorry
and the three-dimension-clasping limbs are crushed flat into the sheet
    of an asphalt-album scrawled with skid-marks
in happy mother's present time the green blades of the earth besieged
    the world's ice
and the scarlet of Viking lips swam on the shoreless sea of a cushion
and the bodiless starpelt panther lolled and clanked in its planet-kennel
    retracting its workaday claws
Downy creatures dusty earth-chicks your firm flesh and your elegance
the tongues chirping with "I says" and "I don't want none"
but I plan to live forever on a dilapidated iron bed admiring the
    expertise of your professor fingers
with you away sky and memory shiver shudder bleak
but strolling the world on the leash of your arms among the machine-
    gunpitted walls was wonderful
wrinkling at the grave my nose picked up immortal scent from the
    embers of your bodies
I watched my enchanted ones grunt over the mud of bombs in the
    besieged sty
and the wartime Circe had neither chiton nor curls of a goddess
    and Greek urn-figures were not her style
nothing is more perilously beautiful than the live mines of your laps
the history of your hair whispers pleasure in this bomb-crater rolling
    round the sun
the spinning-wheel of fate has threaded your arms about my vertebrae
    for good
to step from the burning bush of your slips you mutter to me and it's
    hoarse GIVE ME A LIGHT
while our shivering cells devour each other in a sweat of honey
and embers of spring of creation-the-destroyer hiss through our fingers.

(Edwin Morgan)

JUDIT TÓTH
(1936–   )

TO THE NEWBORN

Like a round loaf, that's how small you were.
I rolled you on the board with my palm,
I kneaded you, patted you,
greased you smooth, floured you.
I shaped your roly body.
You slept in the palm of my hands.
You'd hardly dawned, your slight bones
were still soft under your skin, yet
how vehemently your vulnerable life
pulsed in your tiny torso, your folded limbs
closed about you like thick petals,
beneath, you slept like the still of a rose.

*

What kind of well is the newborn's dreams.
Where do the minute dreamers descend?
Do they summon up their seas?
Among familiar algae, again
they hide, they swim back
to timelessness' cave,
to this grotto's constant quivering dark,
the blood-red fern's nest,
down, under the blood, under destiny,

And their awakening. The breath's
labored stirring,
until finally the will blasts
into terror's bantam blaring.

To what despair
do they wake from their indifferent seas?
This wild crying, this endless
gasping, a mnemne still of their fish-life,
yet with what a voice
is their vernal despair blessed.
They sob, they clamor, they praise,
hardly alive, they meet with their throats
the assaults of reality, the million
afflictions and pleasures of matter.
And they grab what they clamored for,
they grasp what every being grasps,
theirs the air, the earth, the milk,
the death, the lullaby, the glory.

                    *

Wrapped in a shawl you lay in your basket,
you slept, you grew plump in your dreams.
You didn't know that I took you in my arms.
I scanned your face for my lover;
the image of his face wandered across yours,
drifting like a moon in a windy sky.

                    *

What a loveliness to hold.
What a loveliness to lift.
Light as a plume, round as the sun.
My joy that drowns out everything.
The victory of intertwining limbs
against time.
He rounded in the oven of hope,
detached at the gates of expectancy.
Yet he still floats in the boundless
past, and is here too
in the still of this shawl,
in the still of this rose
he dreams his bright dream.

                              (Laura Schiff)

JUDIT TÓTH

DEAD EMBRYOS

They sit in a glass egg,
the begun and abandoned flowering,
their bodies poised in a stiff shell,
millimeter ghosts.
They too slept in star wells,
dark vessels soaked up their dreams.

Oval-shaped pillows cradled
the creation, the beginning,
their microscopic sprout-solitude.
The glass-spun bony structure,
small wild-apple skulls,
hearts, arms, kidneys
could still begin their budding.

But they dont't receive anything.
The air doesn't reach their lungs;
no spoon reaches their lips.
What kind of mourning does
pre-natal death deserve?

They were scraped also of decay,
naked buds, paper-thin cartilages.
Here the start and the continuum
eternally estranged.
They didn't demand their deaths,
didn't beg for anything,
didn't want flesh, bones, minerals;
they returned to nothingness' well.
The useless night peels off them,
the heavens, time—

They bow their heads to their chest,
knees tucked in, curled up,
they age in a glass egg
flung on the sands of a sunless eternity.

(Laura Schiff)

NOTES ON SAINT MAURICE

Other rules had to be learned.
In the double paths of
binding-parting,
in the pull of two faces,
two lives, two landscapes'
opposite gravities.

You weren't there in the February night,
in the brandyreek,
in the reels of dejection.

But later I had to learn
the multi-meaning laws—
that for your sake
I must forsake everything
and I must keep everything,
the land, the language,
(what acid could wash it from my veins?)
a city, a clime's traditions, a clime
that enclosed me like a motherly cave.

When the time came, and I had to depart
(the departures! how many kinds of murmurs,
cleavings in the iron coats of humming cars)
to a land, other than birth had charted,
and to find newer roots,
these differed from the old,
only in distance, in surface—
For one who severs himself
from a spot still is not freed,
he learns that presence
isn't needed to be present.
And if he wants, he can be
where he's not. With those
whom he left.

(Naturally, they don't know I'm there.
I pass them on the street,
I peer up into their flats,
chat or squabble with them.
And I bid adieu. Naturally no one answers.)

This never-ending
November rain.
This steady dripping, rustling, splashing.
The aluminum threads tangling the trees,
the brass plate dead leaves
that never wing, for they never dry out,
and past the dark nets of branches
half-fallen facades.
The wet, the falling, the ooze,
another kind of rain, another kind of ache.

(Laura Schiff)

ISTVÁN CSUKÁS
(1936–   )

THE MACADAM ROAD REMEMBERS

The remembering macadam road rolls
tanks in Its dream, soldiers shot in the head
march and streamers of gauze trail after them:
moonlight; machine-gun nests, warm as laps,
call on It in the curves, at rheumatic milestones,
at village-end, and It by-passes, time and again, the wrecked
airplane and charred pilot with glittering teeth,
and pauses for awhile at the mass grave full of scrambled bones,
and It knows that not far off the spines of their
murderers, like white fish-bones, lodge in a ditch,
It hurries to find that tiny footprint
which hurts the most; it belonged to a fleeing child
whom the charred pilot with glittering teeth mowed down
from behind with a machine-gun, It hurries for day is breaking.
In winter It dreams of salt-colored bones, in summer of scents.
Smell of burnt flesh, stench of sweat, nauseating fume of gasoline,
armpit odor of jasmine, lung-scent of sainfoin,
rotting-throat scent of lavender, liver-scent of anemone.
In spring chloroform pours down the trees, a bullet-riddled
Red Cross truck stinks, hyperdermic syringes rattle,
white-smocked medical orderlies molder among sickly-sweet reeds,
smell of the beach, and officers in shorts tumble out
of the dressing cabins like hermit crabs from the shell.
When was it? When was it? It can remember no longer
exactly and the dream washes everything together, but It knows
the spot, there, where now fishing-rods hang down into the water,
behind the quiet holiday home, on the river bank, the army
having already marched away, two fugitives, pursuer and pursued,

wrestled in silence, and one of them—pursued or pursuer—bit through
the other's throat; It can still hear the gristle crack.
It hurries, for day is breaking and It still has a lot to dream,
though It is but a side road with little traffic, and for some distance
It follows the river, sniffs the alcohol breath of willows,
tempts long-distance truck drivers to bathe
and women in light sandals to have brief affairs;
and while the truck waits, water in the apoplectic
radiator comes to a boil. Now it shakes itself: land-mines
crawl over It clumsily like smooth-bellied turtles
and barbed wire barriers gallop through on knock-kneed legs,
and presently It is strewn with corpses, soldiers' caps,
a mess-tin is knocked about, caught, like a cow-bell,
It can hear this monotonous music a long time; in autumn It dreams
of sound, the cricket-chirring of volleying pistols,
in the eardrum-shattering silence of an explosion, trench mortars bark
in throaty voices and a howitzer belches from the stomach, its echo
resounds for a long time, under fraying skies the airplane
gurgles, the throaty microphone sound of wild geese crackles,
and It knows that autumn has come, straw carts sway,
honey-sweet pumpkins shake in the forage rack, the hamster,
cheeks full, stands up straight, watches gophers whistle
in solitary fields, silver foil slips from the horizon:
hoar-frost; the sky whitens and turns blue,
and the macadam road, remembering, finds what had hurt
most, the tiny footprint, and sighs. Day breaks.

(Barbara Howes)

DEZSŐ TANDORI
(1938–   )

"AND BRIEF, GOOD MOTHER?
FOR I AM IN HASTE? WHITHER??"

(cca.: R:.. III [...] No, no!)

Wednesday. February 9th. 9:35 A. M.
(Where possible let's use round figures.)
Why get worked up, 10 minutes before going out? 10 more
minutes at home, and while I feel O.K. now, I know
it's going to shake me up. Why do I bother writing this down?
(What?) Of course I ask myself. I sit down just the same and write,
though I must be ready by 9:45. Good thing I called the cab for 10.

Or should I call you up and tell you about it?
(I've still got 7, 8 minutes, and our phone calls always disturb me.
But why am I disturbed? "I called you only because
by the time I get home... I want to get started... all right, then
                                           I'll talk to..."
And one of you hands the phone to the other.)

As a matter of fact I call you up often, no one could say...
My calls aren't cut short like this which is all I could manage now
(5 or 6 minutes). It's better, too, that I sit down instead...
though I know it disturbs me, and perhaps
I'd better cancel the cab; my nervousness
will betray itself later, a sudden uncertainty grips me.

"I'll talk to you..." "I'll talk to you then": sometimes the voice is
                                           the man's,
sometimes I can almost see *the face*, the 76-year-old face
as in the elevator mirror when I'm riding up to you
to the 6th floor, as I see my own face, soon to be 36.
"Someone went this way before me, someone who I almost am,
so different from me, yet I grow more like him..." (And shall be.)

Sometimes the woman answers... (and here we really must
pare things down to age; it's 9:44.) As early as '45
just after the war you took me to B—l for the vacation.
It was the woman's voice that said goodbye to me;
and from the tool-shed—that's where they locked me up because
I didn't want to stay alone there, and cried—I watched
it. Strange that I'm almost as old as he (and you) were then,
36, and that even now, with any 10 minutes to wait I still can see
through the shed windows after the rain that deep green—I guess—
　　　　　　　　　　　　　　　　　　　　　　　　garden.

　　　　　　　　　　　　　　　　　　　　　　　　(*Daniel Hoffman*)

HOMAGE

Who as he rides is weighed down by the burden
of all the bodies of his fallen steeds?
Who follows his own tracks toward their beginning
to seek the beasts that bore him, though in vain?

On either side of the sword's-edge path you ride,
though sliced in half, those chargers wait for you,
their pace slowed down to pace your plodding gait
until the saddle-horse that bears you drops:

And now, not yet disguised in boards and earth,
you still should gaze back toward those cooling crops
so that their sobs will shake in your skull like dice
and the fall of their broken walnut eyes will knock.

　　　　　　　　　　　　　　　　　　　　　　　　(*Daniel Hoffman*)

DETAILS

Let me grow older! I would become
duller and more complete.
My life longs for its lesser half,
discarded though unused.

The details, all the details!
They devour my soul.
What's left of me is not enough
to make me whole.

(Daniel Hoffman)

SADNESS OF THE BARE COPULA

I'd have liked it to have been so.
It wasn't so.
I asked that it be so.
It was so.

(Kenneth McRobbie)

ISTVÁN ÁGH
(1939–)

THE DEAD OF MY SONGS

*For Rudolf Vig, who collected folksongs
in my village in July 1959*

1

A redolent song, the sheaf-smell of dusk
draws the utterance out of the throat,
their ordeals ended, voices release
a garland of songs, cackling like geese
the women gather with coughing men,
sing for the stranger, collector of voices
immortalizing the days of youth,
as if the identical dog in a bush,
the ancestral hens bathing in dust
and the barrel have all been drawn on since,
the tune is still the tune we know
as if herd and castle and ball at Somló
and the three Magi live in the old man,
at the kermis they kick the dust in him,
the old woman's shriek of joy is a crowd of girls,
and barking dogs put the record right,
the hum and creak of vehicles,
the quail's quic-ic-ic in the sultry night
move in beneath the leaves of song
as if a quail could also say it,
as if a car too could convey it,
as if a dog also barked into our future.

2

The oakum of our hair, as white as lime,
falls, stopping the machine, which spills
the songs before us onto our table,
freely disgorged the songs are whips,
they eat each other, they spread squirming

on this winter plain, children's songs,
girls' songs of farewell, keenings,
soldiers' songs, chants,
and a tune gathers again
to shape the prayer of the woeful mouth:

Deliver me, Lord, from eternal death...
a change of clothes can't fend away
death, which unbuttons pelisses,
the gold braid tarnishes, the shako slips
off skulls through jaunty angles,
the unassisted stick rattles its chains
and scythes without the help of hands
harvest the unsown crop, in Mother's coif
we need to weep, our pearls are shed,
it is easier to weep than to laugh:
Deliver us, Lord!

3
Collector! place your machine on graves,
push rusty wreath-wires down
from snow-filled cypresses to record the tones
of bones which were never silenced,
collect the songs of the bones!

you knew them, where has that girl gone
who displayed her toys in the dust?
and all the ancient men:
Christ in his passion, Peter,
Gizella, dead, Károly the hussar,

Béla the intoning throat, Imre the gypsy,
let them sing to you from their hollows,
the deeper singers need no wine to free
their long constraints, their bold
songs will burst out from subterranean cold.

(Alan Dixon)

MIKLÓS VERESS
(1942–   )

SELF-PORTRAIT AT THIRTY

In his sockets there were eyeballs full of thirst
and there were pockmarks three upon his brow
but not such leanness in the face since now
alas his empty cup had dropped and burst:

he smiled at moments hesitant and quaint
and when he had consoled some fellow-being
he stared disconsolate in the mirror seeing
poor Don Quixote on his poor old Paint

wearing what seemed a sword-inflicted gash
in the back—memento of a drawn-out clash
and private war in which his youth had died

and all sad wines been emptied to the lees
and trampled down all noble mysteries
leaving a surf of silence deep inside.

(Richard Wilbur)

GYÖRGY PETRI
(1943–)

YOU USUALLY COME IN THE MORNING

I often wake up as though after my death

This is a (slightly more profound) way
of saying what in everyday language
would be: I feel like a new man.

Narrow half-light above a thimbleful of wine,
uncertain edge light on some distant metal object:
All this is articulated—like a sentence
though no more than the impression of one.
A fragment of an epigraph on a porous stone
which ought certainly to be rolled aside.

In the unending morning I attempt
to infer who I am
from my surroundings. Meanwhile, need
naturally necessitates activity:
I throw open the window, drink water, empty my bowels,
and although all this definitely disturbs my speculative inquiry,

it also has advantages. A toothbrush helps
to fix (within a period of some fifty years) the age in which I live;

the marks that I find scrawled
on a piece of paper: call G. B. at 9 A.M.
are not only convincing evidence of literacy
but also of a (relatively) high level of civilization. Furthermore, the writing
indicates that the writer knows Hungarian (which, in itself,
does not indicate the place of origin.)

Then the bell rings, and you arrive.
And I—could I do otherwise?—postpone
the final satisfactory answer
to the question, and:—I am who I am
—I must, after all, be somebody, mustn't I?—
trusting my instincts, I set down the coffee for you
and ask: How is it?
although I realize that question is just as unanswerable.

(William Jay Smith)

WITH THE THIN GIRL

In my dream I embraced
the thin girl with a childish passion
her small breasts like taut tomatoes
nestled in my cupped hands,
we did not perspire our hair did not get matted
in a slippery amorous tussle

Her spine a delicately jointed reed
which my sensitive fingertips caressed shyly
her shoulder blades frisking her shoulders
a responsive nape suggesting the woman she would become
boyish thighs spread out unabashedly
her thin legs well-bruised knees tasting of earth
her lap emanating not steaming heat but the gentle warmth
of a protected bay
the mound with its fair down rising clearly above it

Nevertheless we were not children
or pastoral creatures Our light love
took place not on grass but in my room
larger and lovelier with many windows
all overlooking the river whose waters slowly
colored in the early dawn

And propping our heads on each other's arms
we smoked stared at the ceiling
happy and spent as though we'd been
after it And in the wind-blown sphere
white clouds swam past fluttering
floated on towards the left corner of the window
but new ones came drawing
the eye drifting in the blue field
back to a narrower space Speechless we drank
in the changing sights And fell asleep

I dreamt our sleep I slept our dream
Above us like a white nail dangling
the moon descended The light
oozed in a menacing pink
About this time the paper
is slipped in under the door the shutters bang
open the lorries go thundering
through the empty cold
Gas taps water taps begin to hiss
Kettles boil slices are cut from dry bread
The time of flushes and rushes
                              The waking varicose
pain of charwomen Chairs in apparent death
the soda-fountain tap rattles on the counter
like a plucked chicken head resurrected
Green as Lazarus it goes on
where it had left off because it like all the city can do nothing else
You carefully free your arms gone to sleep
from under my head heavy with double sleep
You slip out quietly Two hours later I wake up
By then all is irreparable

(William Jay Smith)

GYÖRGY PETRI
SONG.

I long for nothing more
than delicate functional
forms of bottles and glass

Let
sorrow take away her corrupt favors
I no longer weep for anyone

Our age seeks empty
harmony
its goal securely in the future

Between the end of one culture
and the start of the next
it would be so good to frolic with you
on the sun-swept grass beside a pool

(William Jay Smith)

SZABOLCS VÁRADY
(1943-)

AN OUTSIDER,
IF THERE WERE SUCH A MAN

An outsider, if there were such a man,
a baby born with a fully developed brain,
or a Martian perhaps,
an outsider, if there were such a man,
would hardly understand
why for his own sake,
for his own, and, well, the world's sake,
for the sake of the entire history of the world, and what's more, the
                                                      whole universe,
it is desirable that
advisable that
and likewise commendable that

An outsider, if there were such a man,
if it were that he would not understand,
if he understood it that way, this outsider,
he would not quite be an outsider.

Some even farther-outsider, one
from some other solar system or from the womb
but in possession of human language—though in its most primitive
                                      form—would rather think,
this farthest-outsider would rather think,
indicating the obsolete traditional
lexicological meaning of words:

nothing more desirable than the
nothing more advisable than the
and hardly anything more commendable than the

This farthest-outsider
would believe such things from the farthest side out.

But we who to a certain degree
(the whole thing may cost us our skins)
are inside and obliged to pay attention
and follow the revelations of the most
superior superiors, our sense of language has changed
so that we now perceive directly the indirect meaning
of words, we stand on the ground allotted to us
for want of anything better and would be content for the time being
if things didn't go from bad to worse—
we don't, as a matter of fact, understand
the degrees of outsideness if things go on like this,
nor does the scent of metaphors irritate
our nostrils to such an extent that we can suitably abhor it.

(William Jay Smith)

CHAIRS ABOVE THE DANUBE

Those two chairs were not really
all that ugly. Too bad the springs
protruded from them and the upholstery
was so hopelessly filthy.

But chairs they were, all the same. And right for that apartment.
So we carried them, mostly on our heads,
from Orlay Street across the former
Francis Joseph, now Liberty, Bridge,
to Number 2 Ráday Street where P. lived
at the time (as some of his poems will show.)

A chair, not to say two, has
many uses. "Two Poets on a Bridge
with Chairs on their Heads"—one can imagine
a painting so entitled. I hope it would be
a down-to-earth painting and not one of those

transfigurations. Those two chairs—
and it's important to make this clear—were by no means
just halos around our heads. About halfway across the bridge—
and not for the purpose of proving anything—
we sat down on them. The springs protruded more prominently from
one—I don't recall which of us
got it. Doesn't matter, since what happened later
can hardly be explained by that. It was a pleasant
summer evening. We lit cigarettes,
enjoying this one might say
unusual form of coziness.
                  The chairs later served
nicely for a while: at the P.s' they
were *the* chairs. But man wants something better
than what is: the chairs were sent to an upholsterer. Then the P.s
moved also, the first time, because they had to, the second,
because they hated their apartment. Nowadays
we meet less often at their place. Several things
brought this about: G. left A.
(P.'s wife) and then M. (B.'s wife)
broke off with me, and the other M. (G.'s wife)
divorced G. and married me (while the B.s
also separated) and P. attempted suicide and
has been living more or less in a sanatorium ever since,
not to mention the changes in the world situation,
so anyway: there's nothing left to sit on.

                                 (William Jay Smith)

BIOGRAPHICAL NOTES

ÁGH, ISTVÁN, b. 1939, Felsőiszkáz, a small village in Western Hungary. The younger brother of the poet László Nagy (q. v.). Studied Hungarian and librarianship at the University of Budapest, has been a librarian, journalist, poetry editor of *Új Írás* ("New Writing"), a Budapest literary monthly. Now supports himself by writing. Of his four volumes of poems, *Jóslatok az újszülöttnek* ("Oracles for the Newborn"), 1973, is the latest; also published a volume of collected articles.

BENJÁMIN, LÁSZLÓ, b. 1915, Budapest. Had to drop out of school at fifteen and go to work in factories to support himself. Worked in journalism, occupying a number of editorial positions after World War II and is at present librarian in the Budapest Municipal Library. Of his fourteen books of poems, *Sziklarajzok* ("Cave Drawings"), 1973, selected and new poems, is the latest. Has translated French fabliaux, some of the *Canterbury Tales*, and various modern poets.

CSANÁDI, IMRE, b. 1920, Zámoly, Western Hungary, the child of a landless peasant family. Studied in Budapest during the war but was drafted. Spent years in a POW camp in the Ukraine. Returning, went to work as a publisher's editor. At present editor of *Új Tükör* ("New Mirror"), a popular cultural weekly. His collected poems appeared in 1975. In 1954 edited an important collection of Hungarian folk ballads.

CSOÓRI, SÁNDOR, b. 1930, Zámoly, Western Hungary, of peasant stock. Studied in the now defunct Lenin Institute (a language academy) in Budapest, published his first volume in 1954. *Párbeszéd sötétben* ("Dialogue in the Dark"), 1973, was his fifth collection. On the staff of various magazines; has been script reader and artistic advisor at the MAFILM Film Studios in Budapest for a number of years. Wrote the scripts of several of Ferenc Kósa's films. Has also published collections of his journalism, a journal of his trip to Cuba, essays and filmscripts.

CSUKÁS, ISTVÁN, b. 1936, Kisújszállás, on the Great Plains. Got his elementary schooling at the now defunct village music boarding school at Békéstarhos, an institution founded to educate peasant children in the Kodály method of music education; some former pupils now occupy important positions in musical life. Studied law and literature in Budapest but took no degree and devoted himself to writing. In addition to four volumes of poems—of which *Ima a vadevezősökért* ("Prayer for Free-rowers"), 1975, is the latest—has written children's books and television plays and programs for children. "Top Hat and Spuds Nose," a television film for children for which he wrote the script won the "Best Children Dramatic Series" award at the 1975 Hollywood television festival.

DEVECSERI, GÁBOR, 1917–71, b. Budapest. His first poems appeared when he was fifteen. Studied Greek and Latin at the University of Budapest, and under Karl Kerényi. Was assistant professor of Greek 1946–48, taught Hungarian at a military academy 1948–54, was Secretary General of the Hungarian Writers' Union 1949–53. His collected poems appeared in 1974, collected verse plays in 1975. Other works include essays on antiquity, travelogues, translations of the complete Homer and many other classical Greek, Latin, as well as modern English and Soviet poets. *A hasfelmetszés előnyei* ("The Advantages of Guts-ripping"), 1974, is a posthumous volume of diaries, essays, remembrances and poems, written in hospital during his prolonged terminal illness. Robert Graves included his translation of "Women and Masks" in his own latest volume of poems.

EÖRSI, ISTVÁN, b. 1931, Budapest. Studied Hungarian, English and philosophy at the University of Budapest, was a pupil of György Lukács; translated some of Lukács's later works into Hungarian from the original German. Served a prison term 1957–1960 for his activities in 1956. Has published three volumes of poems, as well as short stories, journal-ism, essays, and has written plays. Translations from American, English, French, Ger-man, Russian poets include work by Allen Ginsberg, Gregory Corso and Lawrence Ferlin-ghetti.

FÜST, MILÁN, 1888–1967, b. Budapest. Studied law, taught economics in a Budapest secondary school for some years. Traveled all over Europe between the wars. In 1947 became professor of aesthetics at the University of Budapest. His first volume of poems appeared in 1913, and was followed by three others and a collected volume. Author of novels, short stories, an autobiography, plays, and *Látomás és indulat a művészetben* ("Vision and Emotion in Art"), 1948, a volume based on his university lectures. There are French and German selections of his poems, and *A feleségem története* ("My Wife's Story"), 1942, his most successful novel, has Czech, Dutch, French, three German, Polish, Serbo-Croatian, Slovene and Spanish editions.

GARAI, GÁBOR, b. 1929, Budapest. A clerk in the catering company of the Hungarian State Railways before taking a degree in Hungarian at the University of Budapest. After various editorial positions, became Secretary General of the Hungarian Writers' Union. Member of the Central Committee of the Hungarian Socialist Workers' Party since 1966. Has published eleven volumes of poems, *A szenvedély évszakai* ("The Seasons of Passion"), 1973, collected poems, essays and journalism, a verse-play, and a volume of translations from American, English, French, German, and Soviet poets. Traveled to many countries, including Cuba and India.

GERGELY, ÁGNES, b. 1933, Budapest. Studied Hungarian and English at the University of Budapest. Was secondary school teacher, producer for Hungarian Radio and feature editor of a literary weekly; now editor at a Budapest publishing house. In 1973–74 spent six months in the USA as member of the International Writing Program at the University of Iowa. Author of three novels and four books of poems, of which *Válogatott szerelmeim* ("My Selected Love Affairs"), selected poems and translations, 1973, is the latest.

GÖRGEY, GÁBOR, b. 1929, Budapest. Studied English and German at the University of Budapest but took no degree. A staff writer for a national daily paper since 1959, has published a great amount of criticism, reviews, essays, articles, in addition to three volumes of poems—of which *Köszönöm, jól* ("Fine, Thank You"), 1970, is the latest—and a collec-tion of verse translations. Author of several plays for the stage and television.

HAJNAL, ANNA, b. 1907, Gyepűfüzes, Western Hungary. Studied English at a language academy in Vienna. Co-edited an important literary journal in Budapest in the late thirties. Has published thirteen volumes of poetry, of which *Elhiszed nekem?* ("Do You Believe Me?"),

1976, is the latest. Has translated Shakespeare, Edward Lear, Walt Whitman, and many others, and also published several volumes of verse tales and nursery rhymes.

ILLYÉS, GYULA, b. 1902, Rácegrespuszta, Western Hungary. Son of a machine operator on a huge estate; got his schooling by the combined effort of his entire family. Served in the army of the Hungarian Republic of Councils in 1919, and subsequently fled the country, lived in Paris 1921–26. His first volume of poems appeared in 1928. In the thirties took part in the important village-research movement of writers and sociologists which resulted in a series of descriptive sociological works on the largely ignored miserable conditions that prevailed in the countryside. His most noteworthy contribution was *A puszták népe* ("People of the Puszta"), 1934, a partly autobiographical work combining sociology and literature, to which he added a sequel in 1962, *Ebéd a kastélyban* ("Luncheon at the Mansion"), about changed conditions on the puszta of his childhood. Was editor of *Nyugat* and *Magyar Csillag*, its successor, the most important literary magazine before World War II. Visited the United States in the sixties. Collected poems appeared in two volumes, 1920–1945 and 1946–1968, in 1972 and 1973, *Minden lehet* ("Anything Possible"), new poems, 1971. Published a volume of unfinished poems in 1971, a collection of travel notes, two volumes of collected essays and two of translations. His plays were also collected. There is a selected volume of poems in English, from Chatto and Windus, 1971, and a French and German selection. *People of the Puszta*, in English, Corvina Press, 1967; also in Bulgarian, Czech, Finnish, French, Polish, Serbo-Croatian, Ukrainian; *Petőfi*, a life of the nineteenth century poet, Corvina Press, 1973, in English; also in Czech, French, German, Italian, Polish, Serbo-Croatian; *Luncheon at the Mansion*, in French, German, Japanese, Polish, Serbo-Croatian, Slovak; *Kháron ladikján* ("In Charon's Boat"), a prose volume of notes on aging, in Czech, French, German and Slovak editions.

JÉKELY, ZOLTÁN, b. 1913, Nagyenyed (Aiud), Transylvania, now in Rumania. Son of the poet Lajos Áprily. Spent his childhood in Kolozsvár (Cluj-Napoca); studied French, Hungarian and art history at the University of Budapest, worked as librarian, traveled in France and Italy, returned to live in Kolozsvár in 1941, came back to live in Budapest after World War II, a librarian once again until 1954, since when has been devoting himself to writing. Published nine volumes of poems, of which *Az idősárkányhoz* ("To the Time-dragon"), 1975, is a large collection of old and new poems. Author of novels, short stories and a play. Translations include Dante, Shakespeare, Racine, Part One of Goethe's *Faust*, and many modern English, French, Rumanian poets.

JUHÁSZ, FERENC, b. 1928, Bia, a village near Budapest, son of a stonemason. Attended a business secondary school and spent a few terms at the University of Budapest as member of the People's College Movement in the late forties, but took no degree. Was for many years reader at a Budapest publishing house and contributing editor to *Új Írás* ("New Writing"), a literary monthly, of which he is now the editor. His huge output, consisting of more than a dozen volumes of poems—lyrical and narrative—has recently been collected in two volumes under the title *A mindenség szerelme* ("Love for the Universe"), 1946–1970, Vol. 1: *A szarvassá változott fiú* ("The Boy Changed into a Stag"), 1971, Vol. 2: *A titkok kapuja* ("The Gate of Secrets"), 1972, each nearly of a thousand pages. His collected prose writings appeared in two volumes. *A megváltó aranykard* ("The Redeeming Golden Sword"), 1973, contains recent poems. There are two selected editions in English: *The Boy Changed into a Stag, Selected Poems 1949–1967*, translated by Kenneth McRobbie and Ilona Duczynska, Oxford University Press, Canada, 1970, and Sándor Weöres–Ferenc Juhász: *Selected Poems*, Penguin Modern European Poets, 1970, Juhász translations by David Wevill. There is also a German and a Finnish selection: Suhrkamp, Frankfurt, 1966, and Otava, Helsinki, 1974.

KALÁSZ, MÁRTON, b. 1934, Somberek, Western Hungary, in a landless peasant family. Went to school in the Southwestern city of Pécs, held various jobs, including radio reporter, director of a village cultural center, publisher's editor, before becoming lecturer in Hungarian at Humboldt University in Berlin. Returned from Berlin in 1974, lives in the city of Székesfehérvár, and commutes to Budapest where he works on the staff of *Új Irás* ("New Writing.") *Megszámított vigasz* ("Calculated Sympathy"), 1976, was his seventh volume of poems. Has translated many German and Soviet poets.

KASSÁK, LAJOS, 1887–1967, b. Érsekújvár, now Czechoslovakia, in a poor working-class family. As a young poet and worker walked through Austria, Germany, Belgium, to Paris, from which he was forcibly repatriated. Walt Whitman was an early formative influence on him. A poet, novelist, short story writer, editor of journals, painter and organizer of exhibitions, a leader of the Hungarian avant garde in all these respects, and a socialist. Author of many novels, a multi-volume autobiography, *Egy ember élete* ("The Life of a Man"), collections of short stories, books on art and painting, and many volumes of poems. Collected poems appeared in 2 volumes in 1970, collected short stories in 1974, collected articles and criticism in 1975. After his 1960 exhibition in Paris, a great number of his constructivist paintings went into private and public collections in France and elsewhere. There are several French selections of his poems, and also Czech and Slovak editions.

KÁLNOKY, LÁSZLÓ, b. 1912, in the Northeastern city of Eger. Studied law in Eger, Pécs and Budapest. A minor government official and librarian before World War II, was publisher's editor before devoting himself to writing and translating starting with the late fifties. Published three volumes of poems and a selection, *Letépett álarcok* ("Masks Torn"), 1972. His vast output as a translator includes Goethe's *Faust*, Part Two, Racine, Molière, Marlowe, and several volumes of lyrical poems from American, English, French, German, Italian, Russian, and other poets, classical and modern.

KÁROLYI, AMY, b. 1909, Budapest. Wife of the poet Sándor Weöres (q. v.). The latest of her six volumes of poems, *Pakli kártya* ("Pack of Cards"), appeared in 1975. Has also published several volumes of nursery rhymes, and written the book for an opera, based on a tale by Hans Christian Andersen. Her translations include poems by Emily Dickinson.

KORMOS, ISTVÁN, b. 1923, Mosonszentmiklós, Western Hungary, of peasant stock. Published his first volume in 1947, while still a grocer's assistant in Budapest. Later became editor at a publishing house for children's literature. In the sixties spent several years in Paris. *Szegény Yorick* ("Poor Yorick"), 1971, was a book of collected and new poems, and *N. N. bolyongásai* ("The Wanderings of N. N."), 1975, contains new poems. Author of numerous extremely popular books of nursery rhymes, editor of poetry anthologies. Translations include Chaucer, Molière, Burns, a volume of Russian folk poetry, as well as many American, English, French, Spanish, and other poets.

LADÁNYI, MIHÁLY, b. 1934, Dévaványa, of village artisan stock. Studied Hungarian at the University of Budapest, but took no degree. After working for years as editor, teacher, journalist, and director of the cultural center in a provincial town, has been devoting himself to poetry since 1964. *Seregek mögött* ("Behind Armies"), 1976, selected poems, is his eleventh volume.

NAGY, LÁSZLÓ, b. 1925, Felsőiszkáz, Western Hungary, of peasant stock. Husband of the poet Margit Szécsi (q. v.). In 1946–49 studied to become a painter, and also attended a few terms at the University of Budapest as a member of the People's College Movement, but took no degree. In 1949–52 lived in Bulgaria on a state scholarship. For some time edited an illustrated children's paper, later was art editor, and is now contributing editor of *Élet és Irodalom* ("Life and Literature"), a Budapest literary weekly. His entire work, poems and translations, appeared in four volumes in 1975. Translations include folk poetry from Balkan countries, notably Yugoslavia, Bulgaria, Albania; the Eastern Finno-Ugric peoples, and songs from Hungarian Gypsies; has also translated Burns, Garcia Lorca, Dylan Thomas. Latest book of new poems: *Versben bújdosó* ("Hiding in Poems"), 1973. There is a volume of selected poems in English, translated by Tony Connor and Kenneth McRobbie: *Love of the Scorching Wind*, Oxford University Press—Corvina Press, 1973, and a German selection from Neues Leben, Berlin, 1971.

NEMES NAGY, ÁGNES, b. 1922, Budapest. Studied Hungarian, Latin and art history at the University of Budapest; for some time on the staff of an educational magazine, taught secondary school for years before devoting herself entirely to writing. *A lovak és az angyalok* ("The Horses and the Angels"), 1969, her fourth book, was a selected volume. *Hatvannégy hattyú* ("Sixty-four Swans"), 1975, is a volume of essays on poetry. Translations include plays by Corneille, Racine, Molière, Brecht, poems by Rilke, St. John Perse, and many other English, French, German, classical and modern poets.

ORBÁN, OTTÓ, b. 1936, Budapest. His father was killed in a concentration camp; he spent his childhood in a Budapest school for war orphans. Studied Hungarian and English at the University of Budapest but left without a degree and has since been devoting himself to writing. Of seven volumes, *Szegénynek lenni* ("To Be Poor"), 1974, is a book of selected poems, and *Távlat a történethez* ("Perspective for the Story"), 1976, contains new poems. Translations include a volume of selected poems and plays by Robert Lowell, and many American, English, French, German, Russian, Spanish poets, collected in *Aranygyapjú* ("Golden Fleece"), 1972. Has traveled in France, Switzerland, England, Finland, the Soviet Union, and India—the latter trip resulting in a volume of travel notes in prose. Also writes nursery rhymes.

PETRI, GYÖRGY, b. 1943, Budapest. Worked in various odd jobs, including a work therapy institute for the mentally ill, before studying philosophy at the University of Budapest. Published two volumes of poems, of which *Körülírt zuhanás* ("Circumscribed Fall"), 1974, is the latest. Supports himself by writing and translating.

PILINSZKY, JÁNOS, b. 1921, Budapest. Attended university in Budapest. Was drafted toward the end of World War II and taken to Germany where he saw the concentration camps while making his way back to Hungary in 1945. After various other editorial jobs, now on the staff of *Vigilia*, a Roman Catholic monthly in Budapest. *Nagyvárosi ikonok* ("Metropolitan Ikons"), 1970, is a volume of collected poems, *Szálkák* ("Splinters"), 1972, new poems, *Kráter* ("Crater"), 1976, contains selected and new poems. A selected volume in English is in preparation at the Carcanet Press, England, translated by Ted Hughes in collaboration with János Csokits. There is a German edition, Otto Müller, Salzburg, 1971.

RÁKOS, SÁNDOR, b. 1921, Újfehértó-Kálmánháza, Northeastern Hungary, son of a village teacher. Studied economics in Budapest, took no degree, worked in various administrative, journalistic and editorial jobs; has been devoting himself to writing since 1952. Heads the Translators' Section in the Hungarian Writers' Union. Collected poems, *Meztelen arc* ("Naked Face"), appeared in 1971; *Az emlék jelene* ("The Present of Memory"), 1973, contains new poems. *Elforgó ég* ("Turning Sky"), 1974, a volume of essays. Translated *Gilgamesh* and other pieces of ancient Mesopotamian poetry, and and a volume of folk poems from the South Sea Islands.

RÓNAY, GYÖRGY, b. 1913, Budapest. Studied Hungarian and French at the University of Budapest. Reader for a publishing house 1937–47; now editor of *Vigilia*, a Roman Catholic monthly. Besides many volumes of poetry, has published novels, short stories, essays, a book on French Renaissance poetry, another on Hungarian poetry in the late nineteenth century, an important anthology of French poetry in his own translations. *Nyár* ("Summer"), collected poems, appeared in 1957. His latest volume of poems is *A tenger pántlikái* ("Ribbons of the Sea"), 1969. Has also translated poems by Michelangelo, Hölderlin, Novalis, Rimbaud, and many other poets.

SIMON, ISTVÁN, 1926–1975, b. Bazsi, a small village in Western Hungary, of peasant stock. While still in high school, was drafted toward the end of World War II and served on the Eastern front; returned from a POW camp in 1947. As member of the People's College Movement in the late forties, studied at the University of Budapest, and took a degree in Hungarian and German. Worked in various editorial positions, before becoming editor of *Kortárs* ("Contemporary"), a literary monthly, and a Secretary of the Hungarian Writers' Union. Until his death from cancer in 1975, represented his home district in Parliament. His output consists of more than a dozen books of poems, collections of journalism, translations from German poets. His last volume, *Rapszódia az időről* ("Rhapsody on Time"), appeared in 1975.

SOMLYÓ, GYÖRGY, b. 1920, Balatonboglár, son of the poet Zoltán Somlyó. Studied at the University of Budapest and the Sorbonne, with an emphasis on French, philosophy, and folklore. Jobs include administrative positions, playreader, script editor, magazine editor, director of the Literature Department of Hungarian Radio, etc. At present editor of *Arion*, a multilingual poetry yearbook published by Corvina Press in Budapest. Has traveled in East and West Europe and China. The three volumes of *Hármastükör* ("Treble Mirror"), 1970, were selected writings. Recent poems appeared in *A mesék könyve* ("The Book of Tales"), 1974, of which a French selection appeared at Gallimard in Guillevic's translation, *Contre-fables*, 1974 and in *Épp ez* ("Just This"), 1976. Author of a book on the poet Milán Füst (q. v.), and a four-volume collection of essays on poetry. Translated many American, English, French and other poets.

SZABÓ, LŐRINC, 1900–1957, b. Miskolc, Eastern Hungary, son of a railroad engineer. Studied mechanical engineering, then switched to literature and philosophy, but took no degree. Published his first volume of poems in 1922. Was a journalist and writer all his life. Collected poems appeared in 1960, selected poems in 1963, posthumous poems, letters, journals, notes, and criticism in the seventies. His huge output of translations, contained in a two-volume collection which ran to several editions, includes lyrical poetry from many languages. Also translated the complete Sonnets and five plays of Shakespeare, as well as "The Ancient Mariner," "The Rubaiyat," *et al.*

SZÉCSI, MARGIT, b. 1928. in an industrial slum district in Budapest. Wife of the poet László Nagy (q. v.). Did office work, then studied Hungarian at the University of Budapest but took no degree. In 1951 volunteered to help build the Dunapentele (later Sztálinváros, now Dunaújváros) steel mill complex and town; was director of a town cultural center, and also on the editorial staff of a literary magazine in the early fifties before devoting herself to her own writing. Author of seven books of poems, of which *Birodalom* ("Empire"), 1976, is the latest.

TANDORI, DEZSŐ, b. 1938, Budapest. Studied Hungarian and German at the University of Budapest, for years taught German at a military academy. In 1966 a poem of his won first prize in an international competition for young poets organized by P.E.N. International. Has published three volumes of poems, of which *A mennyezet és a padló* ("The Ceiling and the Floor"), 1976, is the latest. His translations include, in addition to many poems, plays and novels, a volume of selected poems by John Berryman.

TORNAI, JÓZSEF, b. 1927, Dunaharaszti, near Budapest, son of a railroad switchman. Attended a business secondary school, worked afterwards in a truck plant as grinder and later as technician, before devoting himself to writing. Also writes criticism, book reviews, essays, does broadcasting work, translates English, American, French poetry and folk poetry from various countries, and contributes regular film criticism to *The New Hungarian Quarterly*. Of nine books of poems, *A bálványok neve* ("The Name of the Idols"), 1970, was a selection, and *Tizenhét ábrándozás* ("Seventeen Pipedreams"), 1976, contained new poems.

TÓTH, JUDIT, b. 1936, Budapest. Her parents were both killed in a concentration camp, and she was raised by relatives. Studied Hungarian and French at the University of Budapest, was for six years poetry editor of *Nagyvilág* ("Wide World"), a Budapest monthly devoted to foreign literature in translation. In 1965 married a French architect and has been living in a southeastern suburb of Paris since 1966. Has published three volumes of poems and numerous verse translations from English, French, German, Russian.

VAS, ISTVÁN b. 1910, Budapest. Studied at a business academy in Vienna, returned to Budapest in 1929, worked in various minor clerical jobs before World War II, has been editor at a publishing house since 1946. Has traveled to most countries in Europe. A two volume edition of his collected poems, *Mit akar ez az egy ember?* ("What Does This Single Man Want?"), appeared in 1970. *Önarckép a hetvenes évekből* ("Self-Portrait from the Seventies"), 1975, contains new poems. *Nehéz szerelem* ("Difficult Love"), 1972, is his autobiography in progress. *Az ismeretlen isten* ("The Unknown God"), 1974, is a volume of collected essays and criticism. His major translations include plays by Shakespeare, Molière, O'Neill, novels by Thackeray, as well as a volume of lyrical poems, classical and modern, from many languages.

VÁCI, MIHÁLY, 1924–70, b. Nyíregyháza, Northeastern Hungary. Went to teacher's college, taught for several years in a *puszta* school; later occupied various administrative and editorial positions, was editor of *Új Írás* ("New Writing") at the time of his death. Since 1963 had represented his home district in Parliament. Died of a heart attack in Hanoi, Vietnam, while member of a writers' delegation. *A sokaság fia* ("Son of the Multitude"), 1970, was his last volume of poems, published posthumously, and *Százhuszat verő szív* ("Hundred and Twenty Heartbeats per Minute"), 1971, a volume of selected writings. Also published volumes of his articles.

VÁRADY, SZABOLCS, b. 1943, Budapest. Graduated from the University of Budapest in Hungarian and English. So far his verse has only appeared in collections of work by young poets. Editor at Európa, a Budapest publishing house specializing in foreign literature in translation. His own translations include essays by Susan Sontag, a volume of selected poems by Archibald MacLeish (with István Vas, q. v.), and a volume of selected poems by William Jay Smith.

VERESS, MIKLÓS, b. 1942, Barcs, a village in Southern Hungary. Studied Hungarian and Russian at the University of Szeged. At present editor of *Mozgó Világ* ("Moving World"), a new monthly magazine for young writers. His two volumes of poems are *Erdő a vadaknak* ("Woods for the Beasts"), 1972, and *Bádogkirály* ("Tin King"), 1975.

WEÖRES, SÁNDOR, b. 1913, Szombathely, a town in Western Hungary. Husband of the poet Amy Károlyi (q. v.). Studied law, geography, history, but eventually took a doctorate in philosophy and aesthetics at the University of Pécs. In 1941–50 librarian in the cities of Pécs, Székesfehérvár and Budapest. Has been living in the capital and devoting himself to writing since 1951. Published his first poems at the age of fourteen, his first volume in 1934. Collected works appeared in three volumes in 1975, containing the complete poems, prose poems, narratives, verse plays, nursery rhymes, and also his doctoral dissertation *A vers születése* ("The Birth of the Poem"). His huge output as a translator—collected in three volumes—includes works by Shakespeare, Rustaveli, Shevchenko, Mallarmé, folk poetry and countless classical and modern poets from East and West Europe, as well as Africa and the Orient. His travels took him to most of Europe, the United States, Egypt, India, and China. A selection in English appeared in Edwin Morgan's translation in Sándor Weöres–Ferenc Juhász: *Selected Poems*, Penguin Modern European Poets, 1970.

ZELK, ZOLTÁN, b. 1906, Érmihályfalva (Valea lui Mihai, now Rumania), son of a village cantor. Supported himself by odd manual jobs before World War II, was imprisoned and subsequently expelled from the country for his communist activities, returned and lived for years under an assumed name. Served in a forced labor battalion 1942–44. Began publishing in 1925. Served a prison term 1957–58 for his activities in 1956. *Sirály* ("Seagull"), 1973, a volume of collected poems, also contains the long poem of the same title, written in prison in 1958 on the death of his wife. His latest volume, *Ahogy a kötéltáncosok* ("Like Tightrope Walkers"), appeared in 1975.

INDEX OF POETS

Ágh, István, 268

Benjámin, László, 122

Csanádi, Imre, 130

Csoóri, Sándor, 233

Csukás, István, 263

Devecseri, Gábor, 126

Eörsi, István, 238

Füst, Milán 5

Garai, Gábor, 229

Gergely, Ágnes, 240

Görgey, Gábor, 225

Hajnal, Anna, 47

Illyés, Gyula, 14

Jékely, Zoltán, 118

Juhász, Ferenc, 196

Kalász, Márton, 244

Kassák, Lajos 1

Kálnoky, László, 84

Károlyi, Amy, 52

Kormos, István, 161

Ladányi, Mihály, 246

Nagy, László, 168

Nemes Nagy, Ágnes, 156

Orbán, Ottó, 251

Petri, György, 271

Pilinszky, János, 142

Rákos, Sándor, 140

Rónay, György, 87

Simon, István, 188

Somlyó, György, 136

Szabó, Lőrinc, 8

Szécsi, Margit, 221

Tandori, Dezső, 265

Tornai, József, 192

Tóth, Judit, 258

Vas, István, 56

Váci, Mihály, 165

Várady, Szabolcs, 275

Veress, Miklós, 270

Weöres, Sándor, 88

Zelk, Zoltán, 41

INDEX OF TRANSLATORS

Connor, Tony, *168, 176, 180, 181*

Davie, Donald, *71*

Dixon, Alan, *140, 158, 159, 160, 165, 168, 235, 236, 268*

Graves, Robert, *126, 127, 128*

Hamburger, Michael, *87*

Hoffman, Daniel, *32, 41, 42, 43, 49, 50, 116, 136, 137, 138, 140, 141 156, 157, 230, 231, 233, 241, 265, 266, 267*

Howes, Barbara, *43, 44, 45, 46, 263*

Hughes, Ted, *142, 143, 144, 144, 149, 150, 152*

Kessler, Jascha, *225, 244*

Land, Thomas, *242*

Lourie, Richard, *88*

MacBeth, George, *177, 178, 182*

McRobbie, Kenneth, *14, 183, 197, 206, 218, 221, 248, 267*

Morgan, Edwin, *1, 2, 3, 5, 6, 8, 9, 10, 12, 48, 52, 62, 72, 84, 85, 86, 88, 99, 105, 106, 110, 118, 122, 124, 130, 131, 134, 135, 148, 161, 162, 163, 166, 169, 188, 229, 232, 234, 238, 240, 246, 247, 249, 250, 251, 252, 253, 254, 256*

Redgrove, Peter, *110*

Schiff, Laura, *223, 224, 258, 260, 261*

Smith, William Jay, *14, 21, 22, 24, 25, 26, 27, 28, 29, 30, 31, 39, 47, 49, 56, 64, 69, 75, 77, 79, 80, 114, 117, 150, 151, 152, 153, 154, 155, 192, 193, 194, 239, 252, 271, 272, 274, 275, 276*

Tomlinson, Charles, *23*

Wevill, David, *196*

Wilbur, Richard, *194, 270*

CO-TRANSLATORS

The poet-translators have been assisted in making their final versions by the following Hungarian-language Informants, who have worked with them, often very closely, either in Hungary, Britain, Canada, or the United States:

László T. András
Margot Archer
János Csokits
Ilona Duczynska
George Gömöri
Júlia Kada
Gyula Kodolányi
Mária Kőrössy
Miklós Vajda
Tünde Vajda